Immigration in Americ

MW00787794

Immigration in American History is a concise examination of the experiences of immigrants from the founding of the British colonies through the present day.

The most recent scholarship on immigration is integrated into an accessible narrative that embraces the multicultural nature of U.S. immigration history, keeping issues of race and power at the center of the book. Organized chronologically, this book highlights how the migration experience evolved over time and examines the interactions that occurred between different groups of migrants and the native-born. From the first interactions between the Native Americans and English colonizers at Jamestown, to the present-day debates over unauthorized immigration, the book helps students chart the evolution of American attitudes towards immigration and immigration policies and better contextualize present-day debates over immigration. The voices of immigrants are brought to the forefront in a poignant selection of primary source documents, and a glossary and "who's who" provides students with additional context for the people and concepts featured in the text.

This book will be of interest to students and scholars of American immigration history and immigration policy history.

Kristen L. Anderson, Ph.D., is Associate Professor of History at Webster University, USA where she specializes in the history of immigration, slavery, and the Civil War.

Introduction to the series

History is the narrative constructed by historians from traces left by the past. Historical enquiry is often driven by contemporary issues and, in consequence, historical narratives are constantly reconsidered, reconstructed and reshaped. The fact that different historians have different perspectives on issues means that there is often controversy and no universally agreed version of past events. *Seminar Studies* was designed to bridge the gap between current research and debate, and the broad, popular general surveys that often date rapidly.

The volumes in the series are written by historians who are not only familiar with the latest research and current debates concerning their topic, but who have themselves contributed to our understanding of the subject. The books are intended to provide the reader with a clear introduction to a major topic in history. They provide both a narrative of events and a critical analysis of contemporary interpretations. They include the kinds of tools generally omitted from specialist monographs: a chronology of events, a glossary of terms and brief biographies of 'who's who'. They also include bibliographical essays in order to guide students to the literature on various aspects of the subject. Students and teachers alike will find that the selection of documents will stimulate the discussion and offer insight into the raw materials used by historians in their attempt to understand the past.

Clive Emsley and Gordon Martel
Series Editors

Immigration in American History

Kristen L. Anderson

Routledge
Taylor & Francis Group

LONDON AND NEW YORK

First published 2021
by Routledge
2 Park Square, Milton Park, Abingdon, Oxon OX14 4RN

and by Routledge
52 Vanderbilt Avenue, New York, NY 10017

Routledge is an imprint of the Taylor & Francis Group, an informa business

British Library Cataloguing-in-Publication Data
A catalogue record for this book is available from the British Library

Library of Congress Cataloging-in-Publication Data
Names: Anderson, Kristen Layne, 1979– author.
Title: Immigration in American history/Kristen L. Anderson.
Description: Abingdon, Oxon; New York, NY: Routledge, 2021. |
Includes bibliographical references and index.
Identifiers: LCCN 2020047339 (print) | LCCN 2020047340 (ebook) |
ISBN 9780367416362 (hardback) | ISBN 9780367415723 (paperback) |
ISBN 9780367815448 (ebook)
Subjects: LCSH: Immigrants–United States–History. |
United States–Emigration and immigration–History. |
United States–Emigration and immigration–History–Sources.
Classification: LCC JV6450 .K62 2021 (print) |
LCC JV6450 (ebook) | DDC 304.8/73–dc23
LC record available at https://lccn.loc.gov/2020047339
LC ebook record available at https://lccn.loc.gov/2020047340

ISBN: 978-0-367-41636-2 (hbk)
ISBN: 978-0-367-41572-3 (pbk)
ISBN: 978-0-367-81544-8 (ebk)

Typeset in Sabon
by Newgen Publishing UK

Contents

PART 2

Documents

List of figures

List of tables

List of maps

Acknowledgements

As with any project of this length, I have incurred many debts during its creation. I am indebted first of all to my fellow immigration historians whose work formed the basis for this volume. Those works on which I have relied most heavily can be found listed in the References. These scholars revealed the great complexity of immigrants' lived experiences, which I have tried to distill into this brief overview. Any errors in the text are of course my own. I also owe a debt to my colleagues at Webster University for providing a supportive and collegial environment in which to work. The staff of Webster University's Emerson Library, including Christine Dugan, Matt Wier, and many others, were instrumental to this project, fulfilling my seemingly endless interlibrary loan requests. This project could not have been completed without their help. And finally, I am indebted to my family for their love and support. My husband David and daughter Samantha have been very patient while mommy works on her book, and I'm so grateful to have them in my life.

Chronology

1848	Treaty of Guadalupe Hidalgo ends Mexican–American War, transferring a large portion of Mexico's territory to the U.S.
1848	Revolutions in Central Europe attempt to create a unified, democratic Germany
1849	Gold rush in California
Late 1840s–1850s	Nativist Know Nothing Party active in state and local politics
1856–1858	Second Opium War in China
1861–1865	U.S. Civil War
1862	Homestead Act allows farmers who were citizens or who had declared their intention to become citizens to claim 160 acres of land in the West
1865	Thirteenth Amendment to the U.S. Constitution ratified, forbidding slavery everywhere within the United States
1868	Fourteenth Amendment to the U.S. Constitution ratified, establishing that everyone born in the United States is a U.S. citizen
1868	Meiji Revolution in Japan
1868	Burlingame Treaty signed with China, stating that Chinese could migrate to the U.S. without restriction
1870	Fifteenth Amendment to the U.S. Constitution ratified, establishing that the right to vote could not be denied based on "race, color, or previous condition of servitude"
1870s–1880s	Warfare between U.S. Army and Native American nations in the West, gradually forcing them to go to reservations
1875	The Page Act passed
1876	Reconstruction officially ends
1879–1880	Black migrants known as Exodusters leave the South for Kansas
1882	The Chinese Exclusion Act effectively ends immigration from China
1882	First general immigration law in U.S. history stipulates that "any convict, lunatic, idiot, or any person unable to take care of himself or herself without becoming a public charge" could be excluded
1885	Chinese residents expelled from a large number of Western towns
1886	The Great Upheaval, the year when nearly 10,000 strikes took place and almost 700,000 workers went on strike
1890s	Southern states gradually create "Jim Crow" segregation ordinances and make laws to disfranchise Black men
1892	Geary Act renews Chinese Exclusion
1896	Supreme Court case of Plessy v. Ferguson upholds segregation laws

1898	Spanish–American War results in the U.S. acquisition of Puerto Rico, Guam, and the Philippines
1898	U.S. annexes Hawaii
1898–1902	Philippine–American War, as Filipinos fight for their independence against U.S. rule
1898	Supreme Court case of U.S. v. Wong Kim Ark establishes that anyone born in the U.S. was a citizen regardless of race
1901–1904	The Insular Cases—Supreme Court rules that the Constitution did not automatically extend to Puerto Rico and the Philippines
1907	Gentlemen's Agreement with Japan effectively ends the immigration of Japanese workers
1907	Expatriation Act of 1907
1910–1920	Mexican Revolution
1914–1918	World War I. U.S. enters in 1917.
1917	Congress passes a literacy requirement for immigration
1917	Asiatic Barred Zone created
1917	Jones Act makes Puerto Ricans U.S. citizens
1921	Emergency Quota Act of 1921 passed
1922	Cable Act allows American women to keep their citizenship if they married a foreign man, provided he was not an alien ineligible to citizenship
1922	Supreme Court case of Ozawa v. U.S. upholds Asian ineligibility for naturalization
1923	Supreme Court case of Thind v. U.S. upholds Asian ineligibility for naturalization
1924	Johnson–Reed Act passed
1929–1941	The Great Depression
1929–1936	Mexican Americans "repatriated" to Mexico, many of them actually U.S. born citizens
1934	Tydings–McDuffie Act schedules Philippine independence for 1945
1939–1945	World War II. U.S. enters in 1941
1942–1945	Japanese American internment
1942	Bracero program brings Mexican guest workers into the U.S.
1943	Magnuson Act repeals Chinese Exclusion
1943	Zoot Suit Riots in Los Angeles
1944	Korematsu v. United States—the Supreme Court upholds Japanese internment
1944	President Roosevelt creates War Refugee Board
1945	President Truman issues Truman Directive, an executive order that gave preference to victims of Nazi persecution for immigration quotas

1946	Philippines declared independent
1946	Luce–Cellar Act gives Filipinos and South Asians a quota and makes them eligible for naturalization
1947–1991	Cold War with Soviet Union
1948	Displaced Persons Act creates a system for admitting refugees, although not entirely outside of the existing quota system
1952	Immigration and Nationality Act of 1952 (McCarran–Walter Act) passed
1953	President Truman's commission to study immigration releases their report, titled "Whom Shall We Welcome"
1954	"Operation Wetback" begins
1954	Brown v. Board of Education of Topeka—Supreme Court rules that segregated schools violate the equal protection clause of the Fourteenth Amendment
1955	Vietnam War begins
1956	Hungarian Revolution creates refugee crisis in Europe
1959	Fidel Castro takes power in Cuba
1964	Civil Rights Act of 1964 passed
1965	Voting Rights Act of 1965 passed
1975	Fall of Saigon ends Vietnam War
1980	Congress passes a new refugee act, allowing people to qualify as refugees even if they were not fleeing communism
1980	Mariel Boatlift
1986	Immigration Reform and Control Act (IRCA) passed
1990–1991	Gulf War
1992–1995	Bosnian War creates major refugee crisis in Eastern Europe
1994	Operation Gatekeeper and Operation Safeguard
1994	President Clinton ends special treatment for Cubans trying to reach the U.S. illegally
1994	California adopts Proposition 187, denying undocumented migrants access to state services
1994	North American Free Trade Agreement goes into effect
2001	September 11 attack on the World Trade Center and the Pentagon
2002	National Security Entry–Exit Registration System (NSEERS) created to track nonimmigrants in the U.S. from certain, mostly Muslim, countries
2003	Department of Homeland Security created, including immigration and naturalization services
2004	Minutemen Project founded

Who's who

Adams, Henry: (1843–?) A former slave and Black leader in Louisiana who advocated for Black migration from the South after Reconstruction, both to Kansas and to Liberia.

Aldrich, Thomas Bailey: (1836–1907) American writer, poet, and editor. Wrote the poem "Unguarded Gates" warning of the potential dangers of unrestricted immigration.

Aoki, Richard: (1938–2009) Japanese American civil rights activist and member of the Black Panther Party.

Austin, Moses: (1761–1821) American businessman who was the first to receive a land grant to settle Anglo-Americans in Spanish Texas, although he died before his plans came to fruition, leaving his son, Stephen Austin, to lead the colony.

Austin, Stephen: (1793–1836) Led the colony of Anglo-Americans in Mexican Texas, following the plans his father, Moses Austin, had made.

Blaine, James G.: (1830–1898) A Republican politician from Maine. Served in the House of Representatives 1863–1876 and in the Senate 1876–1881. While in the Senate, he advocated in favor of Chinese exclusion on the grounds that Chinese workers were unfair competition for white workers due to their low standard of living.

Bolton, John: (1948–) As ambassador to the United Nations during the Presidency of George W. Bush, Bolton maintained that the U.S. had no additional obligation to admit refugees from Iraq after the overthrow of Saddam Hussein.

Bouey, Harrison N.: (1849–1909) A teacher and Baptist minister who advocated Black emigration from the United States after Reconstruction, in particular supporting migration to Liberia, where he himself moved in 1878.

Brinch, Boyrereau: (c. 1742–1827) Born in West Africa around 1742, Boyrereau Brinch (also known as Jeffrey Brace) was enslaved and brought to the British colonies, where he later fought in the American Revolution and received his freedom.

Bulosan, Carlos: (1913–1956) Filipino novelist and poet who immigrated to the United States in 1930. Bulosan worked as a migrant farm worker and was a labor organizer. His most famous work is his autobiography, *America is in the Heart*.

Bush, George W.: (1946–) U.S. President 2001–2009. During his administration, Operation Streamline detained people caught crossing the U.S.–Mexico border illegally for future prosecution.

Carmichael, Stokely: (1941–1998) Civil rights activist and Pan-Africanist. Carmichael was one of the leaders of the Black Power movement and served as a leader both of the Student Nonviolent Coordinating Committee (SNCC) and of the Black Panthers.

Carter, Jimmy: (1924–) U.S. President 1977–1981. During the Mariel Boatlift, due to the large numbers of Cuban refugees arriving, Carter refused to grant them the full resettlement benefits that Cubans usually received.

Castañeda de Valenciana, Emilia: (1926–2020) Born in Los Angeles to Mexican parents, Emilia Castañeda was forced to "repatriate" to Mexico after her mother died and her father lost his job during the Great Depression. She was ultimately able to return to the United States and shared her experiences in an oral history.

Castro, Fidel: (1926–2016) Cuban revolutionary who led the communist revolution in that nation in 1959, and served as Cuba's prime minister during 1959–1976 and president during 1976–2011. In the wake of the Cuban revolution, many anti-Castro refugees sought to come to the United States.

Clements, George P.: (1867–1958) One of the organizers of the Agricultural Department of the Los Angeles Chamber of Commerce, Clements served as the group's manager from its founding in 1918 until 1939, in which position he expressed the belief that Mexican laborers were uniquely suited to seasonal farm work due to their "crouching and bending habits."

Clinton, Bill: (1946–) U.S. President 1993–2001. With the Cold War over, President Clinton announced that Cubans trying to reach the U.S. illegally would no longer receive special treatment. He also authorized $540 million for the construction of barriers at the U.S.–Mexico border and more than one thousand new border patrol agents to try to reduce unauthorized immigration.

Cohen, Rose: (1880–1925) A Russian Jewish immigrant who came to the U.S. in 1892. Cohen worked in garment sweatshops and was active in unionizing efforts. She later became an author and published an auto-biography titled *Out of the Shadow*.

Compeán, Mario: (twentieth century) civil rights activist who was one of the founding members of the Mexican American Youth Organization (MAYO) and La Raza Unida Party.

Cortina, Juan: (1824–1894) Led an uprising of Tejanos (Mexican Texans) in protest of how many of them were losing their land after Texas statehood.

Curtis, Hannah: (nineteenth century) Irish woman living in Mountmellick who sought to emigrate to the United States during the Irish Potato Famine.

DeWitt, John L.: (1880–1962) The commanding general of the Western Defense Command during World War II, General DeWitt advocated for the removal of Japanese Americans from the West Coast to internment camps on the grounds of national security.

Diaz, Porfirio: President of Mexico 1877–1880 and 1884–1911, the entire period of which is often referred to as the Porfiriato. His economic policies spurred migration from Mexico, as did the violence and instability that followed his reign during the Mexican Revolution.

Díaz, José: (1919–1942) Young Mexican American man found unconscious and dying in Los Angeles near the Sleepy Lagoon. His death led to an investigation into Mexican American gangs in Los Angeles, with hundreds of young men and women being questioned. Hostility towards "pachucos" ultimately led to the Zoot Suit Riots in 1943.

Dillingham, William: (1843–1923) Republican Senator from Vermont 1900–1923. Dillingham chaired the Senate committee on immigration which recommended quotas to cut down on the number of "new" immigrants from Southern and Eastern Europe.

Eire, Carlos: (1950–) Historian and Yale University professor, Eire was born in Havana in 1950 and came to the U.S. as a refugee at age eleven as part of Operation Peter Pan, a program that brought refugee Cuban children to the U.S.

Eisenhower, Dwight D.: (1890–1969) U.S. President 1953–1961. During the Hungarian Revolution of 1956, Eisenhower used the President's parole power to admit 38,000 Hungarian refugees.

Emi, Frank: (1916–2010) A native-born Japanese American (Nisei) who protested internment during World War II. Emi was one of the leaders of the Heart Mountain Fair Play Committee, which protested the drafting of native-born Japanese Americans who had been interned, and served eighteen months in federal prison for conspiring to violate the Selective Service Act.

Ford, Henry: (1863–1947) American automotive industrialist whose factories offered English-language classes featuring a mandatory graduation ceremony with workers marching into a large "melting pot" in traditional garb and coming out clothed as Americans.

Franklin, Benjamin: (1706–1790) Well-known American statesman and inventor from Pennsylvania. Although he subsequently supported immigration, he expressed qualms about the numbers of Germans moving to Pennsylvania in his *Observations Concerning the Increase of Mankind* in 1751.

Frethorne, Richard: An indentured servant in early seventeenth century Virginia. Frethorne died before finishing his term of service, despite efforts to convince his parents to raise money to buy him out of his contract.

Garvey, Marcus: (1887–1940) Jamaican political activist who founded the Universal Negro Improvement Association and African Communities League (UNIA-ACL). Garvey was a pan-Africanist who advocated unity between Africans and the African diaspora and pushed for an end to colonialism in Africa. He was also a Black separatist who supported the Back-to-Africa movement.

Grant, Madison: (1865–1937) Known primarily for his work as a eugenicist and promoter of scientific racism, Grant wrote *The Passing of the Great Race* in 1917, lamenting the supposed decline of the "Nordic" race in the United States.

Gual, Florence Bain: (twentieth century) New York City school teacher who faced the loss of her job over her marriage to a Cuban man, which under the terms of the Expatriation Act of 1907, revoked her U.S. citizenship.

Gutiérrez, José Angel: (1944–) A civil rights activist who was one of the founding members of the Mexican American Youth Organization (MAYO) and La Raza Unida Party.

Hirabayashi, Gordon: (1918–2012) An American-born sociologist of Japanese descent, Gordon Hirabayashi challenged Japanese internment and the curfews placed on Japanese Americans on the West Coast during World War II. The U.S. Supreme Court ruled in Hirabayashi v. U.S. (1943) that such restrictions were legal.

Huie Kin: (1854–1934) Emigrated from China to the United States in 1868 at the age of fourteen. Huie Kin converted to Christianity and, after working his way through college, became a Presbyterian minister. Reverend Huie founded the first Chinese Presbyterian Church in New York.

Johnson, Anthony and Mary: (seventeenth century) Originally appearing in historical records as a slave known as "Antonio, a Negro," Anthony

Johnson gained his freedom, married Mary, and purchased land in Virginia in the early 1600s.

Johnson, E.H.: (1841–1906) Prominent Baptist theologian and minister who taught at Crozer Theological Seminary. Johnson advocated for immigration restriction in the late nineteenth century.

Johnson, Lyndon Baines: (1908–1973) U.S. President 1963–1969. Johnson signed the Hart-Cellar Act of 1965 into law, which substantially changed U.S. immigration policy.

Kipling, Rudyard: (1865–1936) Prominent British journalist, novelist, and poet. Among his poems is "The White Man's Burden." This phrase, regardless of whether that was Kipling's original intention, was used by some Americans to support annexing the Philippines.

Korematsu, Fred: (1919–2005) During World War II, Korematsu challenged the legality of Japanese internment. The Supreme Court ruled in Korematsu v. U.S. (1944) that internment was legal, although the dissenting minority argued that internment violated Korematsu's rights as a U.S. citizen.

Krasnow, Miriam Gether: (twentieth century) Emigrated from Russia to the United States in 1910 at age eleven. In 1983, she participated in the Ellis Island Oral History Project, telling of her migration experience.

Laughlin, Harry: (1880–1943) Prominent sociologist and eugenicist who served as the superintendent of the Eugenics Record Office from its inception in 1910 to its closure in 1939. Laughlin provided extensive testimony to Congress in support of the Johnson-Reed Act of 1924.

Lazarus, Emma: (1849–1887) American author and poet who wrote the poem "The New Colossus" which is engraved on the base of the Statue of Liberty.

Lili'uokalani: (1838–1917) Hawaiian Queen who was overthrown by an American coup in 1893. She was imprisoned and Hawaii declared a republic.

Mai Zhouyi: (early twentieth century) Wife of a Chinese businessman and missionary from Canton who struggled to enter the U.S. when her husband was classified as a laborer despite his status as a restaurant owner. She spent more than forty days in detention on Angel Island, finally being released when she became too sick to remain in confinement.

Massasoit: (c. 1581–1661) The sachem or leader of the Wampanoag confederation during the initial English colonization of New England. The alliance he formed with the Puritans at Plymouth Colony helped them to survive their difficult first years.

McCarran, Pat: (1876–1954) Democratic politician from Nevada who served in the Senate in 1933–1954. McCarran was one of the authors of the McCarran-Walter Act of 1952, which reformed the immigration policies of the U.S. to remove the most overt racism, while still essentially keeping the racially-based system of quotas intact.

McKinley, William: (1843–1901) President from 1897 until his assassination in 1901. McKinley was President during the Spanish–American War and advocated for keeping the Philippines afterwards.

McWilliams, Carey: (1905–1980) American author and journalist who wrote widely about conditions in California, including the experiences of migrant farm workers and Japanese internment.

Meir, Golda: (1898–1978) Born in Kiev, Meir immigrated to the United States in 1906. She moved to Palestine in 1921, where she became a politician and served as prime minister of Israel in 1969–1974.

Metacom: (c. 1638–1676) Also known as King Philip, Metacom was a Wampanoag leader who led a coalition of the Algonquin peoples of New England against the English in 1675.

Mittelberger, Gottlieb: (1714–1758) German from the duchy of Württemberg who moved to Pennsylvania in the 1750s. He wrote a popular account of his travels there, titled *Journey to Pennsylvania*, before ultimately returning to Europe.

Morales, Beatrice: (twentieth century) Mexican immigrant who took a war job during World War II, despite her husband's disapproval, to prove that she could do her part.

Morales, Carlos: (twentieth century) Mexican immigrant who entered the U.S. as part of the World War II era bracero program, and debated "skipping out" on his contract to find work on his own, despite the risk of deportation for being in the U.S. illegally.

Obama, Barack: (1961–) U.S. President 2009–2017. A record 1.5 million people were deported during Obama's first term. Obama supported the Development, Relief, and Education for Alien Minors Act (DREAM Act) and provided some assistance to these undocumented youth through the Deferred Action for Childhood Arrivals program (DACA).

Ogawa, Louise: (twentieth century) A young Japanese American woman from San Diego who was interned at Poston, Arizona, during World War II. Ogawa was one of many in the camps who wrote letters to Clara Breed, the children's librarian at the San Diego Public Library.

Ono, Kimiko: (twentieth century) Emigrated from Japan to the United States, where she and her husband ran a tomato farm in California.

Opechancanough: (1554–1646) Brother of Wahunsonacock (Powhatan), who succeed him as leader of the Powhatan Confederacy. He led the confederation in war against the English in 1622, and warfare continued on and off until his death in 1646.

Opler, Morris: (1907–1996) American anthropologist and advocate for Japanese American civil rights during World War II. Opler worked as a community analyst at the Manzanar internment camp during the war, documenting the conditions of the Japanese Americans living there.

Otis, Harrison Gray: (1765–1848) Massachusetts politician and member of the Federalist Party who supported a higher tax on naturalization certificates as a way to keep out potentially dangerous radical immigrants from Europe.

Ozawa, Takao: (1875–1936) Japanese immigrant who sued when denied the right to naturalize. In the 1922 Supreme Court case of Ozawa v. U.S., the court ruled that as non-Caucasians, Japanese immigrants were not eligible for naturalization.

Prager, Robert: (1888–1918) A German immigrant who worked as a coal miner in Collinsville, Illinois. Prager was the only foreigner to be lynched during the nativist outbreak during World War I.

Purdy, Lupe: (twentieth century) Mexican immigrant who naturalized so that she could get a war job during World War II and do her part for the war effort.

Ranciglio, Alessandro: (late nineteenth–early twentieth century) Italian immigrant from Cuggiono who settled in the Italian neighborhood in St. Louis, known as "the Hill," where he worked as a blacksmith shoeing mules.

Reagan, Ronald: (1911–2004) U.S. President 1981–1989. Fighting communists in Central America was a major part of his foreign policy, with the result that refugees from non-communist dictators received little welcome in the United States.

Redal, Olav: (1882–1937) A Norwegian journalist who emigrated to the United States and settled in North Dakota, where his writings contributed to preserving the history of the Norwegian pioneer communities.

Rivera, Sandy: (late twentieth–twenty-first century) Undocumented youth and DACA recipient, Sandy Rivera became an advocate for the DREAM Act, giving a speech at the Indianapolis Women's March in 2018.

Roosevelt, Franklin D.: (1882–1945) Thirty-second U.S. President, 1933–1945. During World War II, Roosevelt created the War Refugee Board to provide some assistance to refugees in camps in neutral or allied nations, but otherwise did not take much action regarding refugee policy.

Roosevelt pushed Congress to repeal Chinese exclusion during the war, since they were an ally.

Ruiz, Francisco: (1783–1840) Mexican soldier and politician who supported the settlement of Anglo-Americans in Texas, and would later support Texas independence in 1836.

Schultz, Alfred P.: (twentieth century) Eugenics expert and author who wrote *Race or Mongrel* in 1908, warning that immigration was a threat to the racial purity of the United States.

Sikand, Sarabjit (Beenu): (late twentieth–early twenty-first century) Indian Sikh who immigrated to the U.S. in the 1990s after her marriage.

Singleton, Benjamin "Pap": (1809–1900) Born into slavery, Singleton managed to escape at age thirty-seven. He assisted other fugitive slaves, and after emancipation, became an advocate for Black migration from the South. He is considered the father of the Exoduster movement.

Takei, George: (1937–) Prominent actor, best known for his role as Hikaru Sulu on *Star Trek*. During World War II, George Takei and his family were forced to go to internment camps, first the camp in Rohwer, Arkansas, and then to Tule Lake, California.

Tape, Mamie: (late nineteenth–early twentieth century) American-born daughter of Chinese immigrants, Joseph and Mary Tape. When she was denied entry to the all-white Spring Valley School in San Francisco due to her race, her parents sued, on the grounds that she was being denied access to the public schools. Although they won their case before the California Supreme Court (Tape v. Hurley, 1885), the outcome was not the admission of Chinese students to the white schools, but rather the creation of segregated public schools for the Chinese.

Terrell, Mary Church: (1863–1954) Noted African American educator and civil right advocate, Mary Church Terrell was one of the first African American women to receive a college degree and became an activist campaigning for desegregation and Black women's suffrage.

Thind, Bhagat Singh: (1892–1967) An Indian immigrant who served in the U.S. Army during World War I, Thind sought naturalization afterwards and sued when he was denied. The Supreme Court ruled in the case of Thind v. U.S. (1923) that although Indians were defined as Caucasians by the science of the time, they were not considered white by the public when the law was made, making him ineligible.

Thomson, Alexander: (eighteenth century) A Scottish immigrant who settled in Pennsylvania during the eighteenth century and wrote a series of letters about his experiences which were subsequently published as a pamphlet, titled *News from America*, in 1774.

Tisquantum: (c. 1585–1622) Better known to history as Squanto, Tisquantum was a member of the Patuxet tribe of the Wampanoag confederation. He was captured by English sailors and sold into slavery in Spain, and later gained his freedom and lived in England for a while before making his way back to his homeland.

Truman, Harry: (1884–1972) U.S. President 1945–1953. During the aftermath of World War II, Truman used an executive order, sometimes referred to as the Truman Directive, to give refugees first priority in immigration quotas. Truman also pushed Congress to eliminate the racial basis of U.S. immigration policy, vetoing the McCarran-Walter Act of 1952 for essentially leaving the racial hierarchy of immigration quotas intact. He also created a commission to study immigration. Their report, titled "Whom Shall We Welcome" advocated replacing quotas with an overall cap on immigration.

Trump, Donald: (1946–) Forty-fifth U.S. President, elected in 2016 partially on a pledge to construct a wall along the border with Mexico to prevent unauthorized immigration. President Trump also signed an executive order shortly after his election placing a temporary ban on immigration from a number of predominantly Muslim countries.

Turnau, Julia: (nineteenth century) Emigrated from Bremen to the United States in 1842 at the age of twenty-three to marry Reverend George W. Wall. She left a detailed diary of her nine-week voyage.

Ulibarri, Sabine R.: (1919–2003) American poet and writer born in New Mexico who is regarded by many as one of the great thinkers of modern Latino literature. Ulibarri served with the U.S. Army Air Corps during World War II.

Vallejo, Salvador: (1813–1876) Prominent Californio whose family ultimately lost their entire estate in the Napa Valley after California was acquired by the United States, despite treaty protections that were supposed to prevent such loss.

Vélez, Manny: (twentieth century) Puerto Rican immigrant who moved to Chicago in 1949, due to "la fiebre" (the fever) for America that so many in his hometown of San Sebastián were experiencing. He lived in Chicago for twenty years before finally returning to San Sebastián in the early 1970s.

Wahunsonacock: (c. 1547–c. 1618) Also known as Powhatan, Wahunsonacock was the leader of the Powhatan Confederacy when the English first arrived in 1607 and founded Jamestown.

Walker, Francis Amasa: (1840–1897) American economist and first president of the American Economic Association, Walker advocated for immigration restriction to prevent migration of Southern and Eastern Europeans.

Wamsutta: (c. 1634–1662) Son of Massasoit who succeeded him after his death in 1661. He was taken into custody by the English in 1662 under suspicion of leading a plot against them and died shortly after this release, making his brother Metacom the new sachem of the Wampanoag.

Warrior, Clyde: (1939–1968) Native American civil rights activist and one of the founders of the National Indian Youth Council. He was a member of the Ponca Tribe of Oklahoma.

Warren, Earl: (1891–1974) American politician and judge who served as Governor of California during 1943–1953 and as Chief Justice of the Supreme Court in 1953–1969. During World War II, he was attorney general of California, in which position he supported the removal of Japanese Americans to internment camps.

Waxman, Al: (twentieth century) Editor of *The Eastside Journal*, an East Los Angeles community newspaper, that reported on the Zoot Suit Riots, serving as an exception to the rule that the Los Angeles Press was generally sympathetic to the rioting servicemen.

Wong Kim Ark: (1873–mid-twentieth century) Born in 1873 in San Francisco, Wong Kim Ark sued to claim his citizenship after he was refused reentry to the country. The Supreme Court ruled that the Fourteenth Amendment did apply to Asians and that Wong Kim Ark was thus a citizen.

Yasui, Minoru: (1916–1986) A lawyer from Oregon, Minoru Yasui was the son of Japanese immigrants. During World War II, he challenged Japanese internment and the curfew laws placed on Japanese Americans on the West Coast. The U.S. Supreme Court ruled in Yasui v. U.S. (1943) that such restrictions were legal.

Zangwill, Israel: (1864–1926) British author and playwright whose 1908 play "The Melting Pot" popularized the use of that term to describe the assimilation of immigrants into America.

Glossary

Alien and Sedition Acts: Passed in 1798, the Alien and Sedition Acts extended the waiting period for naturalization and allowed the President to arrest or deport aliens from nations with which the U.S. was at war or who were deemed dangerous.

Angel Island: The immigration station in San Francisco Harbor. It was the main entry port for Chinese immigrants and became a place of detention for many after the Chinese Exclusion Act was put into place.

Asian–Pacific triangle: Created by the Immigration and Nationality Act of 1952. Immigrants from this region were eligible for naturalization, and each nation received a quota of approximately one hundred, although there was an overall cap of two thousand for the region.

Asiatic Barred Zone: Created in 1917, excluding all Asians from the United States, except for residents of the Philippines, since it was a U.S. territory, and Japan, since the Gentlemen's Agreement was still in effect.

Asylum: People already in the United States who fear persecution if they returned to their home nation can apply for asylum.

Birthright citizenship: Enshrined in the Fourteenth Amendment, this establishes that anyone born in the United States is a citizen.

Braceros: Mexican guest workers during and after World War II who came to the United States on contracts to do agricultural and railroad work.

Burlingame Treaty of 1868: Treaty with China which explicitly stated among its provisions that Chinese people could migrate to the United States without restrictions.

Cable Act of 1922: Act which stated that women who married a foreign man would not lose their U.S. citizenship, unless they married a man who was ineligible for citizenship.

Chain migration: Occurs when migrants encourage friends and family to join them in America, thus resulting in people from specific locations in the Old World clustering together in the New World.

Chicano movement: 1960s movement to fight for Mexican American rights. Chicanos emphasized their pride in their indigenous roots, and that they were not immigrants, but rather conquered people living in their traditional homeland.

Chinese Exclusion Act: Law passed in 1882 that suspended the immigration of Chinese workers for ten years. Merchants, tourists, teachers, and students were still allowed to enter the U.S. The act was renewed for ten years in 1892, and ultimately made permanent.

Civil Rights Act of 1964: Act which outlawed segregation in restaurants, schools, and many other public places and forbade employers from discriminating based on race.

Cold War: The conflict between the Soviet Union and the United States, during the 1950s–early 1990s. Framed as a struggle between rival political and economic systems (authoritarian communism vs. democratic capitalism), this conflict was referred to as the "Cold War" since the rival powers did not confront one another directly in a "hot" or shooting war, but rather made war through propaganda and the use of proxies.

Cubic Air Ordinance: San Francisco ordinance which required all lodging houses to provide at least five hundred cubic feet of air per resident. Ostensibly a racially neutral health measure, this law was primarily enforced against the residents of Chinatown, where overcrowded boarding houses were commonplace.

Deferred Action for Childhood Arrivals (DACA): This program, created in 2012, allowed undocumented people to apply for a two year deferral of deportation and eligibility for a work permit and driver's license, provided they were under thirty-one, had arrived in the U.S. before age sixteen, were in school or had graduated from it, and did not have a criminal record.

Dillingham Commission: 1907 Congressional commission, headed by Senator William Dillingham, which investigated the issue of immigration, laying the groundwork for the Johnson-Reed Act of 1924.

Displaced Persons Act of 1948: The first specifically refugee legislation ever passed by the U.S. Congress, this act allowed 200,000 refugees to enter the U.S. over two years, although they were not admitted separately from the quota system, instead "mortgaging" quotas into the future to allow the admission of eligible refugees.

DREAM Act (Development, Relief, and Education for Alien Minors Act): Undocumented youth and their allies have been lobbying Congress for this since 2001. If passed, it would put undocumented minors on a path to citizenship or permanent residency, provided they met the eligibility requirements and completed either a college degree or two years of military service.

Emergency Quota Act of 1921: Set quotas for each nation limiting immigration to three percent of the total number of foreign born people from that nation in the U.S. in 1910.

Enemy aliens: Term used to refer to immigrants from a nation with which the U.S. was at war.

Eugenics: Movement to improve the genetics of the human population, often by attempting to either keep populations judged "inferior" out of the country or prevent them from reproducing.

Executive Order 13760 "Protecting the Nation from Foreign Terrorist Entry into the United States": Known informally as the "Muslim ban," this executive order issued by President Donald Trump banned entry from a number of predominately Muslim countries for 90 days and suspended refugee admissions for 120 days.

Exodusters: Black Southerners who sought to move to Kansas in the late 1870s and early 1880s, seeking to escape segregation and racially based violence in the South.

Expatriation Act of 1907: This act stated various ways in which Americans could forfeit their citizenship, which included women marrying a foreign man.

Fifteenth Amendment: Constitutional amendment, ratified in 1870, which forbade denying someone the right to vote based on their "race, color, or previous condition of servitude."

Foreign miners tax: Tax during the Gold Rush of 1849 that forced non-citizen miners to pay a fee. It was designed in particular to target Chinese and Latino miners.

Forty-eighter: Term used to refer to the German revolutionaries who led uprisings in central Europe in 1848, in an attempt to create a unified, democratic Germany out of the diverse German states.

Fourteenth Amendment: Constitutional amendment ratified in 1868 which established, among other things, that anyone born in the United States was a citizen.

Geary Act of 1892: This act renewed the Chinese Exclusion Act for another ten years, and also provided that all Chinese residents of the United States had to register with immigration officials and carry a certificate of residence with them.

General Immigration Act of 1882: The nation's first general immigration law placed a head tax on immigration and stipulated that "any convict, lunatic, idiot, or any person unable to take care of himself or herself without becoming a public charge" could be excluded.

Gentlemen's Agreement: Informal agreement between the United States and Japan in 1907. The United States agreed not to pass legislation forbidding immigration from Japan, and in exchange, the Japanese government agreed to stop issuing passports to Japanese workers seeking to go to the United States.

Homestead Act: Passed in 1862, this act allowed American citizens and immigrants who had declared their intention to become citizens to claim 160 acres of land for free. Immigrants not eligible for citizenship would not be eligible to stake claims under the Homestead Act.

Immigration Act of 1965: Also known as the Hart-Cellar Act, this act sought to create a less racially discriminatory immigration policy. 170,000 quota slots were given to the eastern hemisphere and 120,000 to the western, with no nation being allowed to use more than 20,000 slots. Priority was given to family reunification and job skills.

Immigration and Nationality Act of 1952: Also known as the McCarran-Walter Act, this act represented the first attempt to remove the racist features of the 1924 National Origins Act. However, although all nations did receive a quota and all immigrants were eligible for naturalization, the quotas were still very unequally distributed, with about eighty-five percent of quota slots going to Northwestern Europe.

Indentured servant: Someone who had sold their labor for a period of years (usually five to seven) to finance their journey across the Atlantic.

Immigration Reform and Control Act: 1986 law which sought to address the issue of unauthorized immigration by making it illegal to employ undocumented workers and providing a path to citizenship for those who had arrived before 1982.

Insular cases: Series of Supreme Court cases between 1901 and 1904 in which the Court ruled that the Constitution did not automatically extend to the territories, meaning that residents of Puerto Rico and the Philippines were not U.S. citizens.

Irish potato famine: Famine that occurred in 1845–1852 when a fungal blight destroyed much of the potato crop of Ireland several years in a row, killing between one and one and a half million people and forcing another two million to emigrate.

Japanese American internment: During World War II, the U.S. government forced 120,000 Japanese Americans, more than two-thirds of whom were native-born citizens, into ten concentration camps across the West, ostensibly as a protection against potential sabotage or spying.

Jim Crow Laws: Legislation created in the late-nineteenth century to maintain white supremacy by requiring segregation in public places and limiting the political and civil rights of Black Americans.

Johnson-Reed Act of 1924: Also known as the National Origins Act, this act created a restrictive immigration system by allocating quotas to each nation based on the percentage of the U.S. population each nation made up in 1890, before much of the "new" immigration from Southern and Eastern Europe took place.

Jones Act of 1917: Act which reorganized the Puerto Rican government and granted all Puerto Ricans U.S. citizenship.

Know Nothing Party: Nativist political party during the 1850s, which was particularly concerned with the effect that Catholic immigrants might have on American politics.

Korematsu v. U.S.: 1944 Supreme Court case which upheld the legality of Japanese American internment.

Ku Klux Klan: White supremacist organization created during Reconstruction to maintain white supremacy by intimidating Black Southerners. The group had a second resurgence in the early twentieth century, at which time it took on anti-immigrant and anti-Semitic stances as well as being anti-Black.

La Raza Unida Party: Chicano political party which attempted to make civil rights gains for Mexican Americans by working outside of the traditional two party structure.

Luce-Cellar Act of 1946: Gave the Philippines and India quotas of one hundred and made them eligible for naturalization.

Magnuson Act of 1943: Repealed the Chinese Exclusion Act, giving China a quota of 105 and making Chinese immigrants eligible for naturalization.

Mariel boatlift: In 1980, Fidel Castro announced that anyone who wanted to leave Cuba could do so from the port of Mariel, resulting in tens of thousands of people taking to the sea in boats, with about 130,000 crossing over the course of six months.

"Melting pot": Term referring to the idea that immigrants to the United States over time would "melt" into the general American population as they assimilated.

Middle passage: The portion of the slave trade crossing the Atlantic Ocean. Enslaved people were often tightly packed into slave trading vessels, leaving little room to move or even sit up.

Minutemen Project: A civilian organization that sought to patrol the U.S. border themselves, to report any illegal border crossings.

National Security Entry–Exit Registration System (NSEERS): Created in 2002 in response to 9/11, this program required nonimmigrant men from certain countries, nearly all majority Muslim, to report to immigration officials at regular intervals while they were in the United States, as well as whenever they took certain actions like changing a job, school, or address.

Nativism: Feeling of hostility towards immigrants—i.e. people perceived as being "non-native."

Naturalization: The process by which an immigrant becomes a citizen.

Naturalization Act of 1790: The first U.S. naturalization law, this act limited naturalization to free white persons who had lived in the U.S. for at least two years, a period which was increased to five in 1795.

"New" immigrants: Term created by the Dillingham Commission in 1907 to describe the racial suitability of immigrants. "New" immigrants were perceived as less desirable, and less white migrants, coming from Southern and Eastern Europe or Asia. The actual shift in immigration was more gradual and does not align neatly with these categories.

"Old" immigrants: Term created by the Dillingham Commission in 1907 to describe the racial suitability of immigrants. "Old" immigrants were perceived as more desirable, and whiter, migrants, coming from

Northern and Western Europe, including Great Britain, Germany, and Scandinavia. The actual shift in immigration was more gradual and does not align neatly with these categories.

One hundred percent Americanism: Sentiment during World War I that all immigrants should assimilate completely, and abandon any "hyphenated" identity they had as Irish Americans, Italian Americans, etc.

Operation Gatekeeper, Safeguard: Border Patrol operations in 1994, each focused on one portion of the U.S.–Mexico border, designed to cut down on unauthorized immigration.

Operation Streamline: 2005 Border Patrol operation that implemented a zero tolerance policy towards illegal entry and detained those caught attempting it for criminal prosecution.

Operation Wetback: 1954 Justice Department program that sought to use mass expulsion as a solution to unauthorized immigration, arresting and deporting thousands of undocumented workers.

Ozawa v. U.S.: 1922 Supreme Court decision ruling that Takao Ozawa, who was born in Japan, was not eligible for naturalization since he was not Caucasian.

Page Act of 1875: Act that forbade the "importation into the United States of women for the purposes of prostitution," particularly targeting women from "China, Japan, or any Oriental country," making it much more difficult for women from these groups to enter the country.

Plessy v. Ferguson: 1896 Supreme Court case ruling that segregated accommodations were acceptable, giving rise to the pro-segregation doctrine of "separate but equal."

Proposition 187: A 1994 ballot initiative in California, also known as the "Save Our State" initiative, which made undocumented immigrants ineligible for any public social services, public health care, and public education.

Puritans: Puritans maintained that the Church of England had not "purified" itself enough of Catholic elements during the Reformation. Founded colonies in New England.

Repatriation: When an immigrant returns to their home nation.

September 11: Also referred to as 9/11, this term refers to the 2001 attacks on the World Trade Center and Pentagon by terrorists backed by Al Qaeda flying hijacked airplanes.

Spanish–American War: In 1898, the U.S. went to war with Spain to help Cuba gain its independence, and acquired several of Spain's colonies, including Puerto Rico, the Philippines, and Guam.

"Tacoma Method": Refers to the violent expulsion of the Chinese population of Tacoma, Washington, in 1885.

Thind v. U.S.: 1923 Supreme Court case ruling that Bhagat Singh Thind was not eligible for naturalization because although Indians were considered Caucasian by the science of the time, they were not included in the popular definition of "white."

Third World Liberation Front: A coalition of various civil rights organizations, including Blacks, Latinos, Asians, and Native Americans, who went on strike in 1968 to protest the lack of diversity in academia.

Thirteenth Amendment: Constitutional amendment ratified in 1865 after the Civil War which forbade slavery or indentured servitude, except as punishment for a crime, in the United States.

Treaty of Guadalupe Hidalgo: 1848 treaty which ended the Mexican–American War, giving the U.S. a large portion of Mexico's territory and made Mexicans residing in the area U.S. citizens.

Truman Directive: Executive order which gave preference to victims of Nazi persecution for immigration quotas.

Tsenacommacah: An alliance of roughly 30 Native American tribes in the Chesapeake Bay region in the early seventeenth century. Also referred to as the Powhatan Confederacy.

Tydings-McDuffie Act: 1934 act that stated that the Philippines would be granted independence in 1945 and that effective immediately the Philippines would be treated as a foreign country for immigration purposes and be given a quota of fifty.

Unauthorized immigration: Immigrants who enter or remain in a nation without receiving the proper authorization. Also referred to as undocumented immigration or illegal immigration.

U.S. nationals: Status of Puerto Ricans and Filipinos after the U.S. acquired those territories. They were not U.S. citizens, but neither were they foreigners.

U.S. v. Wong Kim Ark: 1898 Supreme Court case ruling that Wong Kim Ark was a citizen, despite being of Chinese descent, because he had been born in the United States.

Voting Rights Act of 1965: Act which outlawed racial discrimination in voter registration.

Wampanoag Confederation: Native American confederation encountered by the Puritans in New England.

War Refugee Board: Created in 1944 by Franklin Delano Roosevelt's administration to assist refugees in neutral or allied nations during World War II.

"Wetbacks": Insulting term used since the early twentieth century for Mexican immigrants who crossed the border for work without going through proper immigration proceedings.

"White man's burden": Named for the poem by Rudyard Kipling, this term referred to the idea that, as the superior race, whites had a duty to protect and lift up inferior races, making colonialism thus a moral obligation.

"Whom Shall We Welcome": Report issued in 1953 by the commission on immigration created by President Harry Truman, which recommended doing away with national quotas for immigration, and replacing them with an overall cap on immigration.

Zoot Suit Riots: Riots that took place in Los Angeles in 1943 during World War II, when U.S. Navy men on shore leave rioted in Mexican neighborhoods, attacking Mexican and Black youth wearing zoot suits, as well as young people of color generally.

Part 1

Analysis and assessment

1   Migration to the British colonies

When the English first arrived in Tsenacommacah and named it Virginia, they were encountering a land that had been settled for millennia and where civilizations had risen and fallen, cultures had evolved and vanished, wars had been fought and peace had been made—in short, where all the activities of human life and "history" had taken place. Too often in American history we talk about the Americas as though they were sparsely populated before the Europeans arrived, and as though the Native Americans had static, unchanging societies that left the landscape largely unaltered—that is, almost as though they did not experience "history" in the same sense as Europeans did. We know this is not true, but more work is necessary to rectify the long omission of Native peoples from United States history.

This chapter, which examines the foundation of the British colonies and migration to them, will not refer to this process as "settlement" for that reason, since it creates the perception that this land was essentially empty and unused when Europeans arrived, when in reality, it had been "settled" thousands of years earlier. Far from encountering an empty land, the Americas were populated by millions of people when Columbus discovered them in 1492. Many scholars estimate that there were between six and seven million people living north of the Rio Grande in 1492, and some think as many as ten to twelve million. The numbers are difficult to estimate, partly because contact with Europeans was a demographic disaster for Native Americans. Conquest, war, and enslavement killed many, and the introduction of European diseases killed many more. Scholars estimate that many regions lost between fifty and ninety percent of their populations to disease epidemics. In that sense, the land the Europeans came to "settle" was not "empty" but rather had been at least partially "emptied" by the impact of colonization. Only on the eve of independence would the population of Europeans and Africans in the future United States east of the Mississippi surpass two million—thus bringing the population of the region back to the level it had been before the Europeans arrived.

The English arrive in Tsenacommacah—the Chesapeake

In the early 1600s, Tsenacommacah was an alliance of roughly thirty tribes under one paramount chief—a man named Wahunsonacock, better known to history as Powhatan—in what is now the tidewater area of Virginia. Wahunsonacock had created a powerful alliance during his lifetime. He became chief in the late 1500s, when he inherited the rule of six tribes on the James and York rivers, and by 1608, he had assembled an alliance of thirty tribes through warfare and diplomacy. The people of Tsenecommacah were farmers, with the women of the tribes growing corn, beans, and squash, among other crops. As was common in the Americas, they had no domesticated animals, so the hunting and fishing that the men performed was a crucial source of protein for their diets.

Wahunsonacock's empire was somewhat unusual in that time and place—most Native American confederacies in northeastern North America in the seventeenth century were smaller and looser than this. Any number of things might have inspired Wahunsonacock to take on the challenge of assembling this alliance, but the changes his people experienced during the 1500s because of contact with Europeans likely played a major role. European traders and explorers had been to the area, and the diseases they left behind killed many, making it harder for villages and tribes to maintain a viable population. Uniting for defense was thus useful, both against their native enemies in the interior, and against the Europeans, who occasionally kidnapped people when they stopped to trade.

This was the nation the British encountered when their ships arrived in the Chesapeake Bay in 1607 and established the colony of Jamestown. Historians estimate that there were about 14,000 subjects and 3,200 warriors living in Wahusonacock's territory when the English arrived. The paramount chief himself was in his sixties by this point, and as an experienced politician and leader, knew he had to manage these English carefully. He pursued a dual strategy towards them—on the one hand, he sought to keep the English weak enough that they would not seek to acquire too much land or spread out enough to trade with nations other than his own. On the other hand, he could not let them become so weak that they would abandon the colony entirely. By monopolizing access to English goods, Wahunsonacock could increase his own people's power at the expense of his enemies—an important consideration in a world of population decline.

Lack of food combined with a poor location made the survival of the English colony uncertain. Given the large number of colonists who expected to find gold or other mineral wealth, farming was not prioritized, with the result that the colony depended on assistance from the Native Americans, voluntary or forced, for its survival. Furthermore, the colony was located on an island in the James River at the point where the tidal flow from the ocean met the freshwater from the James. This meant the water was often quite stagnant, especially during dry weather, and pollutants were not flushed away quickly. Saltwater also seeped into the water table, making wells on the island slightly brackish. Starvation, salt poisoning, and diseases like typhoid and dysentery killed many.

During the winter of 1609–1610, known as the "starving time," more than half the 220 colonists in Jamestown perished, mostly due to starvation. George Percy, who had the misfortune to be Jamestown's leader at the time, described how men first ate their horses and dogs and then their "boots, shoes, or any other leather some could come by." He described them foraging in the woods for "serpents and snakes" and much more disturbingly, turning to cannibalism. Starving colonists did "those things which seem incredible, as dig up dead corpse out of graves and to eat them, and some have licked up the blood which hath fallen from their weak fellows." One man named Collines "murdered his wife, ripped the child out of her womb and threw it into the river, and after chopping the mother into pieces...salted her for his food." The survivors burned him at the stake.

Conditions began to improve by the late 1610s, when the colonists at Jamestown finally came upon a crop they could produce that would make a profit back in England—tobacco. Despite the fact that King James had dismissed smoking as "a custome lothsome to the eye, hatefull to the Nose, harmefull to the braine, daungerous to the Lungs," his subjects were gradually becoming addicted to the tobacco they obtained through trade with the Spanish empire. The amount of tobacco being imported to London increased rapidly during the early 1600s. In 1615 and 1616, merchants in London imported 2,300 pounds of tobacco from Virginia, and 57,000 from the Spanish. By 1617, Virginia exported 20,000 pounds, and by 1629, 1,500,000 pounds. The tobacco boom was underway.

Soon nearly everyone was planting tobacco, to the extent that when the new governor of the colony, Samuel Argill, arrived in 1617, he was astonished to find "the marketplace, and streets and all other spare places planted with tobacco" and most of the colonists "dispersed all about planting tobacco." This troubled the Virginia Company, which tried to convince its colonists to diversify, referring to tobacco as a "deceivable weed" and warning that the profits being obtained from its growth "might soon vanish into smoake." The same was true in the other Chesapeake colony, Maryland, which was founded in 1632 by a royal charter that had been granted to George Calvert, Lord Baltimore. It was never his intention that the colony become devoted to tobacco—as he put it, "I came not hither for toe plant...this stinking weede of America"—but tobacco had become the major crop of the colony within a decade.

Colonists' demands for land to produce tobacco increased dramatically, to the detriment of relations with the Powhatan Confederacy. Given the rapidity with which tobacco depleted the nutrients in the soil, and the rapid growth of the population after the tobacco boom started, the demand for new land was nearly insatiable. This ultimately led to bloodshed in 1622, when Opechancanough (Wahunsonacock's brother who had succeeded him) led the confederation in a major uprising against the English. Of the roughly 1,240 colonists in Virginia, 347 were killed. Warfare between the English and the people of Tsenacommacah continued off and on over the next twenty-odd years, finally ending in 1646 when Opechancanough was captured and killed.

The need for labor in the Chesapeake and the desire of poor people to move there resulted in the creation of an extensive system of indentured servitude, wherein a migrant would sign a contract agreeing to work for a period of years, generally five to seven, to pay off the cost of their voyage. Roughly 100,000 Britons, most of them English, migrated to the Chesapeake region during the seventeenth century, and approximately three-quarters of them went as indentured servants. Early on during the tobacco boom, when tobacco prices were still extremely high and good land was widely available, selling oneself into servitude was a gamble that could pay off handsomely, allowing the landless poor of England the opportunity to obtain land in America and ultimately buy their own indentured servants to work it. It definitely was a gamble, however. Although death rates improved over the "starving time" of the earliest years, life expectancy in the Chesapeake remained shorter than the English average for the remainder of the seventeenth century. Roughly one-quarter of indentured servants would not survive their term of service.

Many during the seventeenth century were willing to take this risk, however, given the economic distress of the times. England had experienced a long period of combined population growth and inflation in the late 1500s, with real wages dropping steadily through the 1620s. The economic distress was worsened by a decline in manorial obligations as landowners began managing their estates more like private property, ending customary practices like allowing tenants to gather firewood or graze animals on the common green. Furthermore, some tenants were being evicted entirely, as landowners switched land from farmland to sheep pasture to produce England's major export, wool. In the eyes of some elite Britons, one potential benefit of the American colonies was to remove some of this growing population of transient poor from Britain. As one contemporary put it, "what can be more beneficial to a commonweal, than to have a nation and a kingdom to transfer unto the superfluous multitude of fruitless and idle people (here at home daily increasing) to travel, conquer, and manure another land, which by the due intercourses to be devised may and will yield infinite commodities?"

This system of migration resulted in a society that looked very different from that of England. Not only were certain classes not represented, like the aristocracy and many types of artisans, but men were vastly overrepresented, outnumbering women six to one during the early years. As a result, family formation was difficult and people tended to marry late, men because of the difficulty of finding a woman to marry, and women because they often were not free to marry until they had fulfilled the terms of their indenture. Given the high death rates, marriages often did not last long, and were generally followed by one or two more. As a result, families were more complex than in England, with assorted step-parents raising children from multiple marriages. Most children had lost at least one parent by the time they reached adulthood, and more than one-third of the children born in Virginia lost both.

Indentured servitude in the Chesapeake was a more brutal system than it had been in England. [Document 1] Servants would receive "freedom dues" after serving their term, generally including a suit of clothes, some food and tools, and a claim on fifty acres of land. But during their time of service, indentured servants had little control over their lives. Their owners could impose any discipline they wanted on them, including physical beatings, and could sell them at will, at least for the time remaining on their contract. Food and housing were often rudimentary. Additional time could be added by the courts, for "crimes" including being unruly, trying to escape, or having a child. For female servants, this presented a double form of punishment, since they were vulnerable to sexual abuse from masters and if they had a child as a result, would be sentenced to spend more time with their abuser.

As late as 1660, the vast majority of unfree people coming to Virginia were indentured servants. There were a few African slaves as well—about nine hundred out of a total non-Native American population of twenty-five thousand. Forced migrants from Africa first arrived in Virginia in 1619, when a Dutch trader sold twenty individuals in exchange for supplies. Given that the English colonists in Virginia had no direct experience with slavery to guide them, the experiences of these first Africans in America varied widely. For much of the seventeenth century, at least some Africans were able to obtain their freedom and live in near equality with the English population. By 1668, for example, roughly one-third of the fifty-nine Africans living in Northampton County, Virginia, were living as free men and women, and a few of them also owned property. One of the best known examples was the man known as "Antonio, a Negro" when he was sold into slavery at Jamestown in 1621. Although he worked as a slave for many years, he ultimately was able to gain his freedom and obtain land. He and his wife assimilated to English culture, baptizing their children in the established church and Anglicizing their names, to become Mary and Anthony Johnson. During his lifetime, Anthony Johnson was not only able to obtain a farm for himself, but to win court cases in disputes with his English neighbors, indicating that he had at least some standing as a member of the community.

During much of the seventeenth century, enslaved Africans—and some enslaved Native Americans—worked and lived alongside indentured servants. There were not yet major differences in their treatment, with both groups being treated extremely poorly. We know that African slaves and British indentured servants worked, lived, and socialized together, and that they sometimes made common cause together in resisting their ill treatment. Advertisements for runaways sometimes mention that groups were composed of both enslaved people and indentured servants, and a

1661 Virginia law punished any English servant who "shall run away in company of any negroes who are incapable of making satisfaction by addition of time"—i.e. because they were already serving for life—by making the English servant work the additional time for the slave's master.

Slavery ultimately became more important in the Chesapeake as the supply of indentured servants began to decrease. Conditions in southeastern England had improved by the late 1600s, with the result that fewer people were willing to sell themselves into servitude. As forced migration through the African slave trade increased, the demographics of the African population of the Chesapeake changed. Tobacco planters preferred to purchase men rather than women, so the sex ratio was skewed, with roughly two men being brought to the region for every woman. The death rate also increased, as people who had already been weakened by the experience of enslavement and the Middle Passage finally succumbed to disease and overwork in the New World. Roughly one-quarter of the enslaved people who arrived in the Chesapeake in the late seventeenth century were dead within a year. [Document 2]

This demography gradually changed, as a new generation of native-born African Americans came of age and started having children. By the 1740s and 1750s, African Americans were coming to outnumber Africans in the enslaved population of the Chesapeake, although there were still parts of the region where the situation was reversed. Nonetheless, there still were many people being forced into slavery and brought to the English North American colonies throughout the 1700s, with more than 134,000 arriving during that century. Most of those brought to the mainland went to either the Chesapeake region or to Carolina. Many more enslaved people went to the British West Indies—more than 609,000 during the eighteenth century—where their labor produced at first tobacco and over time, the even more valuable commodity of sugar. Barbados alone received more slaves than all the continental British colonies in any given year, and Jamaica nearly twice as many. Together, Africans and African Americans became an increasingly important part of the population of the Chesapeake. In 1680, there were roughly 4,300 Africans or African Americans in Virginia and Maryland, making up about seven percent of the non-Native American population. By 1750, that number had grown to 151,000, or forty percent of the non-Native American population of the Chesapeake.

The creation of racially based slavery involved the limitation of the rights of free Africans and African Americans as well as those who were enslaved. By the 1670s, free Blacks in the Chesapeake were forbidden to carry weapons, or to hire white indentured servants. By 1705, they had lost the right to testify in court. Free Black people were barred from serving in the militia, holding office, or voting. They faced different and more severe punishments for crimes than whites. The governor of Virginia made the goal of these laws explicit in 1723, when he described their intention to fix "a perpetual Brand upon Free-Negros & Mulattos by excluding them from that great Priviledge of a Freeman" in order to "make the free-Negros sens-ible that a distinction ought to be made between their offspring and the Descendants of an Englishman, with whom they never were to be Accounted Equal."

New England—a Puritan "city on a hill"

The migration stream that went to the New England colonies was smaller in number and shorter in duration than that which went elsewhere—roughly thirteen thousand people migrated to the area during the 1630s and 1640s. Despite its relatively small size, however, the descendants of these immigrants commemorated this as the Great Migration, because they saw the first colonists of New England as having a unique religious mission. They were members of a group sometimes known as the Puritans, from their desire to "purify" the Church of England of what they perceived as excessive Roman Catholic features. The first colonists to go to New England had given up hope of purifying the Church of England directly, either out of concern that their opposition would be punished or out of the belief that their purifica-tion efforts were futile. Instead, they decided to separate from the Church of England, and cross the Atlantic to set up their own society in America.

There were non-Puritans present in New England from the beginning, although in small enough numbers that leaders could still feel like they were creating a Puritan society. Known as "strangers" or "particulars," these indi-viduals were a source of strain on communities. The anarchic tendencies within Puritanism also resulted in internal splits; Puritans were far from unanimous in their diagnosis of the problems of the Church of England or their solutions for how to fix them. As a result, New England was made up a number of colonies, some founded by groups of Puritans with slightly different ideas. Some dissenters were ultimately banished from the region altogether, and migrated to Long Island in the Dutch New Netherlands.

As with all the English colonies, the Puritans were moving onto land inhabited by Native Americans. In this case, the area was controlled by the Wampanoag confederation, a group which formed part of a tripartite alliance with the Nauset on Cape Cod and the Massachusett farther north. All three groups spoke some variant of Massachusett, and referred to their home as the Dawnland—i.e. the place where the sun rose. Themselves, they called the "People of the First Light." The Wampanoag were farmers living in permanent villages, although they did shift from their "summer place" by the coast to a "winter place" farther inland, to avoid the worst of the winter storms.

Europeans had been visiting the Dawnland at intervals since the 1500s, with enormous impacts on the lives of the indigenous population. In some cases, people were hauled away into slavery—Tisquantum, better known to American history as Squanto, was one such individual, kidnapped with at least nineteen others by English sailors and sold into slavery in Spain.

Disease was another impact; by the time Tisquantum obtained his freedom and returned to his homeland, disease had so ravaged the population that many villages had been entirely abandoned. Particularly bad epidemics in 1617 and 1618 had reduced the population from an estimated fifteen thousand to only about one thousand by the time the first group of Puritan migrants—commonly known as the Pilgrims—arrived. The Pilgrims actually lived initially in the abandoned remnants of Tisquantum's hometown of Patuxet, and ransacking the abandoned Wampanoag homes in the area helped them to survive their first difficult winter.

The Wampanoag also assisted the Pilgrims directly. Their leader, Massasoit, was seeking allies because of the devastating impact the epidemics were having on his people. These epidemics had also devastated the Wampanoag's allies while mostly missing their traditional enemies to the west, the Narragansetts. This is possibly why Massasoit approached the Pilgrims about making an alliance in the spring of 1621. Their assistance helped the Puritans to establish themselves, and also allowed the Wampanoags to gain some power by serving as middle men for trade goods for nations to the west.

The colonies that the Puritans created were different in many ways from the other British colonies, particularly the plantation colonies farther south. The initial migration was much more homogeneous than that of any of the other English colonies. The majority of the population was composed of Puritans of middling means from England, most of whom migrated in family groups, thus resulting in greater gender and generational balance than other English colonies experienced early on. Nearly eighty-eight percent of New England migrants came as part of a family and forty-three percent were women, making the migrant population look much more like that of England, especially compared with colonies like the Chesapeake where the migrant population was overwhelmingly young, male, and unmarried.

Economically as well, there were some differences. The New England colonies were too far north to grow many of the most profitable crops. Most migrants to New England became farmers, seeking what they called a "competency"—i.e. to have enough resources to support their family in safety and some degree of comfort—rather than to grow wealthy. The colonists ultimately found resources they could export, including timber, agricultural produce, and fish that were sent to southern Europe and the West Indies. As this commerce increased, so did shipbuilding and the other maritime trades, until by the end of the seventeenth century, the New England colonies had successful economies that combined a diverse set of trades, including farming, shipbuilding, fishing, and commerce.

Ultimately, as New England grew, continued demand for land strained the Puritans' relationship with their Native American neighbors to the breaking point. By 1662, English suspicions of a rumored plot against them led them to take Wamsutta, who had taken over as ruler from his father Massasoit, into custody for interrogation. They released him, but he was very ill and died on the way home, making his brother Metacom, known as King Philip to the English, the ruler. Metacom ultimately went to war with the English in 1675, leading a coalition of the Algonquin peoples of New England, to try to restore balance. They had some success at first, attacking more than half the English towns in New England. The English countered by attacking Native American villages and destroying their food supplies. As starvation led to increased illness in the summer of 1676, the war came to an end.

The Lowcountry—a colony of a colony

Farther south in Carolina, the process of colonization looked very different than in the Chesapeake or New England. The colony was officially chartered in 1663, and the first major wave of English colonists were divided roughly evenly between England and the West Indies, particularly Barbados, in terms of their origin. The English colonies in the West Indies had been going through a transition period, as sugar replaced tobacco as the major crop being produced. Planters who could not get land or who lacked the capital to purchase the expensive equipment needed for sugar production went to Carolina seeking better opportunities. They brought their enslaved people with them, so African slavery was a part of Carolina from its founding.

Indentured servitude was also a presence, at least during the colony's earliest years, and about three-fifths of the migrants coming from England were indentured servants. This situation would not last, however, since the supply of indentured servants was already decreasing during the last decades of the seventeenth century. Slaves from Africa and the West Indies made up the bulk of unfree migrants to Carolina.

At first, the main economic purpose of the Carolinas was to produce supplies to support the valuable sugar plantation colonies of the West Indies. In particular, grain and cattle were among the major crops, with the enslaved population of the Carolinas laboring to feed the enslaved people of the West Indies. Things changed abruptly when planters discovered the much larger profits they could produce in the Carolina Lowcountry by growing rice and indigo. As with the tobacco boom in the Chesapeake, the shift to rice cultivation in the Lowcountry led to an increase in the importation of enslaved people directly from Africa and a deterioration of the conditions in which they lived. By 1700, there were almost 2,400 Africans in the colony, by 1730, almost 23,000, and by 1750 there were 40,000 Africans and African Americans in South Carolina, making up almost forty percent of the total non-Native American population.

Enslaved people were more likely to be isolated and formed a larger percentage of the population than in the Chesapeake, since rice plantations were fairly unhealthy areas that were avoided by the white population, aside from a few overseers who were hired to run the plantations for the often absentee masters. This resulted in the creation of slightly different African American communities in the Lowcountry—in particular, a unique creole African American culture and language known as Gullah-Geechee developed in the South Carolina and Georgia Sea Islands, and continues to exist to the present day.

The major dependence on slavery affected relationships with Native Americans in the Lowcountry. In particular, planters feared that Native Americans might make common cause with enslaved people in case of rebellion, or at the very least, might shelter runaways. As a result, English policy sought to establish barriers between Native Americans and African Americans by forbidding African Americans from entering Native American lands and rewarding Native Americans for returning fugitive slaves. A 1763 treaty with the Creeks promised them goods in the value of five pounds for each fugitive they returned. Such efforts were not always successful, however, and African Americans and Native Americans did meet, live together, intermarry, and resist English domination together.

The colony of Georgia was almost an exception to the rule of the early importance of African slavery in the Lowcountry. Founded partly to serve as a buffer against threats from Spanish Florida and partly to assist the poor, the colony was chartered in 1723, well after the plantation revolutions in the Chesapeake and the Lowcountry led to massive dependence on enslaved labor. By keeping land grants small and forbidding slavery, Georgia's trustees hoped to make their colony a refuge for the poor of Britain. Instead, they found that few wanted to move there—only a few thousand had done so by 1752—and that migrants complained that not being allowed to own slaves was limiting their economic opportunities. The trustees surrendered their charter to the crown in 1752, and with all restrictions removed, the colony quickly came to resemble South Carolina closely in its dependence on the production of rice and indigo using enslaved labor.

The middle colonies—diverse European migration

The middle colonies—usually taken to include New York, Pennsylvania, and New Jersey—had the most diverse population of any of the British North American colonies. This is partially because of how they were founded. New York began as the Dutch colony of New Netherlands, which was founded in the early seventeenth century by the Dutch West India Company in hopes of creating a base for trade with the Native Americans. Unlike the British colonies, New Netherlands had no land policy that would encourage small farmers to migrate. Furthermore, conditions in the Netherlands were good enough that few people were interested in crossing the Atlantic seeking opportunities. As the directors of the West India Company put it in 1644, they could not attract migrants, "not so much for want of population, with which our provinces swarm, as because all those who will labor in any way

Figure 1.1 This sketch by Joost Hartgers, while probably not a historically accurate representation of the layout of New Amsterdam, does illustrate the presence of both Native Americans and Europeans in the colony.

Source: Joost Hartgers, "t' Fort nieuw Amsterdam op de Manhatans," in *Beschrivinghe van Virginia, Nieuw Nederlandt, Nieuw Engelandt*, Amsterdam, 1651. JCB Archive of Early American Images, John Carter Brown Library, Brown University.

here, can easily obtain support, and therefore, are disinclined to go far from home on an uncertain outcome."

As a result, only about half of the nine thousand residents of New Netherlands were actually from the Netherlands. Other residents of the colony included Belgian Walloons, Sephardic Jews, subjects of a number of different German states, and a few Swedes and Finns, particularly in the Delaware Valley. Migrants from the neighboring English colonies were also a presence, particularly on Long Island, where colonists who were disgruntled over religious dissention or struggles over land in the neighboring New England colonies came to start anew. Father Isaac Jogues, a French Jesuit priest visiting Manhattan in 1646, reported that eighteen different languages were being spoken there—including European, Native American, and African tongues—by a population of about four hundred to five hundred.

African slavery was a part of that diversity almost from the very beginning of New Netherlands, with accounts as early as 1625 mentioning the presence of enslaved Africans. By 1639, there were perhaps one hundred Africans in the colony. In New Amsterdam, the colony's main city, there were about 150 Black people in 1655 and 375 in 1664, seventy-five of whom were free. Africans and African Americans thus formed roughly twenty to twenty-five percent of the town's population and about four percent of the colony's. Some enslaved people belonged directly to the Dutch West India Company, which used them to create much of the infrastructure for the new colony, including clearing land to make farms, constructing buildings, and creating ship yards. Some company-owned slaves held the status of "half-freedom," in which they were allowed to live and work at liberty, but were required to pay a substantial annual fee to the company, as well as provide them with labor if required. Given that the company did not have work for their enslaved labor force to do all the time, this allowed them to avoid the cost of feeding them, while still profiting from their labor and having the ability to summon them when needed.

Because New Netherlands was under Dutch law instead of English, the lives of women there differed in some significant legal aspects from those of their sisters in neighboring colonies, given that women were not subordinated as completely to their husbands as they were in England. They could continue to own property after marriage and have a civil identity— that is, they could sign contracts, conduct business in their own name, and sue and be sued in the courts. After England took over New Netherlands in 1664 and named it New York, those in the colony gradually began to acculturate to English ways, until the situation of women in New York was no different from that in the other English mainland colonies.

Slavery, on the other hand, survived the transition, and even continued to grow. By 1664, when the English took over, there were about 1,500 people living in New Amsterdam, and ten percent of them were African. By 1737, a census showed 8,666 people in New York, 6,947 of them white and 1,719 Black, nearly all of whom were enslaved. In fact, for much of the eighteenth century, the only city in the British North American colonies that had a higher percentage of enslaved people in its population than New York City was Charleston. Under British rule, the slave code of New Netherlands was made stricter and more slaves were brought in—between 1700 and 1774, about 6,800–7,400 enslaved people were forcibly imported, about thirty percent straight from Africa and the rest from the Caribbean, although it is possible they had only stopped there briefly on the way, given that many had African names.

Another of the middle colonies—Pennsylvania, chartered in 1681— would also add diversity to England's New World colonies. William Penn, the proprietor, had hoped to create a colony dedicated to complete religious toleration, in accordance with Quaker principles. Penn did a good job of convincing people to move to his colony—by 1684, about four thousand people had done so. Most of the migrants came from England, Wales, and parts of the European continent that had substantial Quaker populations, including the Netherlands, the southwestern German states, and the German-speaking parts of Switzerland. By 1700, there were about eighteen thousand colonists in Pennsylvania.

Religious toleration motivated these immigrants, but so did the chance to obtain cheap land. During Penn's lifetime, he insisted that all land taken by colonists was first purchased legitimately from the Lenni Lenape chiefs, who controlled the area. As a result, Pennsylvania had a much better relationship with its Native American population than many other English colonies, to the extent that Native Americans from surrounding colonies sometimes fled to Pennsylvania seeking refuge or justice. As one Native American told the government of Pennsylvania, "The People of Maryland do not treat the Indians as you & others do, for they make slaves of them & sell their Children for Money."

Colonists in Pennsylvania found that they could prosper well by producing things to meet the needs of the rest of the British Atlantic world. Much of the grain grown for export in Pennsylvania, for example, went to feed enslaved people in the West Indies, and flax was grown that was sent to the linen makers in Ireland. This growth put pressure on the good relationships with the Native Americans that Penn had tried to cultivate, however, and by the second quarter of the eighteenth century, many groups were being driven west and out of Pennsylvania altogether. By 1750, Pennsylvania's population included Germans, Irish, Scots, Welsh, Huguenots from France, and enslaved Africans. Not only Quakers, but English themselves were a minority in this colony. Alluding to the difficulties authorities faced in trying to govern such a diverse population, eighteenth century German Gottlieb Mittelberger described Pennsylvania as "heaven for farmers, paradise for artisans, and hell for officials and preachers." [Document 3]

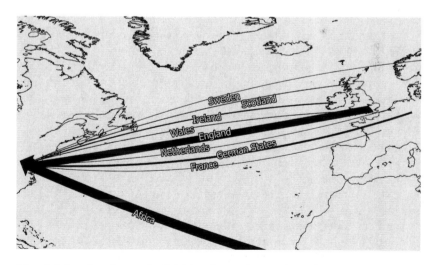

Map 1.1 Immigration to the British colonies during the Colonial Period

Eighteenth-century migration

Migration to the American colonies became even more diverse during the eighteenth century. In 1700, there were about 250,000 non-Native American people resident in the British mainland colonies, nearly all of them either English or African in ancestry. By 1776, that population had grown to 2.5 million, a tenfold increase, and also included many Germans, Scots-Irish, and others, in addition to hundreds of thousands more Africans and African Americans. As a result, by 1776 the English were a minority even of the non-Native American population of their colonies. Migration from England as a whole decreased in the eighteenth century as conditions there improved further. English people formed about nine-tenths of the migration to the mainland British and Dutch colonies in the seventeenth century (about 160,000 people), but only about 72,000 chose to go in the eighteenth century, forming about one-fifth of the migration to the British mainland colonies from Europe during that century. The non-English European migrants changed as well; over ten thousand Dutch, Swedes, and French Huguenots migrated in the seventeenth century, and very few did in the eighteenth. The two single largest groups of European migrants during these years were migrants from the German states and Scots-Irish migrants from Northern Ireland.

Scholars divide the eighteenth century migration of Germans to the British colonies into three waves: one at the end of the seventeenth century and the start of the next (1682–1709), one from 1709–1714, and the largest wave by far between 1717 and 1775. The first wave was primarily due to religious persecution in central Europe, and mostly consisted of organized pietist groups migrating to Pennsylvania to take advantage of Penn's offer of religious toleration. A major agricultural disaster in 1709 encouraged a few thousand more Germans to go to New York's Hudson River Valley. The third migration, in addition to being much larger (about 80,000 as compared to 4,000–5,000 in the first two waves combined) was inspired more by long-term conditions rather than a recent disaster. Land scarcity and overpopulation were beginning to threaten the ability of German families to maintain their status in Europe, making migration elsewhere seem desirable. The majority of these migrants ultimately went to Pennsylvania.

About 100,000 migrants came from the Irish county of Ulster between 1718 and 1775. Naming this group poses some difficulties, and did at the time as well. Most were descended from Scottish Presbyterians who had migrated to the north of Ireland. Today, we tend to identify them as Scots-Irish, although it was not a term they generally used. They did not see themselves as being the same as the mostly Catholic Irish, but also did not identify as Scots, preferring to call themselves northern dissenters. They lived on the cultural margins and faced discrimination both in Ireland and in the American colonies. As Presbyterians, they did not share the dominant status accorded to Irish Protestants who were members of the established church, meaning that they could not participate in government and tended to rent rather than own land. In America, they tended to live on the frontier, beyond the reach of much of society and to be quite mobile. They would face discrimination, particularly from English colonists who held a prejudice against Irish of any kind, seeing them as drunks and criminals.

During the eighteenth century, there was concern, particularly in the more diverse middle colonies, that too many non-English migrants were coming to the colonies. In response to the Scots-Irish migration, James Logan, the provincial secretary of Pennsylvania, wrote that "It now looks as if Irel[an]d or the Inhabitants of it were to be transplanted hither" and that "[W]e may easily believe there are some grounds for the common apprehensions of the people that if some speedy Method be not taken, they will soon make themselves Proprietors of the Province." Some Americans apparently agreed with him, based on the Boston mob that attempted to stop a group of Protestant Irish migrants from landing in the eighteenth century.

Anti-German sentiment was common as well. By the 1750s, the Pennsylvania Provincial Assembly was debating how they should respond to the large numbers of Palatine Germans moving there, worrying that they were bringing with them both disease and crime. In his *Observations Concerning the Increase of Mankind* (1751), Benjamin Franklin expressed his objections to German immigration, many of which would be repeated throughout American history with other groups of immigrants. As Franklin put it,

> Why should the Palatine boors be suffered to swarm into our Settlements, and by herding together establish their Language and Manners to the Exclusion of ours? Why should Pennsylvania, founded by the English, become a Colony of *Aliens*, who will shortly be so numerous as to Germanize us instead of us Anglifying them, and will never adopt our Language or Customs, any more than they can acquire our Complexion.

In general, however, there seems to have been a common assumption among most English Americans that the Germans and Scots-Irish could assimilate. Franklin himself later abandoned these nativist ideas and actually encouraged European immigration. In fact, Thomas Penn, one of proprietors of Pennsylvania said of the Germans that they would "certainly by degrees loose their attachment to their Language, and become English, and as they acquire property I dare prophecy will become good Subjects."

Conclusion

Early migration to the mainland English colonies thus set the stage for the future United States in a number of ways. Although the initial migration from Europe was predominantly English, as time passed a varied group of

European migrants decided to move to the British North American colonies, with the eighteenth century migration in particular setting patterns that would be followed in the nineteenth century as well. Europeans were not alone in these colonies either; hundreds of thousands of forced migrants from Africa formed an increasingly large part of the population and a crucial part of the labor force. Additionally, the indigenous population had not vanished, despite European fantasies about "unsettled" lands, and continued to interact with and fight back against the colonizers. New ideas about race had been developed out of these interactions, as English and other European colonists sought ways to set themselves apart from the "non-white" Native American and African American populations. These developments set the stage for the massive population growth that would accompany American independence.

2   Immigration during the early national and antebellum eras

The American Revolution set up a relatively liberal system of immigration and naturalization, but one that was deeply based on race. As a result, for all migrants to the United States, part of their migration experience included learning their place in the racial hierarchy. For some, this was a place of privilege, even if occasional discrimination made it seem somewhat precarious. Others, however, found themselves in a permanent second-class status, ineligible for naturalization.

This would remain true as immigration to the young United States grew dramatically during middle third of the nineteenth century. Although immigration continued throughout the early national period and increased a bit during the 1830s, this increase was dwarfed by the wave of immigrants arriving in the United States during the 1840s and 1850s. Although the bulk of these migrants arrived from Ireland or one of the German states, the United States also received immigration from elsewhere in Europe and from China on the west coast. Another group—Mexicans residing in the territory annexed by the United States after the Mexican–American War—suddenly found themselves Americans after the border crossed them. All of these groups found themselves living in a young republic that teetered between extending welcome to new immigrants and expressing fears that they were too culturally or racially different from the Anglo-Saxon norm to be assimilated.

Impact of the Revolution

The American Revolution created a new nation, and with it a new national identity. Former subjects of the British Empire were suddenly citizens of the United States, and had to define the process by which future immigrants could become citizens as well. In general, most Americans of the revolutionary era liked the idea that their new country could be a refuge for others fleeing the tyranny of European monarchies, and the prospect of "unsettled" land to the west made population growth seem both necessary and desirable.

The Naturalization Act of 1790, the nation's first naturalization law, made the process relatively easy, but entirely dependent on race. Any free white person could apply for naturalization after living in the United States for two years, a period which was increased to five in 1795. This act set trends that would remain in effect for the next century. A five-year waiting period, with a brief exception during the administration of John Adams, would remain the norm, and race would continue to play a central role in how citizenship was defined well into the twentieth century. [Document 4]

The citizenship status of Black Americans was unclear in the wake of independence. Many drew on the ideology of the revolution, with its inspiring words about all men being created equal, to attack slavery and fight for their own equality. Some white Americans agreed that slavery had no place in a republic, and a few states put slavery on the road to extinction within their boundaries, albeit very gradually. At the same time, however, commitment to the institution of slavery, especially in the Deep South, only grew after the revolution, and when the Constitution was created, the delegates from these states insisted that it contain important provisions to defend the institution. One of those provisions ensured that the international slave trade could not be outlawed until 1808. As a result, there would be another twenty years of forced migration from Africa to the American South.

Free Black Americans also faced challenges to their citizenship. Although they would not have been eligible for naturalization if they had been immigrants, most free Black Americans were native-born, and considered themselves citizens of the new nation. They faced varying restrictions on their rights in different states, however, making their citizenship of a more contested nature than that of white Americans. Some whites doubted that Blacks and whites could live alongside each other without conflict. Their solution was colonization, by which they meant sending free Blacks "back" to Africa—a continent few of them had ever seen—or somewhere in Latin America. The fact that this was seldom if ever referred to as deportation demonstrates the very different view colonization supporters had of the citizenship of white and Black Americans.

For the Native Americans living in the new United States, the revolution put them in a very difficult position. After independence, the United States took a more aggressive approach to dispossessing Native Americans of their land. Furthermore, the new citizenship being defined would not include Native Americans. Their status was left ambiguous, since they were recognized as nations in some ways, but lived within the boundaries of the United States. An attempt to clarify their status finally came from the Supreme Court in 1831 in the case of Cherokee Nation v. Georgia, when Chief Justice John Marshall rejected the Cherokee's claim to be an independent foreign nation and declared them to be "domestic dependent nations" living on United States territory. This status put Native Americans in an incredibly disadvantaged position relative to white Americans, whether immigrant or native born. With a few exceptions, most Native Americans would not receive U.S. citizenship until the twentieth century.

Immigration during the early national period

Immigration, which had largely been cut off by the revolution, began again after the war; however, it remained at fairly low levels. Much of Europe was in a state of war from the French Revolution in 1789 until Napoleon's defeat in 1815, making emigration difficult. Between 1783 and 1815, possibly 250,000 people migrated to the United States, with the majority of them coming in the 1790s. Most were English or Scots-Irish, who were less affected by the war on the continent.

Despite its relatively low numbers, this immigration worried some members of the Federalist Party—one of the first political parties in the United States. In addition to the fact that these immigrants would likely vote for their political opponents, the Democratic-Republicans, some Federalists were concerned that they might be infected with the radicalism of the French Revolution. Similarly, they worried that Irish immigrants might also be radicals, fleeing Ireland's failed revolution in 1798. These fears led to a number of proposals to restrict or police immigration and naturalization. In 1797, Federalists proposed a $20 tax on naturalization certificates, with the goal of making it harder for recent immigrants to naturalize. Those who supported it, like Harrison Gray Otis of Massachusetts, maintained that this tax was necessary to keep out "the mass of vicious and disorganizing characters that cannot live peaceably at home." He warned of the need to protect the United States against the "hordes of wild Irishmen...[who] come here with a view to disturb our tranquility, after having succeeded to the overthrow of their own Governments."

Although that tax did not pass, in 1798 the Federalists managed to pass the Alien and Sedition Acts. The first of these—the "sedition" portion of the Alien and Sedition Acts—dealt with criticism of the government. The other three acts all pertained to immigration and naturalization. The Naturalization Act of 1798 extended the waiting period for naturalization to fourteen years. The Alien Enemies Act allowed the President to arrest or deport non-naturalized immigrants from nations with which the United States was at war. The Alien Act would have required non-naturalized aliens to register with the government, and gave the President the authorization to detain or deport them if they were ever deemed dangerous. Most portions of the Alien and Sedition Acts were revoked or allowed to expire when Thomas Jefferson became President in 1801. However, these laws demonstrate early on that some in the United States feared the impact immigrants might have on American society.

Mass migration from Europe—the Germans and the Irish

The antebellum period saw the first major wave of migration to the United States. From 151,824 arrivals during the 1820s, the number of immigrants

Table 2.1 Antebellum immigration

Decade	Irish Immigration	% of Total	German Immigration	% of Total	British Immigration	% of Total
1831–1840	207,381	34.6%	152,454	25.5%	75,810	12.7%
1841–1850	780,719	45.6%	434,626	25.4%	267,044	15.6%
1851–1860	914,119	35.2%	951,667	36.6%	423,974	16.3%

Source: U.S. Immigration and Naturalization Service, *Statistical Yearbook of the Immigration and Naturalization Service, 2001.* (U.S. Government Printing Office: Washington, D.C., 2003), pp. 16–17.

coming to the United States increased to nearly 600,000 during the 1830s, 1.7 million during the 1840s, and 2.6 million during the 1850s. The vast majority of these immigrants were coming from Europe, and the vast majority of those were either German, Irish, or British. [See Table 2.1] These categories mask considerable diversity—"British" migrants might be English, Welsh, or Scottish, while "Germany" did not even exist as a nation until 1871, so these migrants left dozens of different nations and principalities, some substantial, like Prussia, and others incredibly small.

Economic change in Europe played a major role in the migration of all three of these groups. The Irish, for example, had been facing difficult economic conditions for most of the early nineteenth century. Agricultural prices were generally low and cottage industry, especially woolens, was being hard hit by cheap manufactured goods arriving from England. Furthermore, most land in Ireland belonged to large landowners, who began shifting to livestock grazing due to low grain prices, resulting in leaseholders being evicted. Ireland's population had almost doubled between 1788 and 1841, going from 4 million to 8.1 million, which further increased pressure on the land. As a result, the number of people emigrating from Ireland increased, and the composition of that migration stream changed. Whereas earlier emigrants from Ireland had been nearly exclusively Protestants, by 1840, ninety percent of them were Catholic.

All of these economic factors together, although not unique to Ireland, put the country in a vulnerable state when a fungal blight destroyed the majority of the potato crop in 1845. This fungus was also not unique to Ireland—it had likely originated in Peru and spread to Europe via the United States. However, it thrived in the damp weather that prevailed in Ireland, and nowhere else in Europe was there such a large population that was dependent on potatoes for so much of their food supply. Unlike previous potato blights, which were typically short lived and local in scope, this blight affected the entire country and lasted for years, causing a disaster of truly epic proportions. Historians estimate that between one and one and a half million people died from starvation or starvation-related diseases during the years between 1845 and 1852. Another two million left Ireland, of whom approximately three-quarters would go to the United States. [Document 5]

Migrants from Ireland during the famine tended to have a slightly different social profile than Irish emigrants before or after. They were more likely to migrate as complete families, whenever possible. Those migrating tended to have limited resources as a result of the famine as well, although they were not the poorest of the poor, who could not afford to leave, and died in Ireland. They were almost all rural laborers, and were disproportionately Catholic, given that Protestants in Ireland were concentrated in areas that were hit less hard by the famine due to higher rates of industrialization and urbanization.

German migrants during the antebellum period, in contrast, were both more diverse than the Irish in religion and national identity and less likely to be extremely poor. Most were migrating for economic reasons, but were generally facing a situation that was less dire than the potato famine. Central Europe was facing a combination of stagnation and rapid change during the nineteenth century, which destabilized the economy. Small producers in town and country struggled to keep pace with industrial production, resulting in an increase in the number of propertyless peasants and artisans seeking work as wage laborers. This situation was additionally complicated by demographic changes, as the population of Central Europe grew rapidly during the second half of the eighteenth century and continued to do so into the nineteenth. This population growth surpassed the ability of the relatively underdeveloped economy to absorb them, especially in the countryside. As a result, many Germans faced the prospect of a declining standard of living during the nineteenth century.

Other Germans came to the U.S. seeking political freedom. A revolutionary movement during the 1840s sought to create a unified, democratic Germany out of the diverse German states, although the uprisings of 1848 ultimately failed in their goals. As a result, the leaders of this movement, known as Forty-Eighters, found themselves having to leave or face arrest. Ultimately we cannot know how many German migrants after 1848 were at least partially inspired to move to the United States since it was already a democracy. For the vast majority, however, economic motives were primary, and the number of actual political refugees, who had to leave or face arrest, is quite small—perhaps only three or four thousand.

The journey to America was not easy, particularly for the Irish escaping the famine who had few resources. The voyage itself took five or six weeks during the 1840s, and ships were frequently overcrowded. In such conditions, disease spread quickly, made worse for those Irish passengers by malnutrition. Typhus, known as "famine fever," was an especially great problem on ships carrying Irish immigrants, and the general expectation was that not everyone would survive the voyage. Conditions began to improve in the

1850s and 1860s as steamships were introduced. In addition to being larger, these ships could make the trip much faster with the aid of their steam engines, reducing it to two to three weeks. [Document 6]

Once in America, most immigrants settled in cities. The Irish fleeing the famine in particular often lacked the resources and the desire to start farming—agriculture had failed their families badly in Ireland, and they sought work that provided an immediate paycheck. Irish women tended to work as domestic servants or in the textile factories of the Northeast. By 1850, three-quarters of the domestic servants of New York City were Irish. Irish men found work in factories, and also in a wide range of mostly unskilled jobs, including constructing railroads and canals, loading and unloading ships, and driving wagons. Letters home sometimes talked about the many opportunities to find work in America, but others warned about how hard and uncertain that work could be. One Irish immigrant warned that "God help any one who has to work for his living in America" and that people in Ireland should not believe "half the favourable letters you see from America." Regardless of such warnings, the positive stories combined with desperation kept migrants coming from Ireland for years to come.

Most Germans also settled in cities, if not as disproportionately as the Irish. In 1860, about one-third of German American men worked in agriculture and the other two-thirds in urban pursuits. About thirty-seven percent of German-born workers held skilled artisan positions in 1870, mostly due to the skills they brought with them from Germany. The 1870 U.S. census found disproportionate numbers of German men working in the building trades (carpenters, plasterers, and masons) and as boot and shoemakers, blacksmiths, furniture makers, cigarmakers, butchers, and bakers. Only one out of twenty-three Americans had been born in Germany, but one in six shoemakers had been, almost one in three butchers, and nearly two in every five bakers.

Although Germans were more heavily represented in the skilled trades than the Irish were, many still did unskilled work. German men built railroads, drove wagons, loaded and unloaded ships, and paved streets. A few urban Germans worked as merchants or professionals, running a store or tavern, or working as a doctor or lawyer. For German women in the cities, many contributed to their family's business, much like women did on the farm. German women who needed to earn wages outside the home frequently worked as domestic servants, dressmakers, or in industry.

Like most immigrants, the Irish and Germans often formed ethnic neighborhoods in American cities. Such neighborhoods were seldom exclusively composed of one ethnic group, but most cities had a neighborhood or neighborhoods that were perceived as being "Irish" or "German" by mid-century. Ethnic neighborhoods could develop for many reasons, including the simple necessity of living near where one was working. They could be places to find assistance, where family or friends from the old country could help a new arrival in finding a place to live or work. And they could also be reminders of home, where shared community institutions could help keep traditions from the old country alive in the new. For the Germans, linguistic differences were an additional driving factor behind such community formation, and German neighborhoods and institutions played a major role in language maintenance for the population.

In addition to housing and businesses, a wide variety of ethnic institutions existed in ethnic neighborhoods to meet immigrants' needs. For the Irish, many of these associations were affiliated with or related to the Catholic Church—which itself was an important institution in Irish neighborhoods. Religious affiliation was more diverse among Germans—there were German-speaking Catholics and a wide range of Protestants, with Lutherans forming the largest group. There were also many secular associations—or "vereine" in German—that played major roles in the community, just as they had in Germany. Societies devoted to charity, theater, music, sports, shooting, politics, and assorted crafts all flourished in America as well. And, whereas institutional life for Irish women tended to be more focused on institutions affiliated with the Catholic Church, German women had an associational life that was just as varied as that of German men, with many sacred and secular associations in which to participate.

One other subset of the migration stream from the German states deserves special mention—German Jews. About 100,000 Jews moved to the U.S. from the German states during the years between 1820 and 1880. Many of them had a strong German cultural aspect to their identity. As the Reform rabbi Bernhard Felsenthal put it in 1901,

> I was born as a Jew....Spiritually I am German. I have been influenced by Schiller, Goethe, Kant, and other spiritual German heroes. I drank from the sources of German literature, and I sat at the feet of German teachers, and with a certain sense of pride I can say: I am spiritually a German.

However, this does not mean that they can be simply lumped in with the rest of the Germans unproblematically, since their identity was more complex than that. Jewishness was an important part of their identity as well, and given that in most German states, Jews did not enjoy full civil or social equality, they faced discrimination that other Germans would not have. In that sense, German Jews during the nineteenth century must be understood both in connection with the general German American community, and as a population that was at least in some ways set apart from it.

The border crossed us: the first Mexican Americans

The U.S. takeover of the region that ultimately became the American Southwest began when Americans first started settling in northern Mexico during the early nineteenth century. From the perspective of Mexico, the

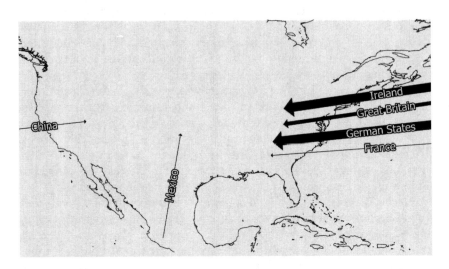

Map 2.1 Immigration to the United States 1820–1860

North was their frontier, and they were interested in seeing this frontier "settled" and integrated into the rest of the nation. As a result, first Spain and then Mexico would offer incentives to settlers who sought to colonize the area—including immigrants from the United States. Encouraging migration made sense from a security perspective, given that there were only about two thousand Spanish-speaking Mexicans living in Texas in the 1820s, and around forty thousand unassimilated Native Americans.

In 1820, Moses Austin went to the Spanish capital of Texas, seeking permission to settle a colony of three hundred American families there. In exchange for a grant of land, Austin agreed that he would be responsible for recruiting settlers, and that the settlers would have to swear allegiance to Spain, convert to Catholicism, and be of good moral character. Slavery was not mentioned in the arrangement, and was still legal although soon to be abolished after Mexico gained its independence in 1821. Given the profitability of cotton production in 1820, slavery was definitely part of the plans of the Americans seeking to relocate to Texas. The cheap price of land lured many to Austin's colony—whereas government-owned land in the United States cost $1.25 per acre in 1820, Austin intended to charge only the cost of surveying, or roughly 12.5 cents per acre, a steal for prime cotton lands.

Moses Austin ultimately died before his ambitions could be realized, and his son Stephen took over the effort. Initially, at least some of the Mexican residents of Texas, known as Tejanos, were enthusiastic about this immigration. As one supporter, Franciso Ruiz, put it, "I cannot help seeing the advantages which, to my way of thinking, would result if we admitted honest, hard-working people, regardless of what country they come from...

even hell itself." Quite quickly, the volume of American immigrants arriving in Texas had a profound impact on the demographics of the area. By 1830, just ten years after Austin sought permission for his colony, the Anglo-Texan population was over twenty thousand, while there were barely three thousand Tejanos.

Trouble began in Texas when leaders took power in Mexico City who were more committed to the idea of a strong central government. This concerned Anglo-Texans, who feared the government would force them to abolish slavery. Many Tejanos were also concerned, and saw centralism as a violation of the Constitution of 1824, which had established strong state governments. Tensions continued to grow throughout the early 1830s, until fighting finally broke out in October 1835, when Anglo-Texans opened fire on Mexican cavalry near Gonzales. Many Anglo-Texans were not initially pushing for independence, but as the fighting continued, their attitudes changed, and a convention officially declared Texas independent on March 2, 1836.

After the war, Anglo-Texans sought annexation by the United States, although it would be nearly ten years before this took place, since many Northerners were uninterested in adding another slave state to the Union, particularly at the price of war with Mexico. War did indeed result from the U.S. annexation of Texas, and as a result of that war, the United States took not only Texas, but a vast stretch of Mexico's territory—the entire northern frontier. Roughly one hundred thousand Mexican citizens lived in the area at the time of annexation. Article VIII of the Treaty of Guadalupe Hidalgo, which ended the war, stipulated that they could remain Mexican citizens if they wished, but that otherwise, they would be considered American citizens. Soon after the annexation, however, Americans were already questioning the extent to which this conferred citizenship rights on Mexicans, as well as what their place in the American racial hierarchy would be. [Document 7]

The post-annexation period witnessed the gradual dispossession of Mexicans from the middle and upper classes, as they lost their property despite treaty protections. In Texas, Juan Cortina led a Tejano uprising along the Texas–Mexico border in protest of how many Tejanos had lost their land after statehood. [Document 8] Similarly in California, there were challenges to Californios' land claims. The 1851 California Land Act established a board of land commissioners to evaluate land claims, and stipulated that after two years, any unclaimed land plus claims that had been rejected would be opened up to Anglo-American settlement. Many Californio land owners had to sell some of their land to pay the cost of legal fees to defend their claims, and many gradually lost their land as a result of this law. For instance, Salvador Vallejo, who owned land in Napa, initially sold some of his cattle to cover the legal costs of defending it. Although his claim was upheld, the decision was appealed and that process combined with Anglo-American squatters moving onto his land, ultimately resulted in the Vallejos losing all their land in Napa Valley.

Californios also faced discriminatory laws during the Gold Rush. By late 1849, many mining regions in California were already making regulations that aimed to prevent foreigners from holding claims and mining gold, including Mexicans. Laws like the Foreign Miners tax, which established a fee that non-citizen miners had to pay, in theory exempted Mexicans who had become U.S. citizens as a result of the Treaty of Guadalupe Hidalgo. In practice, however, Mexican Americans faced challenges to their status, with the prosecution arguing in People v. Naglee that the tax should apply to them, since although the treaty stipulated that Congress would make them citizens, it had not yet done so. Anglo-Americans continued to make this argument for many years, until finally in 1870 in the case of People v. de la Guerra, the California supreme court ruled that the admission of California as a state had been the act that made the Californios into U.S. citizens. But challenges to Mexican American citizenship and the ability of Mexican immigrants to naturalize continued far into the future. In particular, many Americans maintained that Mexicans with indigenous ancestry, which was many of them, would not be able to naturalize given that Native Americans in the U.S. were not eligible for citizenship.

Gold mountain guests: the first Chinese Americans

Although many aspects of Chinese immigration, including why they were migrating, were similar to the experiences of other immigrant groups, they were the only significant group of immigrants during the antebellum period who were completely ineligible for naturalization. While European migrants were simply able to naturalize, and Mexican Americans occupied an uncertain position vis-à-vis their citizenship eligibility, Chinese migrants were not eligible for naturalization under the laws of the time. This is an important distinction and one that would have a profound impact on the experiences of Chinese immigrants in America. But in terms of the reasons why Chinese migrants were leaving their homes and the kinds of work they found once in America, their experiences were fairly typical of nineteenth-century immigrants.

People had begun moving to the United States from China during the 1850s. As in many of the regions of Europe experiencing emigration during that time period, southeastern China was experiencing a rising population accompanied by a decrease in per capita income and standard of living. British efforts to open China to Western trade, particularly by illegally trading opium up the Pearl River in Southeast China, ultimately resulted in two wars—the first and second Opium Wars between 1839–1842 and 1856–1858—that destabilized the political and economic systems of the region. Guangdong province, which included the Pearl River delta and was near both British-seized Hong Kong and the Portuguese colony of Macau, was hit particularly hard by Western interference, and the vast majority of nineteenth-century Chinese emigrants would come from this province.

Around 2.5 million people would leave China during the last six decades of the nineteenth century. [Document 9]

As was generally the case, the United States was hardly the only destination for these migrants. The majority went somewhere in Southeast Asia—to Malaya, Siam, the Philippines, or Singapore, for instance. Others traveled farther afield, going to Hawaii, Australia, Peru, Cuba, Jamaica, or the United States. Those coming to California in the mid-nineteenth century were thus only one branch of a much larger migration network. About 322,000 Chinese people came to the United States between 1850 and 1882, after which Chinese immigration was essentially made illegal. Given that many Chinese migrants returned to China after a time in the U.S., the total does not reflect the size of the Chinese population in the United States at any moment. In 1880, for instance, there were about 105,000 Chinese people living in the United States.

The vast majority of migrants were young men who intended to earn money and return home. They were either unmarried or left their wives in China. In some cases, families encouraged a young migrant to marry before he left, hoping that this would "cement his ties to the village" and ensure his return. As a result, very few Chinese women migrated, particularly during the early years. The California state census of 1852 for San Francisco showed a Chinese population of 2,954 men and nineteen women, for a ratio of about 155:1. This was extreme even by the standards of this frontier city, in which the total population showed three men for every woman. More Chinese women came to the U.S. as time went on, but even as late as 1870, there were still more than thirteen Chinese men for every Chinese woman in the U.S. This was enough, however, that families and children were still a presence—between 1860 and 1920, about eleven percent of the Chinese American population of San Francisco was age sixteen or under, for instance.

Many of the earliest Chinese migrants came to California for the Gold Rush. They were hardly the only people moving to California for that reason—many Americans were going, as were immigrants from Europe, Mexico, South and Central America, and Australia. The 1852 state census found a non-Native American population of about 250,000 in California, with forty-seven percent of those living in the seven major mining counties of the state. About one-third of the residents of those counties were foreign-born. Chinese migrants formed an increasingly large proportion of this, forming about ten percent of the total population and thirty-five percent of the foreign born. By 1860, the Chinese were the largest foreign-born group in California, and made up between twelve and twenty-three percent of the population of the major mining counties.

Particularly during the early years, when miners were competing directly against each other for access to the best claims, foreign-born miners faced hostility, especially if they were not white. Some mining districts created local regulations to limit claims to people who intended to become citizens, which would allow European immigrants to make claims but would make

Figure 2.1 "Mining life in California"
Source: *Harper's Weekly*, v. 1, no. 40 (Oct 3 1857), p. 632. Library of Congress Prints and Photographs Division, Washington, D.C. https://lccn.loc.gov/2001700332.

it more difficult for Mexicans and impossible for the Chinese. Chinese and Mexican miners were also the main targets of the Foreign Miners tax, which placed a tax on non-citizens working as miners. This tax produced a major amount of revenue for the state of California at a time right after statehood when money was short. Despite the shift to wage labor and the hostility they faced, many Chinese workers remained miners, with the result that in 1870, about one-quarter of the miners in California were Chinese.

Another common career path for Chinese migrants was doing service work of some kind, including working as domestic servants. While such positions were not generally held by men in nineteenth-century America, the racist stereotypes that attributed an effeminate, servile nature to Chinese men made it seem appropriate. Many white Americans maintained that Chinese men made ideal domestic servants, since they were supposed to be innately willing to subordinate their own desires and interest to those of their employers. While this was not true—Chinese servants did bargain for better wages and working conditions, just as other servants did—the belief that Chinese men would consent to employment without any negotiation or qualification remained, and would be responsible for some of the hostility white workers felt towards them.

Businesses run by Chinese migrants were often service oriented as well. Some created restaurants, at first to serve familiar food from home to other migrants, and over time, Americanizing some of their food to attract additional customers. Others ran laundries. There was substantial demand for laundries during the nineteenth century, due to the amount of time and effort laundry took, and the disproportionately male population of California only increased it. Laundries were also fairly cheap businesses to establish, requiring only kettles, a water source, soap, and irons to get started, but the work was also hard, hot, and low paying. As a result, it tended to be fairly low status work, usually done by women, and often women of color. The association of Chinese men with laundries became so strong in the minds of white Americans that it was almost a cliché. It also reinforced the American belief that Chinese men were effeminate, since they did women's work—in total disregard of the work Chinese men did in the very "masculine" fields of mining and railroad construction.

Know Nothings and nativism

Nativism has always been part of American society. Such sentiment has waxed and waned over time, however, often in response to economic and social forces. Times of economic prosperity and social stability tend to see lower levels of nativism, while episodes of social turmoil or economic disaster mean more. Immigration rates during the late 1840s and early 1850s were very high; in fact, between 1845 and 1854, about 2.9 million immigrants arrived in the United States, more than in the previous seven decades combined. These immigrants amounted to 14.5% of the 1845 U.S. population, a figure that has yet to be surpassed. Combined with political crises surrounding the collapse of the Whig Party and conflicts over temperance and slavery, the United States was primed for a massive nativist outbreak in the 1850s.

Nativists in the nineteenth century made a number of objections to the foreign presence in the United States. Some raised economic complaints, worrying about the job competition immigrants provided or that they were paupers who would be burdens on society. This concern was aimed at the Irish escaping the Great Famine in particular, many of whom were nearly destitute by the time they reached the United States. Most nativist concerns during the 1850s, however, were cultural or moral in nature. For instance, Americans who had become supporters of the temperance movement were concerned with the important role that alcohol consumption played in the cultures of both the Germans and the Irish. Drinking was part of their social life, and the taverns and beer gardens they frequented were important centers of the ethnic neighborhoods. Temperance supporters considered such activities immoral, and were particularly shocked to see entire families frequenting German beer gardens. Having a pint of beer with one's family while listening to a band was a common way to spend a Sunday afternoon for German migrants, but to some native-born Americans, it was a desecration of the Sabbath to drink and listen to secular music on Sundays.

Even more problematic in the eyes of religiously motivated nativists was the fact that the majority of antebellum immigrants were Catholics. Nearly all of the Irish immigrants during the 1840s and 1850s were Catholic, and roughly one-third of the Germans. Many Protestant Americans in the nineteenth century saw Catholicism as a religion that was fundamentally incompatible with democratic governance, due to the emphasis placed on deference to church hierarchy. As a result, anti-Catholic nativists were particularly concerned with the political impact these immigrants could have. Nativists not only assumed Catholics would vote as a block, but that they would essentially allow their church to make their voting decisions for them.

For the most part, mid-nineteenth century nativists were not pushing for exclusion, with the exception of some in California who hoped to exclude the Chinese. But most nativists were content to allow Irish and Germans to move to the United States, provided their political influence was restrained. The most influential such organization during the 1850s was the group generally known as the Know Nothing Party. Originally founded as a secret nativist fraternity known as the Order of the Star Spangled Banner, this group later came into the open and got involved in politics as a nativist third party alternative to the Democrats and the declining Whig Party. They referred to themselves as the American Party, but many called them the Know Nothings, supposedly because the response of members of the earlier secret society to questions about their organization had been to state that they knew nothing about it. By 1854, the American Party had become fairly popular, winning local and state races across the country.

The solutions Know Nothings proposed demonstrated their belief that the major issue was the immigrants' political influence. They promoted changing the waiting period for naturalization from five years to twenty-one, on the grounds that a new-born American baby had to wait that long before they were able to vote, and that you could not expect an immigrant to master the nuances of American political participation any faster. The ultimate intention of this proposal was to stop many immigrants from naturalizing at all. Know Nothings also proposed restricting all elected offices to native-born Americans. Neither measure ever became law. However, the victories the Know Nothings won in state and local races demonstrate that their ideology did appeal to many Americans. [Document 10] Ultimately, concern about immigrants and Catholicism was swamped by strife over slavery in the late 1850s, as the country moved towards the Civil War. But during the mid-1850s, anti-immigrant sentiment was high enough to support a substantial third party based on the issue.

Immigration and whiteness

Given the large role that race has historically played in shaping American attitudes towards immigration, historians have also investigated whether some of the nativism of the 1850s was based on racial judgements about the arriving immigrants. Race obviously played a major role in the experiences of Chinese immigrants and of Mexicans, whether they crossed the border or it crossed them. Their ability to become naturalized citizens was either completely denied based on their race or at least severely challenged and limited. They faced discrimination in most other areas of life as well—in terms of where they worked and lived, and with whom they could marry and socialize. The question is if this was true for any of the European immigrants as well.

The invented category of race was elaborate and complex during the nineteenth century, with many identifying a hierarchy of more or less advanced white races in Europe. Among immigrants to the United States, the Irish in particular were often seen as less racially desirable, drawing on the centuries-old prejudices that the English founders of America had held against them. Caricatures of Irish migrants often made them look subhuman or ape-like, leading some historians to question if the Irish were entirely perceived as "white" by native-born Americans at the time of their arrival, or if this was a status they achieved at some later date.

The Irish undeniably experienced discrimination in the United States, with employers sometimes specifying in job advertisements that "no Irish need apply." However, in all of the ways that mattered most, the Irish were treated as white from the very beginning. They were able to become naturalized citizens under the Naturalization Act of 1790. They were able to vote or give testimony in court even in states that restricted those rights to white people, and no laws prevented them from intermarrying with the white native-born population. In this, their experience was categorically different from that of the African American, Chinese, and Mexican populations in the United States, all of which were clearly identified as not white by state and federal government. Although nativist Americans might object to their culture or their religion, or even see them as racially inferior, as far as the government was concerned, the Germans and Irish were "white on arrival."

However, there is another sense in which the Irish and Germans did have to become "white." They were moving to a nation with a society based on a racial hierarchy rooted in the enslavement of African Americans. For native-born Americans, being "white" was thus an important identity that brought with it many real privileges, including being able to access full citizenship rights, while even free Black Americans found themselves facing many legal restrictions on what they could do. Once in America, Irish and German immigrants could not help but learn that Black Americans were at the bottom of the social hierarchy in the United States, and that they, simply by virtue of their European heritage, would always have more privileges and rights than Black Americans would. If they rejected this hierarchy—whether by vocally opposing slavery or simply interacting with Black Americans as equals—they would also learn from the anger of white Americans that such behavior was not socially acceptable. Learning what it meant to be "white" in America was thus part of the assimilation process for European immigrants.

The same was true in the opposite direction for people from Mexico or China. Even elite Tejanos, Neuvo Mexicanos, and Californios learned to their dismay after annexation that despite the treaty provisions that were supposed to grant them citizenship, and despite their families' long history and elite status, they were immediately relegated to a second-class status simply by virtue of having some indigenous or African ancestry. Chinese immigrants too found themselves struggling to navigate a world based on a racial hierarchy that relegated all "non-whites" to an inferior position. The American racial hierarchy tended to assume people were either white or Black, leaving Mexicans and the Chinese—and the Native Americans as well—in an ambiguous position. Regardless of how the laws were worded, however, the Chinese were definitely defined as not white in the eyes of white Americans, meaning that they had to join Mexican Americans in learning about what it meant to be "not white" in America. The racialized nature of American immigration would only increase in the wake of the Civil War. Slavery may have been abolished, but the racial hierarchy had not, and new scientific ideas about race would only harden white Americans' commitment to it.

3 Immigration during the late nineteenth century

Immigrants in the late nineteenth century encountered a United States that was rapidly changing and modernizing. The Civil War briefly interrupted, but did not entirely stop, the flow of migration to the United States. In its wake, immigration increased again, much of it coming from the same sources and for the same reasons as before the war. These immigrants entered a nation that was rapidly evolving. Slavery had been abolished, and although Black Americans were now definitively established as citizens, they faced a lengthy struggle for social and political rights, and citizenship itself was still very much defined in racial terms. Industrialization, urbanization, and westward expansion were changing the economic landscape immigrants encountered in profound ways. The origin of immigrants was also gradually changing during these years, as numbers from northwestern Europe declined, and increasing numbers of immigrants entered from other parts of the world—particularly southern and eastern Europe, but also some from Mexico and Japan. Together, these changes made the United States even more a nation of immigrants and its population even more diverse than previously.

A new vision of American citizenship

Although emancipation was not one of the Union's aims at the start of the war, it soon became one as a steady stream of enslaved people came to Union lines, seeking safety, offering help, and making it clear that the war could not be won without destroying slavery. In the aftermath of the war, Congress passed and the states ratified three constitutional amendments in an attempt to secure the freedom of the formerly enslaved. The Thirteenth Amendment, ratified in 1865, forbade slavery in the United States. The Fourteenth Amendment, ratified in 1868, established among other things that anyone born in the United States was a citizen. And the Fifteenth Amendment, ratified in 1870, forbade denying someone the right to vote based on their "race, color, or previous condition of servitude."

The Fourteenth Amendment was a first step towards a new and more expansive vision of American citizenship. In creating the amendment, Congress was focused on establishing definitively that Black Americans were citizens—an important goal, given that the Dred Scott decision of 1857 had called their citizenship into question. The amendment also had major implications for immigrants, however, particularly those who were not themselves eligible for naturalization. The birthright citizenship provision of the Fourteenth Amendment had the potential to make the children of Chinese and Japanese immigrants into citizens, even though their parents were ineligible for naturalization. Citizenship in the wake of the Civil War continued to be defined by race. The new Naturalization Act of 1870, although it extended naturalization rights to Africans and people of African descent, also explicitly stated that Chinese people were not eligible. Nonetheless, the birthright citizenship provision of the Fourteenth Amendment was a first step towards a more racially inclusive citizenship.

Immigration during the late nineteenth century

Historians used to divide late nineteenth century immigrants into the categories of "old" and "new," with the year 1890 roughly serving as a break between the two groups. "Old" immigrants included Germans, Irish, British, and Scandinavians, while "new" included people from southern and eastern Europe (like Italians, Greeks, Poles, and Eastern European Jews) and people from Asia. These categories were created in 1907 by a government commission studying immigration to make a point about the perceived racial suitability of migrants, and are problematic as tools for understanding immigration history. For one thing, the change was more of a gradual transition than a clear break—there were "new" immigrants arriving before 1890, and "old" groups remained prominent into the twentieth century. Also the categories "old" and "new" were based more on perceived racial suitability than time of migration. Scandinavians were almost always put in the "old" group, for instance, and the Chinese, who were actually forbidden from immigrating after 1882, were sometimes placed in the "new" category.

Nonetheless, there was a gradual shift taking place in immigrant origins in the late nineteenth century. Old sources, like Britain, Germany, and Ireland, were declining in importance, although they would remain major senders of immigrants into the twentieth century. Many more migrants were coming from other places, including Scandinavia (particularly Norwegians and Swedes) and southern and eastern Europe (Italians, Greeks, Poles, and Eastern European Jews, among others). Table 2 includes immigration numbers by decade from 1861–1920, demonstrating the gradual, but very significant, change taking place.

For all immigrants, the process of travel was different in the late nineteenth century than it had been earlier. Nearly all were able to travel on steamships, which dramatically reduced their journey. The trans-Atlantic voyage that had taken five to six weeks now took only two or three, and only ten to twelve days by 1900. This made two-way travel much more feasible, and resulted in seasonal migration networks of workers coming to

Table 3.1 Immigration to the United States by nation, 1861–1920

Nation	1861–1870	1871–1880	1881–1890	1891–1900	1901–1910	1911–1920
Germans	787,468	718,182	1,452,970	505,152	341,498	143,945
Irish	435,778	436,871	655,482	388,416	339,065	146,181
British	606,896	548,043	807,357	271,538	525,950	341,408
China	64,301	123,201	61,711	14,799	20,605	21,278
Japan	186	149	2,270	25,942	129,797	83,837
Canada	153,878	383,640	393,304	3,311	179,226	742,185
Mexico	2,191	5,162	1,913	971	49,642	219,004
Scandinavia	126,392	243,016	656,494	371,512	505,324	203,452
Italians	11,725	55,759	307,309	651,893	2,045,877	1,109,524
Austria-Hungary	7,800	72,969	353,719	592,707	2,145,266	896,342
Russia	2,512	39,284	213,282	505,290	1,597,306	921,201

Note: Great Britain includes England, Scotland, and Wales. Scandinavia includes Norway, Sweden, and Denmark.

Source: U.S. Immigration and Naturalization Service, *Statistical Yearbook of the Immigration and Naturalization Service, 2001.* (U.S. Government Printing Office: Washington, D.C., 2003), pp. 17–18.

the Americas in the spring and returning home in the fall. Many different groups would engage in this behavior—both British and German workers were doing so by the 1870s, and Italians, Greeks, and others would in the future.

Despite the greater speed, conditions on board the ships were still not pleasant for those immigrants traveling in steerage. Ships might have between nine hundred and fourteen hundred passengers living on their lower decks. People lived in large dormitories, divided for men, women, and families, where they slept on bunk beds with straw mattresses. Privacy was generally nonexistent and washrooms were fairly limited. Usually there would be one for men and one for women, with some basins where they could wash in cold water. Some food was provided, but it often was not very good, and utensils and dishes sometimes were not provided. With so many people in an enclosed space, the air was often stuffy and foul smelling. Walking on the deck could provide a break from this, but the deck was often crowded in good weather and not accessible during bad.

The entry experience of immigrants arriving from Europe changed when the Ellis Island Immigration Station began operation in 1892. Previously, most immigrants had entered through New York City's Castle Garden immigration station. Ellis Island combined all of the functions of entry (customs, potential quarantine, and immigration processing) into one facility. First class passengers were generally able to simply disembark at the city's docks and bypass much of this process, but steerage passengers were ferried to Ellis Island for inspection and registration. In addition to having their

Figure 3.1 Group of women and children migrating to the United States from Eastern Europe at the end of the nineteenth century

Source: Johnston, Frances Benjamin, photographer. Group of emigrants women and children from eastern Europe on deck of the S.S. Amsterdam, 1899. Library of Congress Prints and Photographs Division Washington, D.C. https://lccn.loc.gov/91482252" https://lccn.loc.gov/91482252

papers checked and their names recorded, migrants underwent a medical inspection, and potential quarantine if they were suspected of carrying a contagious disease. Most were admitted after spending a few stressful hours waiting in lines at Ellis Island, but a few were denied entry on various grounds. They had the chance to appeal, but if their appeal was rejected, they were sent back to Europe. More than twelve million immigrants entered the United States through Ellis Island between 1892 and 1932, when it ceased operations as a reception center for arriving immigrants. [Document 11]

Italians

Many late nineteenth century immigrants from Southern and Eastern Europe came to the United States for essentially the same reasons as earlier migrants. They were predominantly seeking economic betterment, whether through permanent relocation to the United States or temporary work there. Many were leaving regions that were economically poor and relatively under industrialized, making seeking work elsewhere seem like a viable strategy. For many Italian immigrants, their intention was not to stay in the United States permanently, but to earn enough money to return home to a higher standard of living. Between 1880 and 1920, over four million Italians moved to the United States. Because men were more likely in Italian culture to travel for temporary work, about seventy-five percent of Italian immigration to the United States was made up of men. Whatever their initial plans had been, many Italian migrants ultimately stayed in America, although about forty-five percent did return to Italy. For some, the higher standard of living they encountered in the United States ultimately drove their decision to stay. Alessandro Ranciglio moved from Cuggiono to St. Louis, where he found work as a blacksmith, shoeing mules in the city's Italian neighborhood known as the Hill. He explained his decision to stay by saying, "Here I eat meat three times a day, not three times a year!" He wrote home to his wife that "I'm not going to come back there. Cuggiono! I want you to take Tony [his son] and come here on the Hill. There's an abundance, a lot of work and I'd like to live here....If you don't come here, I don't come back!"

Essentially all immigration exhibits some degree of chain migration—when migrants encouraged friends and family to join them in America, thus resulting in people from specific locations in the Old World clustering together in the New. Italian immigrants, however, demonstrated this to a very high extent, partially because of how decentralized Italy was during the nineteenth century, which had the effect of giving people a very strong sense of local identity. The term for this was campanilismo, which referred to the sense of loyalty and affection felt for those who lived in the same village and distrust for those who did not—that is, for those who lived too far away to hear the bells of the local church tower, or campanile. This resulted in a high degree of chain migration, with migrants from certain regions of Italy going to certain places in the United States, or even to certain neighborhoods within a city. One might be populated mostly by people from Palermo, another by Neopolitans, and so on.

Once in America, many Italian men found work in manufacturing, or found themselves doing "pick-and-shovel" work—paving streets, building bridges and elevated rail lines, and digging tunnels for subways. Married Italian women were less likely than some groups to work outside the home, but many Italian women worked for wages prior to marriage. They were especially prominent in the garment industry, and made up about one-third of the workforce, with the rest mostly being Jewish immigrants.

Greeks

Like Italians, Greeks also had a high rate of temporary migration. Many Greek migrants were relatively poor peasants living in a region that still had little industrialization, and saw going abroad as a strategy that could help supplement the income of their family at home. This was essentially taking seasonal labor migration patterns that already existed in Greece, and extending them beyond the country's borders. Between 1880 and 1920, about 370,000 Greeks moved to the United States. Greek migration was even more male dominated that Italian—during the 1890s, nearly twenty-four Greek men migrated for every woman. Once in America, many Greek men found work in the mills of eastern cities, although some also found work in mines and smelters in Colorado and Utah.

Poles

Changes in land use accompanying economic modernization often spurred migration as well. For instance, many Polish peasants in the late nineteenth century found themselves seeking non-agricultural work, in some cases because partible inheritance, where land was divided among all heirs, had made their plots too small to survive on, in others because landlords were shifting to commercial agriculture and evicting them entirely. Although many of them came not intending to stay, they were much more likely to do so than the Italians or Greeks. Although initial migrants were mostly men, Polish women soon joined them, forming families. Polish immigrants predominantly found jobs in industrial cities, where they struggled with American stereotypes that saw Poles as unsuitable for jobs that required complex thought, but excellent at tasks that required brute strength and obedience. As a result, they were often hired for unskilled positions on docks, and in warehouses, mines, stockyards, steel mills, and assembly plants.

Eastern European Jews

Jewish immigrants, in contrast, were much less likely to return to Europe. Nearly 34% of all immigrants to the U.S. returned home, but only 5.2% of Jews did. This was because of the increasing violence Jews were facing, particularly in Russia under the rule of Czar Alexander II. Not only were increasing numbers of anti-Semitic laws being made, but Jews also faced outbreaks of violence, known as pogroms, when Russian peasants and soldiers destroyed their homes and attacked them. Golda Meir described experiencing this violence as a child in Kiev, saying that although she did not know what the word pogrom meant at that age, she "knew it had something to do with being Jewish and with the rabble that used to surge through town, brandishing knives and huge sticks, screaming 'Christ killers' as they looked for the Jews, and who were now going to do terrible things to me and to my family." They were also much more likely to emigrate as entire families, although it wasn't unheard of for a husband to go first to prepare the way and earn money to finance the migration of the rest of the family. As a result, women made up forty-four percent of Jewish migrants, while they were only twenty-three percent of Italian immigration and thirty-three percent of Polish. Late nineteenth and early twentieth century Jewish immigration changed the composition of the U.S. Jewish population considerably. In 1880, there were about 250,000 Jews in the United States, five-sixths of them German in heritage. By 1920, there were four million Jews in the country, and five-sixths of them were of Eastern European descent.

Scandinavians

As elsewhere in Europe, the population of Scandinavia was increasing during the mid-nineteenth century due to declining infant mortality. Norway's population rose from nearly 1.2 million in 1835 to over 1.7 million in 1865. Further complicating the issue of population growth in Norway and Sweden was the fact that both nations were mostly rural during the late nineteenth century, having few cities where people were able to seek work. As in other places where industrialization lagged behind population growth, people were more likely to consider going overseas as an option to seek economic opportunity. During the period 1865–1915, nearly 677,000 Norwegians emigrated to the United States.

The vast majority of Scandinavian immigrants settled in the Midwest. Like the British, Germans, and Japanese, Swedish and Norwegian immigrants were more likely to be middle class, meaning they could afford the additional cost to travel to the Midwest and set up a farm. In 1860, for instance, there were about 55,000 people of Norwegian ancestry (sixty-eight percent of whom were immigrants) in the Midwest, and perhaps a thousand at most in the rest of the United States. Scandinavian communities often exhibited chain migration, sometimes several times over. Migrants from one location in Norway settled near each other in Illinois or southern Wisconsin, and then later as the community grew, some moved again, farther west to Iowa, and then later to Minnesota or the Dakotas.

Japanese immigration

The number of Japanese immigrants to the U.S. also grew in the late nineteenth century as a result of increasing turmoil in that nation. After the Meiji Revolution in 1868, Japan experienced rapid changes as it shifted from being an isolated agrarian society to an industrial one. The pace of the change caused major hardships for farmers during the 1880s: about one-seventh of Japan's rice farmland was foreclosed on during the years 1884–1886 alone. Emigration was one possible solution. Many went to Hawaii, where they could earn roughly six times as much as they could in Japan. During the years from 1885 to 1924, 200,000 Japanese migrants went to live in Hawaii and 180,000 went to the U.S. mainland.

Once in America, many Japanese immigrants worked in mines, railroad construction, and agriculture. Japanese farmers were quite successful in

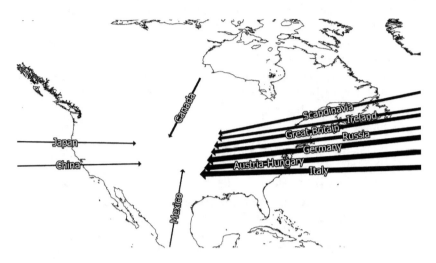

Map 3.1 Immigration to the United States 1860–1920

California, and by 1920, agricultural production on Japanese farms made up nearly ten percent of the total value of California's crops. One Japanese woman, Kimiko Ono, described a typical day on her family's farm:

> I got up before dawn with my husband and picked tomatoes in the greenhouse. At around 6:30 A.M. I prepared breakfast, awakened the children, and all the family sat down at the breakfast table together. Then my husband took the tomatoes to Pike Market. I watered the plants in the greenhouses, taking the children along with me....My husband came back at about 7 P.M. and I worked with him for a while, then we had dinner and put the children to bed. Then I sorted the tomatoes which I had picked in the morning and put them into boxes. When I was finally through with the boxing, it was midnight—if I finished early—or 1:30 A.M. if I did not.

As was common for many women, agricultural labor often meant doing double duty in the fields and the household for Japanese women. As Ono put it, "My husband was a Meiji man; he didn't even glance at the house work or child care. No matter how busy I was, he would never change a diaper."

Mexican immigration

As demand for farm labor continued growing in the West, Mexican immigration also increased. In addition to agriculture, Mexican men also found work in mines, on railroads, and in construction, and women in canneries, laundries, and packinghouses. Employers justified hiring Mexicans in racial terms, claiming that they were uniquely suited to do these types of work, particularly "stoop" labor in agriculture. George P. Clements, head of the Los Angeles County Agricultural Department, claimed that Mexicans had "crouching and bending habits" that made them uniquely suited for work as seasonal farm laborers, while whites were "physically unable to adapt." Employers also maintained that Mexican workers were especially docile and uncomplaining and would work for less due to a lower standard of living. As one Texas farmer put it, "The white people won't do the work and they won't live as the Mexicans do on beans and tortillas and in one room shacks." These characteristics made Mexicans seem like great workers, but not good potential citizens.

Living conditions for migrant farm workers were often very poor. Since the work was migratory, shelters were primitive. Workers lived in shacks made of canvas, burlap, or palm branches, with dirt floors. Water for drinking and cleaning came from the irrigation ditches, and there were no bathing facilities. Wages were also extremely low. Despite their supposed passivity, Mexican farm workers were active in labor struggles trying to improve conditions. Led by groups like the Confederacion de Uniones de Obreras Mexicanas (Confederation of Mexican Labor Unions) or La Union de Trabajadores del Valle Imperial (The Imperial Valley Workers' Union), migrant workers tried to negotiate better pay.

Many were still willing to cross the border to take these jobs, however, because of instability and dangerous conditions in Mexico during the reign of President Porfirio Diaz (1876–1911) and during the Mexican revolutionary period that followed (1910–1920). Porfiro Diaz's policies sought to modernize Mexico's economy and did cause rapid economic growth, but it was very unevenly distributed. The breakup of communal landholdings, combined with a bad drought in 1905–1907, put many farmers in a precarious position. Conditions worsened when a revolution broke out after Diaz was elected to a seventh term in 1910. One-tenth of the country's population died in ten years and in many places farmland was destroyed by the fighting, which further spurred emigration.

Mexican folk ballads, known as corridos, express the hopes and sorrows emigrants felt in leaving Mexico to seek work in the United States. One, titled "An Emigrant's Farewell," expressed the regrets some migrants felt:

Goodbye, my beloved country,
Now I am going away;
I go to the United States,
where I intend to work

Goodbye, my beloved mother,
The Virgin of Guadalupe,
Goodbye, my beloved land,
my Mexican Republic....

> I go sad and heavy-hearted
> to suffer and endure;
> my Mother Guadalupe,
> grant my safe return....
>
> I go to the United States
> to seek to earn a living.
> Goodbye, my beloved land;
> I bear you in my heart.
>
> For I am not to blame
> that I leave my country thus;
> the fault is that of poverty,
> which keeps us all in want....

The United States government expedited migration from Mexico through a policy of "benign neglect" at the border. During the early 1900s, there were only sixty border agents from the Bureau of Immigration operating along the entirety of the two thousand-mile long border with Mexico. Even those patrols that did exist were more focused on preventing Asian immigrants from sneaking into the country than with regulating Mexican immigration. Until the 1920s, it was common for large numbers of Mexicans to cross the border for harvest season, return to Mexico afterwards, and repeat the process year after year.

Urbanization during the Gilded Age

American cities during the Gilded Age were growing with incredible rapidity. In 1860, only one American in six lived in a city with a population greater than eight thousand, and by 1900, one in three did. The urban population roughly quadrupled during these years, while the rural population only doubled in size. The structure of cities changed as well, as increased construction of light rail allowed middle class families to move to the suburbs, while industrial workers, who could not afford to commute, were relegated to living in the increasingly crowded areas around the growing factories. Since so many immigrants were industrial workers, they were particularly likely to wind up living in the city's slums, either in the city core or in industrial districts around the periphery. Streets were often not paved and the trash not collected, so they became muddy and filled with rubbish. The trash combined with human and animal waste created a miasma of bad smells, which mingled with those of local industries: the smells of packinghouses and tanneries, the smoke and soot from industrial smokestacks.

Recent immigrants during the Gilded Age found themselves living in multifamily housing that was often dilapidated. Some of the buildings had been built to be multifamily dwellings, but many were single family dwelling or industrial buildings that had been repurposed to house multiple families. After 1880, some cities started constructing a style of multifamily building known as dumbbell tenements. Wider at the front and back and narrower in the middle, the airshaft formed between these buildings in theory provided ventilation to lower floors. In practice, little air or light reached the lower levels, and the airshaft itself became a place to throw trash, resulting in increased vermin and bad smells. Worst of all were the cellars that were rented as apartments, where residents not only had to cope with overcrowding and no windows or ventilation, but often also faced seepage from sewer lines or outside privies when it rained.

The constant stream of immigrants arriving, particularly men alone, meant there were a lot of people who needed a place to stay temporarily. Taking in boarders could be an invaluable way for a working-class family to bring in some extra revenue and help pay for their apartment or house. All available space was often packed with beds so that more people could fit. In some cases, beds were rented to two different men, one working the day shift and one at night. Women were the ones responsible for handling the work involved in taking in boarders, which included cleaning the apartment, doing laundry, and cooking meals. Sometimes boarders were strangers, but in other cases, families took in extended kin or people from their home village.

As they had done in the early nineteenth century, immigrants in the late nineteenth century continued forming ethnic neighborhoods that nurtured a wide assortment of ethnic institutions, including churches, schools, newspapers, businesses, and social institutions, all of which both helped increase the quality of life of immigrants and aided them in adapting to conditions in the United States. As with the early nineteenth century neighborhoods, saloons and coffeehouses remained popular gathering places. In addition to being places to socialize after work, they were also places to get information about employment opportunities, for other organizations to meet, or just to escape from overcrowded tenements. Butcher shops and grocery stores were often important businesses in the community as well, since they allowed migrants to find the correct ingredients to prepare their favorite foods or meet their dietary laws, such as kosher butchers for Jewish communities. Ethnic newspapers were also important institutions, allowing migrants to read local and international news in their own language and advertise their businesses and ethnic organizations to their compatriots. Many ethnic groups formed their own churches, and some created schools as well, whether to promote language maintenance among the second generation or to avoid the Protestant overtones of nineteenth century U.S. public education.

Large-scale industrialization

The United States underwent massive economic growth during the years after the Civil War. Industrialization had started during the early nineteenth century, but increased in its impact during the second half of the century. The number of people working in manufacturing in America went from 1.3 million in 1865 to 4.5 million in 1900. This rapid industrial growth, although it made some people very wealthy and made a plethora of products available for American consumers, was not without negative consequences. For workers, industrialization was often accompanied by falling wages, loss of job skills, long hours, and dangerous working conditions. It was not uncommon to work ten, twelve, or even more hours a day. Workers in mechanized industry might lose fingers or limbs to the unguarded moving parts of the machines, miners ran the risk of cave-ins and toxic gases, and smelters worked with molten metal on open hearths. To add insult to injury, wages in the late nineteenth century were extremely low, if still higher than immigrants were able to get in their homelands in Europe, and many industries had irregular or seasonal layoffs, with the result that their employees were often unemployed for at least part of the year.

So many immigrants were coming to America in the late nineteenth century seeking industrial work that to many middle-class Americans, manual labor itself was becoming associated with cultural foreignness. "Not every foreigner is a workingman," as one Chicago clergyman put it in 1887, but "it may almost be said that every workingman is a foreigner." This was an exaggeration, but immigrants and their children did make up a majority of the industrial working force in the late nineteenth century. In 1890, fifty-six percent of the workforce in manufacturing and mechanical industries were either foreign born or had foreign-born parents.

Not only immigrant men but women as well worked in industry. Immigrant women were especially dominant in the textile industry. Women made up fourteen percent of the industrial workforce in 1870 and twenty percent in 1910, but in areas where the textile industry dominated, like Fall River, Massachusetts, or Atlanta, Georgia, women made up around thirty-five percent of the workforce. For some groups, like the Irish and Scandinavians, domestic service was still the major source of employment for women who worked outside the home. As late as 1920, eighty percent of Irish women who worked outside the home were domestic servants. Jewish and Italian women, in contrast, preferred to avoid service if possible, and as a result, were more likely to work in garment factories or sweatshops. [Document 12] Both Jewish and Italian women were more likely to marry younger than Irish women, and industrial work would not require them to live away from their husband and children the way domestic service would. Both cultures also had taboos about married women working outside the home in general, and about daughters living outside their father's homes. Nonetheless, many were forced by financial need to accept daughters or wives working in industry, if the family was to survive.

Workers, whether native-born or immigrant, did not meekly accept the long hours, low wages, and dangerous conditions they experienced at work in the late nineteenth century. Some sought to unionize to give them better leverage against their employers in negotiating changes. This was difficult to do, however, given that employers could easily fire people for attempting to unionize, particularly during periods of economic downturn. Organizing efforts were also complicated due to divisions within the working class, between native-born and immigrant, between different ethnic and racial groups, between different religions, and different levels of skill and pay. Employers were very aware of this and sought to use it to their advantage, creating distinctions between different ethnic groups to keep them from cooperating. As a result, most people were not union members during the late nineteenth century—only about ten percent of the employed population belonged to a union in the 1880s and 1890s.

Nonetheless, strikes were common during the late nineteenth century. During the 1880s, there were nearly 10,000 strikes, and almost 700,000 workers went on strike in 1886, the year sometimes known as the "Great Upheaval," alone. Many strikes were spontaneous responses to a local event, like a firing, wage cut, or some other change in working conditions. Immigrants played major roles in strikes, perhaps not surprising given their prominence in the workforce. The predominance of immigrants in strike activity meant that to some native-born Americans, it seemed like alien forces had seized control of the nation, thus decreasing their sympathy with workers' plight.

Industrial-scale resource extraction in the American West

Economic development in the American West was both a major draw for immigrants and a product of their labor. The completion of the first trans-continental railroad in 1869 linked the economies of east and west, allowing larger scale development to take place in the west. Much of the construction was done by immigrants, particularly on the Central Pacific Railroad in the west, where nearly ninety percent of the workforce was Chinese. Although they were not a majority, a large proportion of the workers on the Union Pacific were Irish. Building the Transcontinental Railroad was no easy task, particularly in mountainous areas. Drilling and blasting to create tunnels and footings for the roadbed was a dangerous and laborious process. Nonetheless, despite their importance to the construction of the railroad in the west, Chinese immigrants generally received lower pay than white workers and—to add insult to injury—were excluded from the public cele-bration of the road's completion, including the famous "East-Meets-West" photograph that was taken at Promontory Point.

Western agriculture also underwent major growth after the Civil War. Intensive fruit and vegetable production developed along the lower Rio Grande in Texas, the Gila and Salt River valleys in Arizona, the Yakima Valley in Washington and the valleys of California. Chinese immigrants were involved in this process as well, introducing intensive techniques to grow asparagus, potatoes, and strawberries in California. The Chinese also provided labor for land reclamation work in the Sacramento–San Joaquin delta area, as farmers sought to raise the floodplain and build levies around it, so that the super fertile land could be made into fields. For some Chinese immigrants, this work would not have been entirely unfamiliar, since they had done similar work in the Pearl River Delta of China.

Much of the work of harvesting crops in California was done by migrant farm workers—approximately 200,000 migrant workers were employed in this sphere by the late nineteenth century. Initially, this migrant labor force was about half Chinese, although this proportion decreased after the Chinese Exclusion Act was passed in 1882. Farm owners seeking labor often relied on them, particularly since many white workers objected to the low wages and highly seasonal work patterns. As the work became more associated in their minds with Chinese workers, this further intensified white resistance to it, as they insisted they did not want to do "Chinamen's work" at "Chinamen's wages." As mentioned earlier, many Mexicans worked as migrant farm laborers as well, and the number only increased as the twentieth century began. Employers perceived Mexican workers, like the Chinese, as being people they could pay less than white workers. As one agricultural employer put it, "We want Mexicans because we can treat them as we cannot treat any other living men."

Mining was also growing across the west in the late nineteenth century, with major mining booms taking place in Colorado, Montana, Nevada, and Arizona. Many workers in these mines were immigrants. For example, after the silver boom at the Comstock Lode in Nevada, the 1880 census found 2,770 people working in the mining labor force, and only 770 of them American born. In general, native-born Americans were more likely to be machine operators, maintenance men, and supervisors, with immigrants predominating among the general mining labor force. The population included German, French, French Canadian, Cornish, Irish, Welsh, Scottish, Mexican, and Chinese miners.

Although there were still individual prospectors throughout the nineteenth century, seeking to stake claim to a mine on their own, by the 1860s, most miners were the employees of mining corporations. By the late nineteenth century, most of the profit in western mining was being made in common metals like copper and lead, instead of precious metals like gold and silver. In addition to immigrants, both white and Black native-born Americans worked in the mines, often moving from one to another over time in search of better wages. In general, Black, Chinese, and Mexican miners were paid less than white miners. Sometimes this was because of perceptions of skill, but also due to the prevalent racist belief that non-white workers did not need or deserve to make as much money as whites, even if performing identical work. There was also the perception that if they made more money, they would just waste it. The journalist J. Ross Browne, while visiting the Mowry Silver Mines near Santa Cruz, Arizona, described Mexican miners on payday wasting their money until "The women and children are left dependent upon new advances from the store-houses" and "the workmen are stupefied with mescal and many nights of debauch." Such attitudes made it easy for white mine owners to justify giving Mexican workers lower pay. Doing so also helped keep them working—if a miner owed money to a company store, it made it harder for them to quit and seek work elsewhere.

The Homestead Act and Western agriculture

The Homestead Act, created in 1862, encouraged immigrants who qualified and who had the necessary resources to take up farming in the American West. For just a small fee, farmers were able to stake claim to 160 acres of western land, and gain full title to it after five years of continuous occupation. Any adult citizen, male or female (if she was a household head), was eligible to claim land, as were unnaturalized immigrants who had declared their intention to become a citizen. Any immigrants who were ineligible to citizenship, however, like the Chinese or Japanese, would not be able to make a claim under this act. Women made up between five and fifteen percent of all homestead entries prior to 1900, and roughly twenty percent in the twentieth century.

Many people lacked the resources to stake a claim, however, including most urban workers. African Americans in the South, who had agricultural knowledge and would have loved to escape from the sharecropping system, were often prevented from leaving through debt. Similarly, recent immigrants might not have the resources to set up a farm in the United States. Estimates vary on how much money was required to start a farm on the frontier, but range from $500 to $800—a sum that was beyond the reach of many.

Even in rural areas, immigrants tended to settle in ethnic clusters. For instance, three-fifths of the adults in a small township in southeastern Nebraska were Germans, and similar communities could be found in other parts of Nebraska and Dakota Territory. Germans were the single largest group of immigrants to settle on the plains—from the border with Canada all the way down to Texas. Similarly, Scandinavians were concentrated in the Midwest and on the northern Great Plains. By the early 1900s, Swedes made up about ninety percent of Issanti County in eastern Minnesota, and Norwegians formed seventy to one hundred percent of the population of western Minnesota counties. The Homestead Act was a major draw for these migrants, and encouraged many of them to migrate to South Dakota, North Dakota, Minnesota, and Iowa to claim land. So many did so that the Norwegian journalist Olav Redal, who lived near Minot, North Dakota, referred to the area in northern Bottineau County as a Norwegian "bygd," or community. Even if there were fewer people around than in Europe or the eastern United States, people formed communities and depended on each other for survival. Assisting neighbors with work, helping them through childbirth and illness, borrowing equipment or pooling resources to buy shared oxen or plows, and making joint trips to town were common. The houses they lived in, at least at first, were often fairly primitive—sod houses, constructed from strips of prairie sod, were common, and although they were warm in winter, were small and dark and frequently leaked in the rain. Nonetheless, many immigrants were willing to make the sacrifice. As Redal put it, "At that time it was no disgrace for a hefty girl from the dales of Norway or a Trønder maiden to accompany her strong husband out on the unknown plains and move into a house that perhaps did not cost over \$20."

As a result of the westward expansion encouraged by the Homestead Act and the mining and lumbering booms in the west, Native Americans were losing their land with increasing rapidity in the late nineteenth century. Many groups resisted as long as they could, including fighting against the U.S. military to keep from being removed, but by the 1880s, most groups had been forced to surrender and move to reservations. An elaborate system of boarding schools, promoted by so-called "Friends of the Indian," may have meant well, but its intended purpose was to "detribalize" children by forcing them to abandon their native language, clothing, customs, and even their names, and it brutalized many children. The government was also determined to eliminate traditional tribal landholding patterns, and replace them with individually owned farms. Nonetheless, Native Americans chose land allotments based on their own values and traditional systems of land use that sought to preserve the tribal structure, instead of abandoning it as the government had hoped.

Conclusion

The period after the Civil War thus saw both a continuation of large-scale immigration to the United States, and the rapid changing of the world those immigrants were encountering. Industrialization and urbanization changed the ways immigrants would live and work, at least for the majority of them who would settle in cities. Birthright citizenship had been established, although it remained to be seen how many rights that citizenship would entail for Black Americans. And although immigrants of African descent were now eligible for naturalization, those from Asia still were not. Citizenship was thus just as attached to ideas about race as it had been previously, with Black Americans experiencing second-class citizenship and most Asians and Native Americans still being beyond the bounds of citizenship altogether. White Americans still judged immigration by racial standards, with immigrants from northwestern Europe being more welcomed than those from other areas. Chinese immigration would ultimately become the focus of the first efforts to exclude immigrants from the United States, ushering in an era of immigration restriction based on race.

4   The road to restriction

During the second half of the nineteenth century, American attitudes towards immigration gradually shifted in favor of exclusion. While some still embraced the idea of the United States as a nation that welcomed immigrants, others feared that the new arrivals were too numerous and too different to be incorporated into American society, making exclusion the only viable solution. [Documents 13 and 14] The Chinese were the first group targeted, resulting in the Chinese Exclusion Act of 1882. This act would ultimately become a model for subsequent racially based immigration policy that would seek to keep certain groups out of the country altogether. This immigration legislation was driven by the same growing racial consensus that led to segregation and Jim Crow laws across the U.S. By the late nineteenth and early twentieth centuries, pseudoscientific ideas about race and eugenics emphasized the need to keep the racial stock of the nation strong. Eugenics also shaped how immigration policy affected the disabled, and many immigration restrictions were created that directly or indirectly targeted people with disabilities. Ultimately, in the wake of World War I, the United States put in place restrictive immigration quotas that not only dramatically reduced the number of migrants able to come to the U.S. each year but also were based on the perceived racial suitability of each nation, with "whiter" nations receiving higher quotas and most Asian nations receiving no quota at all.

The Chinese Exclusion Act

The Chinese Exclusion Act of 1882 has been condemned by historians as being one of the most racist pieces of legislation of its era, but it was only the beginning. It represented the start of a new racist consensus on immigration that ultimately led to the exclusion of nearly all Asians from the United States by 1900 and the creation of strict limits for migration from many European nations by the 1920s. The Chinese were the first group specifically singled out for exclusion based on nationality, despite the fact that they made up less than one-twentieth of the migration stream going to the United States during the nineteenth century. There were just over 100,000

Chinese people in the entire country in 1880, as compared to nearly two million Germans.

Anti-Chinese sentiment can be seen in the laws local communities passed in the late nineteenth century that while racially neutral on their face, were specifically designed to target the Chinese. One notorious example was San Francisco's ordinance stating that all lodging houses had to provide at least five hundred cubic feet of air per resident, a standard that was not met by many Chinatown boarding houses. When many Chinese men wound up in jail as a result, the city passed another law, sometimes referred to as the Queue-Cutting Ordinance, which required all prisoners in the city jail to have their hair cut to within one inch of their scalp. In theory a health measure to prevent lice, this law targeted Chinese men who wore the queue, in which the front of the head was shaved and the rest pulled back into a long braid, as was required under the laws of the Qing dynasty.

In 1875, Congress passed the Page Act, which forbade the "importation into the United States of women for the purposes of prostitution." The law went on to specifically instruct inspectors to investigate whether women from "China, Japan, or any Oriental country" were being imported for these purposes. As a result of the supposition that Chinese women were likely to be prostitutes, they were nearly barred from the country altogether by this law.

Supporters of exclusion portrayed Chinese immigration as a threat to American workingmen and the power of the United States itself. [Document 15] As Senator James G. Blaine put it, "either the Anglo-Saxon race will possess the Pacific slope or the Mongolians will possess it." He further contended that "You cannot work a man who must have beef and bread, and would prefer beer, alongside of a man who can live on rice. It cannot be done."

Banning Chinese immigration entirely was complicated by the Burlingame Treaty of 1868, which explicitly stated that the Chinese could migrate to the U.S. without restriction. This was revised in 1880, providing that the U.S. could not entirely prohibit migration from China, but could regulate, limit, or even temporarily suspend it. In 1882, the Chinese Exclusion Act did exactly that, suspending the migration of Chinese laborers to the U.S. for ten years. Merchants, professionals, teachers, students, and tourists were not subject to the ban. When exclusion was renewed by the Geary Act in 1892, it also required all Chinese residents in the U.S. to register with immigration officials and keep a certificate of residence with them. If they did not do so, they could be arrested and potentially deported. [Document 16]

Chinese exclusion thus also had a major impact on the lives of Chinese people already living in the U.S. They were the first people in U.S. history to face suspicion of being illegal immigrants, even if they had been born in the United States. Chinese Americans also faced a general increase in hostility after the passage of the Exclusion Act. It had the effect of making it more acceptable to discriminate against them, since even the government had deemed them unsuitable for U.S. residency or citizenship, and segregation of the Chinese was common as was violence against them. [Document 17]

The fact that anti-Chinese violence continued after exclusion demonstrated that the hostility they faced was not solely about reducing immigration, but also about getting rid of the Chinese Americans who were already living in the country. Many towns in the West expelled their Chinese residents during the years after the Exclusion Act was passed. In February of 1885, the Chinese residents of Eureka, California were given twenty-four hours to leave, before those who remained were forced onto steamships and the Chinese neighborhood destroyed. In September of 1885, twenty-eight Chinese residents of Rock Spring, Wyoming were massacred, and the bunkhouses of another seventy-five burned, with the bodies of the dead and wounded being thrown into the flames. Tacoma in Washington Territory similarly expelled its Chinese population during the fall of 1885. In early November, about five hundred Chinese residents fled the city, before a mob drove out the two hundred who remained. Initially, the mob gave them four hours to leave, but growing impatient, they started breaking down doors and hauling people to the train station. Those who had money were able to buy a ticket, but others were forced to either jump onto freight trains or walk the one hundred miles to Portland. The mob then proceeded to burn down the Chinese neighborhood. People began referring to this method of violently expelling the Chinese as the "Tacoma Method."

For those Chinese people who had the right to enter the United States, either because they had lived here prior to 1882 or belonged to one of the exempt classes, entering the country posed major challenges. Many who sought entry were ultimately sent back to China without ever setting foot on the mainland. At any one time, there were between thirty and fifty women and six times as many men housed at the Angel Island immigration station in San Francisco Harbor, awaiting entry. Any non-Chinese immigrants entering from the port were kept separate from the Chinese migrants, and Chinese men and women lived in separate sex segregated dormitories, and were not allowed to communicate until they had been admitted, to prevent them from coordinating their stories.

Mai Zhouyi, the wife of a Chinese merchant and missionary from Canton, described this experience: "All day long I faced the walls and did nothing except eat and sleep like a caged animal. Others—Europeans, Japanese, Koreans—were allowed to disembark almost immediately. Even blacks were greeted by relatives and allowed to go ashore. Only we Chinese were not allowed to see or talk to our loved ones and were escorted by armed guards to the wooden house. Frustrated, we could only sigh and groan."

The interviews conducted to establish their right to entry could take hours, and returnees might be required to produce testimony from non-Chinese Americans to vouch for their claims. To try to detect falsehoods, family members were interviewed separately, and their right to enter denied if their answers did not match. This was often a challenging proposition,

Figure 4.1 Chinese women and children at Angel Island

Source: Chinese women and children at the immigration station, ca. 1910–1940 [Angel Island, Calif.], CHS2009.091 California Historical Society.

since the questions were very detailed and in some cases, the people in question had been separated from each other for many years. Typical questions to determine if people really were family focused on details about their home town in China, the layout of their house, or events at their wedding. Husbands who had been in America for years might no longer remember what furniture had been in their living room or who had poured the tea at their wedding, and some questions, like how many rooms were in the house, were somewhat ambiguous, given that one individual might count a hallway as a room, and another not. The entire process could drag on for months, during which time a migrant might have to send to China for documents or try to contact people on the mainland to testify on their behalf.

Some Americans who supported exclusion were frustrated by the apparent multitude of means by which Chinese people could still enter the country, and expressed concern that Chinese migrants might sneak across the border from Mexico or Canada, or might lie to bring in fake family members. As early as 1883, an article in the San Francisco *Alta California* referred to the Exclusion Act as "The Chinese Evasion Act" and an "Act to perfect the art of lying among the Chinese and their white auxiliaries." Others, however, agreed with the Chinese that the examinations were too difficult, and actually prevented even legal immigration. When the San Francisco Chamber of

to leave. Due to racially based hiring practices, it was difficult for Black men and women to get jobs in northern factories during the late nineteenth century, meaning that the northern cities that provided so many jobs to European immigrants during the nineteenth century were not a similar draw for Black migrants. It was also difficult to get the resources to start farming in the West, particularly given that Black sharecroppers found themselves living in near debt peonage, compelled to keep working for their land-owners, since that was the only way they would be able to pay them off.

Pseudoscientific ideas about race and nativism

Driving both segregation and the campaign for immigration restriction were new "scientific" ideas about race that developed in the late nineteenth and early twentieth centuries. Nineteenth century scientists who had strong ideas about race and European superiority not coincidentally found "evidence" that supported their preexisting beliefs. Theorists not only maintained that Africans, Asians, and Native Americans were inferior to Europeans but also identified a hierarchy of races within each of these categories. Europeans were divided into Nordic, Alpine, and Mediterranean races, with the former being portrayed as superior by people like Madison Grant, in his book, *The Passing of the Great Race*. He described Nordics as "a race of soldiers, sailors, adventurers and explorers, but above all, of rulers, organizers and aristocrats."

By the early twentieth century, some people worried that the Nordic race was essentially committing suicide by allowing such high numbers of racially different immigrants to come to the United States, and many prominent social scientists endorsed immigration restrictions on racial grounds. They warned that since native-born Americans were having fewer children while immigrants had many, the Nordics were making it inevitable that they would be replaced in their own nation. Francis Amasa Walker, in his presidential address to the American Economic Association in 1890, described immigrants from Southern and Eastern Europe as "beaten men from beaten races, representing the worst failures in the struggle for existence." E.H. Johnson of Crozer Theological Seminary described his visit to the Castle Garden immigration station in New York City by saying, "I have seen these poor wretches trooping out, wretches physically, wretches mentally, wretches morally, and stood there almost trembling for my country."

These racial theories were connected with eugenics, which was devoted to the idea of using science to improve human evolution. Although some supporters maintained that eugenics was only concerned with the health of the population, for most, eugenics was an act of judgment—deciding that some people were more fit than others, and that perhaps those who were less fit should be kept out or prevented from reproducing. This ultimately resulted not only in immigration restriction, but in the sterilization of people who were deemed unfit and, taken to its ultimate conclusion, in the Nazi

Holocaust, when "unfit" Jews, homosexuals, and people with disabilities were sent to death camps to be removed from the population.

We can see examples of these racialized views in the immigration law and court cases of the late nineteenth and early twentieth century, as policy makers and judges sought both to define what was meant by "whiteness" and to preserve the United States as a white nation. In some cases, the birthright citizenship of the Fourteenth Amendment could override ineligibility for citizenship. It had long been established, through court cases and legislation, that Chinese immigrants were not eligible for naturalization. Left unclear, however, was the status of the children of these immigrants born in the United States. This was finally clarified in 1898, when Wong Kim Ark, who had been born in San Francisco in 1873, sued after he was refused reentry to the country. In this case, the Supreme Court's ruling in U.S. v. Wong Kim Ark said that the Fourteenth Amendment's birthright citizenship provision applied to anyone born in the United States, regardless of race, and that Wong Kim Ark was thus a citizen.

In other cases, citizenship was both gendered and racialized. The Expatriation Act of 1907 stated various ways in which Americans could forfeit their citizenship, including for women, marrying a foreign man, since her citizenship was seen as being derivative of her husband's. In general, people portrayed the woman in question as an elite who had been dazzled by some European noble into marrying him for a title. In reality, very few American women who married foreigners were marrying nobility. Florence Bain Gual, a public school teacher in New York City, is a real example of the impact of this law. She had been teaching for fifteen years when she learned, in the early 1920s, that her marriage to a Cuban man threatened her job. The situation was made worse when her husband abandoned her, leaving her as the sole source of support for her family. As she put it, "I am the daughter of an American citizen and the mother of an American citizen, yet I am to be deprived of my livelihood in my own country because of the citizenship of a man."

Women who had married a foreign man and either been widowed or divorced had the option to become citizens again, although they would have to undergo naturalization like an immigrant. Elizabeth Cady Stanton's daughter, Harriot Stanton Blatch, found herself in this position, after her English husband died. However, for Asian American women, marrying a non-citizen meant that they lost their citizenship permanently, since as Asians they would be ineligible for naturalization. Given the relatively small number of women in the Chinese American community, native-born Chinese American women were quite likely to marry older Chinese immigrants, and thus irretrievably lose their citizenship without ever leaving the country. This remained true even after most aspects of women's derivative citizenship were eliminated by the Cable Act of 1922. Women would still lose their citizenship if they married a man ineligible for naturalization—i.e. someone from Asia.

Two later decisions about race and citizenship make clear that Americans defined race in confusing and inconsistent ways. The first case, Ozawa v. U.S. (1922) centered on Takao Ozawa, who was born in Japan and lived in Hawaii. He maintained that he should be eligible for citizenship, claiming both that Japanese were white and that his acculturation should make him eligible for American citizenship regardless. The court maintained that skin color alone did not determine whiteness, since that could vary quite a bit even between people of the same race. Instead they maintained that despite his light skin tone, Ozawa was not "Caucasian" according to the customary scientific definition of the word, and that the words "white person" in the naturalization law meant "Caucasian."

The court would contradict this reasoning the next year, in the case of Thind v. U.S. (1923). Ozawa's decision had given some hope to Indian immigrants, since most Indians were defined as Caucasian by the racial science of the time. Bhagat Singh Thind, an Indian man born in Punjab, was seeking naturalization. This time, however, the court said that "white" did not necessarily mean "Caucasian" in the scientific sense of the word, but rather in the sense it was popularly understood when the law was made. This time, they maintained that not science, but common knowledge, should rule. As they put it, "It may be true that the blond Scandinavian and the brown Hindu have a common ancestor..., but the average man knows perfectly well that there are unmistakable and profound differences between them to-day."

Racialized citizenship was further complicated when the United States acquired overseas colonies after the Spanish–American War in 1898, including Puerto Rico, Guam, and the Philippines. This was not done without debate. Some objected to bringing more non-whites into the country, even on very unequal terms. Others saw keeping these territories as hypocritical, given the U.S.'s supposed commitment to self-government. The counter argument to this was that, as the superior race, whites had a moral obligation and duty to protect and lift up inferior races. Sometimes referred to as the "white man's burden," after the poem by Rudyard Kipling, this condescending attitude appeared in President William McKinley's explanation of his decision to keep the Philippines: "(1) That we could not give them [the Philippines] back to Spain—that would be cowardly and dishonorable; (2) that we could not turn them over to France or Germany—our commercial rivals in the Orient—that would be bad business and discreditable; (3) that we could not leave them to themselves—that they were unfit for self-government—and they would soon have anarchy and misrule over there worse than Spain's was; and (4) that there was nothing left for us to do but to take them all, and to educate the Filipinos, and uplift and civilize and Christianize them, and by God's grace do the very best we could by them, as our fellowmen for whom Christ also died."

The treatment of these territories thus differed considerably from those in the mainland United States, where the assumption was both that the population would be mostly white and that the area would become a state. In the Insular Cases, between 1901 and 1904, the Supreme Court ruled that the Constitution did not automatically extend to these territories. Residents of Puerto Rico and the Philippines were not aliens but also were not U.S. citizens, even if they were born after the U.S. took over the area. Neither Puerto Ricans nor Filipinos were happy with this state of affairs. The Filipinos rebelled against U.S. rule, resulting in a war that lasted from 1898 to 1902.

At the same time that the United States was acquiring land during the Spanish–American War, they were also engaged in a takeover in Hawaii. There had been some Americans, mostly missionaries, in the Hawaiian Islands since the 1820s, not long after the kingdom of Hawaii had been unified by King Kamehameha I. By 1848, foreigners had convinced the Hawaiian government to allow them to purchase land in the islands. As a result, in only two decades, most of the best agricultural lands in Hawaii were in the hands of foreigners. These were turned into large plantations growing sugar and pineapples using not only local Hawaiian labor but that of many immigrants from China and Japan. In 1897, Americans forced King Kalakaua to accept a new constitution, sometimes referred to as the Bayonet Constitution, which forced the king to give up most of his power to a legislature that was dominated by Americans. Six years later, the foreigners, with support from U.S. troops and a warship, successfully overthrew the Hawaiian monarchy, imprisoned Queen Lili'uokalani, and proclaimed Hawaii a republic on July 4, 1893. They immediately asked to be annexed by the United States, although this would not take place until 1898.

Disability and nativism

Many of the earliest federal immigration restrictions focused on ability, whether directly or indirectly. Concern that an immigrant might become a public charge was often based on whether they appeared able bodied or not. Disability also connected with the late nineteenth century obsession with race, since eugenics warned that allowing more people with "inferior" or "defective" genes into the United States might pollute the racial stock of the nation. Immigration restriction in the late nineteenth and early twentieth centuries was thus heavily based on appearance, with those whose appearance did not seem "normal" to the immigration inspectors being much more likely to be singled out for additional screening or deportation.

The first general immigration law (passed in 1882, less than three months after the Chinese Exclusion Act) stipulated that "any convict, lunatic, idiot, or any person unable to take care of himself or herself without becoming a public charge" could be excluded. While offensive, the terms "lunatic" and "idiot" were considered clinical diagnoses in the 1880s, and would refer to people with psychiatric or intellectual disabilities. The specific list of excludable criteria would be expanded upon several times over the next few decades, adding epileptics, "imbeciles," "feeble-minded persons," and those who could not read to the list. The "likely to become a public charge" provision was essentially a catch-all for other types of disability, and could be applied at the discretion of the immigration officials. This provision was also highly gendered, in that it was much more likely to be applied to women than to men. This was particularly true for women who arrived alone, were pregnant or had children to support, had a questionable moral past, or performed work that was not in high demand.

It is hard to judge how many immigrants were excluded by these measures. Only about two percent were sent back, but the measures likely deterred some people from attempting to enter. Furthermore, shipping companies had a vested interest in not bringing over people who would not be admitted, since a law required them to pay a fine for each rejected immigrant, plus return them to Europe for free.

Immigration officials watched the migrants as they progressed through Ellis Island, and if they suspected that one had a disability or disease, they would mark them with chalk on their backs, to signal that they should be pulled out for further inspection. The letter they wrote was a code for what the inspector should look for, with K standing for a hernia, S for senility, CT for trachoma, etc. [Document 19] Inspectors were warned to watch for people trying to hide a disability. For instance, Dr. Allan McLaughlin of the U.S. Public Health Service said that

> The nonchalant individual with an overcoat on his arm is probably concealing an artificial arm; the child strapped to its mother's back, and who appears old enough to walk alone, may be unable to walk because of infantile paralysis...and a bad case of trachoma may show no external evidence and be detected only upon everting the eyelid.

Homosexuals and those who did not conform to cisgender, heterosexual norms also found themselves targeted for exclusion during these years. The rationale for their exclusion tended to include both moral aspects and a portrayal of homosexuality as a disease. Since American physicians at the time characterized homosexuality as an inheritable form of insanity, seeking to exclude them from entry fit with the general eugenics-focused view of immigration restriction. If immigration inspectors suspected someone might be homosexual, they would question the person on whether or not they were married, if they wanted to marry, if they liked the opposite sex, etc.

In all of these cases, a lot of power was placed in the hands of inspectors. Many of the categories excluded were quite vague, leaving inspectors with a lot of leeway to decide who was "feeble-minded" and who was not. Inspectors prided themselves on being able to watch a line of people walk past, and pick out those who had disabilities. As one inspector put it, his job was "to detect poorly built, defective or broken down human beings." This was a very subjective process, however, and immigrants were largely at the mercy of whether or not an inspector thought they appeared disabled. Excluding the disabled was one of the major goals, and not just a side effect, of the immigration laws of the late nineteenth and early twentieth centuries. The Commissioner General of Immigration even said that "the exclusion from this country of the morally, mentally, and physically deficient is the principal object to be accomplished by the immigration laws."

World War I

World War I brought an immediate decrease in immigration, due to the chaos of war. During 1916, for instance, the number of immigrants arriving at the U.S. went below three hundred thousand, with fewer than half being from Europe. Nonetheless, there was a strong nationalistic sentiment in the country at the time, that led Congress to pass a literacy requirement for immigration in 1917 and, when President Wilson vetoed it, to pass it over his veto.

The same law created the Asiatic Barred Zone, which added South and Southeast Asians to the list of those excluded from the U.S. Exceptions were made for the Philippines, which was still a U.S. territory, and Japan, since the Gentlemen's Agreement was still in effect. The law also expanded the mental, physical, and moral defects that could be used as grounds for exclusion, and strengthened the anti-radical provisions of immigration law. Finally, "persons with abnormal sexual instincts" was added to the list of "defects" that could justify exclusion, making it even easier for inspectors to deny entry to homosexuals as well as those who didn't conform to binary gender norms.

Nativists during the World War I era were not only concerned with restricting immigration, however. They also wanted to try to encourage the assimilation of any immigrants who were already in the United States. This wasn't unique to the World War I period—one of the major debates about immigration in the late nineteenth and early twentieth centuries focused on whether or not immigrants could be assimilated. Although the term "melting pot" grew in popularity as a metaphor for assimilation after Israel Zangwill's play by that name in 1908, some nativists doubted that all immigrants were capable of "melting." As one letter writer to a Chicago newspaper put it, "the U.S. has ceased to be a 'melting pot': it is only a 'mixing pot' [and] the scum is running over and extinguishing the flames of pure Americanism burning underneath. Why should we not discriminate between immigrants? Some are more desirable than others. Some cannot be assimilated."

Some thought the public schools could be an important mechanism of assimilation, since they removed children from their parents' influence and put them into a controlled environment where they would play with and learn from American children. Some thought this could work with adults as well, as was symbolized by the mandatory graduation ceremony for the

English classes offered in Henry Ford's factories. Workers dressed in trad-itional garb marched into a large "melting pot" on stage, only to come out in American clothing. Others with more racially based ideas of culture dis-agreed. As eugenics expert Alfred P. Schultz wrote in his 1908 book, *Race or Mongrel?*, "the opinion is advanced that the public schools change the chil-dren of all races into Americans. Put a Scandinavian, a German, and Magyar boy in at one end, and they will come out Americans at the other. Which is like saying, let a pointer, a setter, and a pug enter one end of a tunnel and they will come out three greyhounds." [Document 20]

Americanization efforts took on new urgency for many after the U.S. entered World War I, due to concerns that immigrants might have divided loyalties. Advocates of "100% Americanism" urged immigrants to assimilate completely and abandon their "hyphenated" identities as Irish Americans or Italian Americans to be purely American in their culture and sympathies. Prior to U.S. involvement in the war, most immigrant groups and most of the native-born sympathized with the Allies. The exceptions were German Americans, Irish Americans, and American Jews, all of whom tended to sympathize with the Central Powers. For German Americans, supporting Germany seemed natural, and many were proud of what that nation had accomplished since it had unified in 1870. The Irish and Jewish Americans supported the Central Powers not out of an attachment to any one of them, but out of hostility to one of the Allies—Great Britain in the case of the Irish, and Russia for Jewish Americans.

Once the U.S. entered the war, however, the overwhelming majority of people, regardless of nativity or ethnicity, supported the U.S. and sought to create more enthusiasm for the war effort. The Committee on Public Information was created to help with this effort. At least some of the propa-ganda they created was aimed at making Americans hate Germans—calling them Huns, accusing them of being rapists and baby killers, and generally attacking German culture.

Partially as a result of these efforts, there was a lot of anti-German sen-timent during the war. Such feelings led to many attacks on German cul-ture in the U.S., including the closure of German-language newspapers, the cancelling of German classes in schools, the burning of pro-German books, and even renaming things, making sauerkraut into "liberty cabbage." Some states even sought to forbid the speaking of German in public or on the phone. Newspapers published lists of Germans deemed disloyal, and some people faced violence or humiliation as a result of their presumed disloy-alty. Some people were made to kiss the U.S. flag, or paraded through the streets singing patriotic songs. Some were forced to kneel and denounce Germany or curse the Kaiser. And a few were injured or killed as a result of these actions—John Meints, a farmer living in Luverne, MN, was tarred and feathered, and Robert Prager of Collinsville, IL, was lynched. In response, some Germans sought to perform their loyalty publicly by purchasing large amounts of Liberty Bonds or doing volunteer work, while others sought to hide their German ancestry, abandoning their culture and changing their names.

Crafting the National Origins Act

Immigration reform began in earnest in 1907, when a Congressional investigation into immigration was commissioned. Referred to as the Dillingham Commission, after its chair, Senator William P. Dillingham, this commission was a massive undertaking. Its final report, submitted in 1911, filled forty-two volumes and included testimony from business leaders, sociologists, economists, policy leaders, and diplomats. Heavily influenced by the racial ideas of the era, the commission created the terms "old" and "new" immigration to differentiate between the more desirable immigrants from Northern and Western Europe, and those from Southern and Eastern Europe they hoped to exclude.

Ultimately, the commission recommended a literacy test and the creation of a racially based set of immigration quotas that would limit the number of people coming from each nation. In 1921, Congress enacted the Emergency Quota Act, which limited migration to three percent of the total number of foreign born people in the U.S. according to the 1910 census, with a total cap of 350,000. The Johnson-Reed Act of 1924, also known as the National Origins Act, was even more restrictive. The quota was lowered from three percent to two percent, and the census used to set the baseline was not the 1910 or 1920 census, but the 1890 one. This meant that the quotas for Southern and Eastern Europeans would be substantially lower, since they had formed a much smaller part of the total U.S. population back then. Immigration from Asia, including Japan, was essentially forbidden, since anyone ineligible for citizenship was also barred from immigrating. The restrictionists failed, however, to extend these quotas to the western hemisphere. Agricultural employers in the Southwest ensured this, with their arguments that losing access to seasonal labor from Mexico would ruin them. The law then called for a "scientific" study of the origins of the U.S. population to be used to set quotas after 1929. It would be more accurate to say it was a study of the white population of the U.S., since it excluded any immigrants from the New World and their descendants, Asians and their descendants, descendants of "slave immigrants," and the descendants of "American aborigines." "American" and "white" were essentially synonymous in the eyes of Congress.

Conclusion

Ultimately this legislation had a profound impact on immigration to the United States. The numbers dropped immediately, although still not as low as restrictionists had hoped. The composition of the migration stream changed significantly as well. Prior to World War I, immigrants from the New World were only about seven percent of total immigration to the U.S., and during the six years afterwards, they were nearly half. Germans, British, and Irish had been only about thirteen percent of total immigration to the U.S. during the first decade of the twentieth century, but now made up sixty-two percent. Italy, Russia, and Austria-Hungary had been the three biggest sending nations between 1890 and 1920, and between 1930 and 1960 the largest were Germany and Canada. One prominent eugenicist, Harry Laughlin, summed up the restrictionists' goals when he wrote,

> Henceforth, after 1924, the immigrant to the United States was to be looked upon, not as a source of cheap or competitive labor, nor as one seeking asylum from foreign oppression, nor as a migrant hunting a less strenuous life, but as a parent of future-born American citizens. This meant that the hereditary stuff out of which future immigrants were made would have to be compatible racially with American ideals.

Ensuring that "racial compatibility" was the primary goal of the National Origins Act.

5 Immigration under the National Origins Act

Under the National Origins Act, U.S. immigration policy was designed to encourage immigration from Northwestern Europe and discourage it from the rest of the world. However, other forces affected the operation of this system. The needs of businesses continued to encourage immigration from the western hemisphere. The Great Depression disrupted immigration altogether, as did World War II, which additionally raised new issues that began to crack Americans' commitment to the national origins system. In particular, Americans' desire for an immigration policy that would recognize the needs of refugees increased in the wake of the Nazi Holocaust, as did their distaste for a policy that was so explicitly based on race. As a result, by the 1950s and 1960s, support for replacing the National Origins Act with something that would be racially neutral and more equitable between nations grew immensely.

Reduced immigration under the National Origins Act

To a certain extent, the Johnson-Reed Act did exactly what its creators had hoped, and resulted in both a reduction in the number of migrants coming to the U.S. and a reduction in the percentage of them that were coming from Southern and Eastern Europe. After the act went into effect, only 8,000 Poles and 15,000 Italians were entering each year. Germans, on the other hand, were coming at a higher rate than before World War I, with about 45,000 immigrants. Together, the British, Irish, Scandinavians, and Germans made up thirty-seven percent of total immigration to the U.S., and nearly seventy percent of immigration from Europe—a massive change from the previous trends.

Nonetheless, total immigration was higher each year than the restrictionists had expected. They had predicted immigration would average around 150,000–165,000 per year, but actual totals were closer to 220,000 people per year. This was partially because immigrants from the Americas were not included in the quotas, and New World immigration was increasing during the 1920s. As a result, there was a continual push to extend the quota system to the New World, which failed due to successful lobbying

Table 5.1 Immigration between 1921 and 1950

Nation	1921–1930	1931–1940	1941–1950
Germans	412,202	114,058	226,578
Irish	211,234	10,973	19,789
British	339,570	31,572	139,306
China	29,907	4,928	16,709
Japan	33,462	1,948	1,555
Canada	924,515	108,527	171,718
Mexico	459,287	22,319	60,589
Scandinavia	198,210	11,259	26,158
Italians	455,315	68,028	57,661
Austria-Hungary	63,548	11,424	28,329
Soviet Union	61,742	1,370	571

Note: British includes England, Scotland, and Wales, and after 1925, Northern Ireland. Scandinavia includes Norway, Sweden, and Denmark.

U.S. Immigration and Naturalization Service, *Statistical Yearbook of the Immigration and Naturalization Service, 2001*. (U.S. Government Printing Office: Washington, D.C., 2003), p. 18.

by the agricultural interests in the West, who relied on low-wage migrant labor from Mexico. There were also other opportunities to enter as a non-quota immigrant. For instance, the wives (but not husbands) and children of U.S. citizens (provided they were not aliens ineligible to citizenship) were allowed to enter as non-quota immigrants.

Continued immigration during the 1920s

Mexicans

Closing the door to large-scale immigration from the eastern hemisphere increased the proportion of immigrants coming from the new world, particularly Mexico. In addition to working in agriculture, Mexican immigrants also found work in railroad construction and mining in the West. Others went to industrial cities in the Midwest and Northeast to take factory jobs that had previously been filled by immigrants from Southern and Eastern Europe. Due to employment discrimination, Mexican workers were disproportionately located in unskilled work. In 1918, seventy percent of Mexicans living in Los Angeles held unskilled blue-collar jobs, while only about six percent of Anglos did. This was very frustrating for Mexican workers—as one put it, "I know that if I want to amount to something in any work I will have to do it there in Mexico, because the Americans only despise us."

Although there was no quota for western hemisphere immigration, there were still some laws that could potentially limit it. The 1917 immigration law included both a literacy test and an eight-dollar head tax on entry, and employers worried that these requirements might exclude some Mexican

Figure 5.1 Migratory Mexican field worker's home on the edge of a frozen pea field

Source: Dorothea Lange, photographer. Migratory Mexican field worker's home on the edge of a frozen pea field. Imperial Valley, California, 1937. Library of Congress Prints and Photographs Division Washington, D.C. https://www.loc.gov/item/2017769879/

migrants. Agribusinesses succeeded in having a provision added to the law that would allow the Secretary of Labor to set the law aside if there was a labor shortage. This provision was used almost immediately for agricultural workers as well as those in factories, mining, construction, and railroads. Not all Mexican immigrants entered the country through official channels, however, given how much of the border was unpatrolled and how simple it was to cross without going through immigration proceedings. Some referred to these migrants derogatorily as "wetbacks" or "mojados," since they had supposedly swum the Rio Grande River to enter the country.

As increasing numbers of Mexican immigrants came to the United States during the late 1920s, opposition to them increased. One editorial in the *Saturday Evening Post* asked, "how much longer [are] we going to defer putting the Mexican Indian under the quota law" and expressed concern that Mexican Americans would soon outnumber whites given that "Mexican laborers often have nine children, or even more." Congressman Albert

H. Vestal of Indiana asked "what is the use of closing the front door to keep out undesirables from Europe [while] permit[ting] Mexicans to come in here by the back door by the thousands?"

Mexican Americans faced segregation and discrimination in their daily lives as well. In many communities, Mexican Americans were not allowed to shop in the Anglo-American business district except on Saturdays, or eat in Anglo cafes unless they had a separate seating section. Mexican Americans sometimes objected to having to sit in the section reserved for African Americans, demonstrating their awareness that this was a degradation in the eyes of white Americans. Wenceslao Iglesias described an incident during the 1920s when "a group of us Mexicans who were well dressed once went to a restaurant in Amarillo, and they told us that if we wanted to eat we should go to the special department where it said 'For Colored People.' I told my friend that I would rather die from starvation than to humiliate myself before the Americans by eating with the Negroes."

Mexicans also had to send their children to segregated schools. The wife of a white American ranch manager saw this as a necessary step to keep them in their place. As she put it, "Let him [the Mexican] have as good an education but still let him know he is not as good as a white man. God did not intend him to be; He would have made him white if He had." A white sharecropper put the matter more bluntly when he said "Why don't we let the Mexicans come to the white school? Because a damned greaser is not fit to sit side of a white girl." But ultimately, keeping Mexican Americans minimally educated served the needs of employers who wanted to retain them as a low paid workforce. As one sugar beet grower put it, "If every [Mexican] child has a high school education, who will labor?"

Filipinos

Another major group of migrants working in agriculture in the West during the early twentieth century were Filipinos. Filipinos were able to move to the United States free of any quota and despite the restrictions on immigration from Asia because they were not immigrants—the Philippines was a U.S. colony. At the same time, however, Filipinos were designated as U.S. nationals, not citizens, and were deemed ineligible to become naturalized citizens by virtue of being Asian.

Many Filipino migrants during the early twentieth century went to Hawaii. By 1930, there were more than sixty thousand Filipinos in Hawaii, making up seventeen percent of its population. After the Gentlemen's Agreement with Japan in 1907 cut off their supply of Japanese labor, Hawaiian sugar planters sought to bring in Filipino workers. In addition to being a new source of labor, many planters also saw a turn to Filipino labor as being a way to deal with the increasingly militant Japanese labor movement in the islands. Filipinos were supposedly a docile workforce that would not mind bad work or low pay.

In reality, Filipino workers in Hawaii actively organized to fight for better wages throughout their time working there. A major series of strikes took place in the 1920s in which workers from different ethnic groups united around their common dislike for the "lunas" (plantation foremen). The planters ultimately prevailed, but the strikes were serious enough to make them take action to further diversify the workforce in an attempt to prevent future strikes.

As conditions failed to improve in the islands, some Filipinos decided to move to the U.S. mainland seeking work. Some found work in West Coast cities as domestic servants or in hotels and restaurants as bellmen, cooks, dishwashers, and janitors. However, their major employer, as with the Mexicans, would be agriculture on the West Coast. By 1920, there were 5,603 Filipinos living in the mainland United States, mostly on the West Coast. By 1930, there were about 56,000 Filipinos living on the West Coast, most of them young, single men.

Most were migrant laborers, who followed the harvest and canning season, finding work through Filipino labor contractors. Filipinos worked with a wide variety of crops over the course of the year, picking fruit, cutting asparagus, topping beets, and thinning lettuce. As was common in the industry, Filipino migrant farm workers encountered rudimentary living conditions, with overcrowded and poorly constructed bunkhouses being the norm. They often worked eight to ten hours a day stooped over in the field with only short breaks, and spent much of the day coated in dust. The pay was terrible—generally just fifteen cents an hour before 1933, and twenty after that. According to journalist Carey McWilliams, Filipinos were some of the "most viciously exploited" workers in California.

During the off-season, many Filipino workers went to Alaska to work in the salmon canneries. Again they were hired for some of the hardest and dirtiest jobs, like hauling and cleaning the fish. Canneries struggled to find workers—the work was extremely hard and unpleasant, Alaska was remote, and the canning season only lasted three or four months. By the 1920s, canneries had established recruiting stations in West Coast cities like San Francisco, Portland, and Seattle, to recruit Filipino workers during the off-season for agricultural work. Cannery workers were paid $250 for a four-month season, but much of that could be lost through deductions for food and supplies. As a result of all of these expenses, workers were often left with only thirty or forty dollars at the end of the season.

Cannery workers created unions to fight for better pay and conditions, and Filipinos were active in this effort. The Cannery Workers and Farm Laborers Union (CWFLU), affiliated with the American Federation of Labor, was formed in 1932. The majority of the members were Filipinos, as were all of the leaders. Unionizing was difficult in this industry, since private contractors controlled hiring and ethnic divisions within the workforce caused difficulties. Nonetheless, by the mid-1930s they were able to make some significant gains, including ending the contractor system and winning a closed shop that gave the CWFLU control of hiring through its hiring hall in Seattle.

As the number of Filipinos on the West Coast increased, an anti-Filipino movement developed. Some opponents argued that Filipinos were unfair low-wage labor competition for white workers, while others worried that Filipino men were obsessed with white women and interracial sex. Filipino immigrants faced violence as a result, as the Chinese and Japanese had before them. In some cases, this violence came from law enforcement. As Filipino novelist and poet Carlos Bulosan put it in his memoir *America is in the Heart*, "I came to know that the public streets were not free to my people: we were stopped each time these vigilant patrolmen saw us driving a car. We were suspect each time we were seen with a white woman." In other cases, vigilantes or mobs were the source of the violence. As a child, Connie Tirona saw two Filipino men being dragged away by men on horseback because they had been talking to white women. A group of white youths in Dinuba, California, attacked Filipino workers who were out on dates with local white girls in 1928. During the winter of 1929–1930, at least thirty anti-Filipino acts of violence took place, including several fire bombings and two major race riots. Filipinos were soon referred to as the "third invasion" from Asia.

Filipinos did not accept this characterization of themselves as cheap labor and of interracial relationships as degenerate. They pointed out the hypocrisy of condemning white-Filipino relationships in the United States, given how common relationships between white American men and Filipina women were in the Philippines. They had received U.S. style educations in the Philippines, and emphasized that they were not savages, but Americanized nationals of the United States. As Manuel Buaken put it, "I was born under the American flag, I had American teachers since I was six, I am a loyal American," but nonetheless he found employers would not hire him.

The anti-Filipino movement was also an anti-imperial movement by necessity, since opponents of Filipino immigration could find no way to exclude them unless the Philippines was an independent nation. This led to an odd alliance between Filipino nationalists and anti-Filipino nativists, both pushing for Philippine independence. In 1934, the Tydings-McDuffie Act said that the Philippines would gain its independence in 1945. However, it noted that "the Philippines shall be considered a foreign country" for immigration purposes immediately, and granted them a quota of fifty. Had World War II not intervened, the islands likely would have been added to the Asiatic Barred Zone in 1945. However, the capture of the Philippines by Japan during World War II meant not only that independence was postponed until 1946, but also that the sacrifices of Filipinos during the war were recognized with a token quota of one hundred, and the extension of naturalization rights to Filipinos.

Puerto Ricans

Puerto Ricans, much like Filipinos, did not start moving to the continental United States in large numbers until the 1920s, at which point, they were not immigrants at all in any standard sense of the word. Like Filipinos, they had been U.S. nationals since the United States took control of Puerto Rico during the Spanish American War in 1898. Unlike Filipinos, Puerto Ricans had been made U.S. citizens in 1917. Angry that the Foraker Act that made Puerto Rico a U.S. territory provided no path to self-rule or statehood, Puerto Rican leaders had asked for independence in 1914. Congress replied with the Jones Act of 1917, which made it clear that Puerto Rico would always be part of the United States, and granted all Puerto Ricans U.S. citizenship.

Prior to 1917, the majority of Puerto Ricans moving overseas went to Hawaii to work on sugar plantations. After 1917, when they received U.S. citizenship, more Puerto Ricans came to the mainland U.S. as well. New York City was an especially popular destination, where they filled many of the industrial jobs previously filled by Southern and Eastern European immigrants after they were shut out by the 1924 National Origins Act. Many Puerto Ricans had skilled jobs in industry, with cigar making being an industry in which they were especially prominent. Many Puerto Ricans settled in the neighborhood of East Harlem in New York in the 1920s, which became known as Spanish Harlem or El Barrio as a result. Although identified as a Puerto Rican neighborhood, it was also common for there to be other Spanish speaking groups, including Cubans, living there, as well as Black Americans.

In 1920, there were only about 12,000 Puerto Ricans in the continental U.S., but by 1930, there were 53,000, and 90,000 by 1944. Even more came after World War II, and it was during the 1940s that Puerto Ricans surpassed Cubans to be the most numerous Caribbean group in the U.S. Before that, although there was a lot of poverty on the island and they were not barred from going to the mainland, there had been no easy way for them to go, since no cheap transportation existed between Puerto Rico and the mainland U.S. After 1946, most Puerto Ricans arrived in New York City by plane, resulting in the first large-scale air migration in history. As flights became more frequent, cheaper, and shorter, back and forth migration became more practical, allowing people to move to the mainland while still maintaining close ties in Puerto Rico.

Manny Vélez was a typical example of a Puerto Rican who decided to migrate after World War II. Years later, he attributed his decision to move to Chicago in 1949 to "la fiebre" (the fever for America) that made so many want to leave his hometown of San Sebastián. As he put it, "I don't know why I went [to Chicago]. I didn't really have to go there. There were others who really did have to leave, but not me. I think it was the fever. Yes, the fever to leave...to get to know [a new place]." Despite efforts by his employers in Puerto Rico to talk him out of leaving, Vélez moved to Chicago and lived there for more than twenty years, before finally returning to San Sebastián in the early 1970s—a not uncommon course for Puerto Rican migrants.

Indian Sikhs

A final group that attracted some attention in the early twentieth century were Sikhs from India. Roughly 6,400 had come by 1920. Sikhs often found agricultural work in the West, frequently working alongside Mexican migrants. Native born Americans mocked them as "the tide of turbans" for the turbans that Sikh men wore. This migrant stream was mostly composed of men. In 1914, only 0.24% of the five thousand Asian Indians in the U.S. were women. The population would likely have balanced over time, as was common with many immigrant groups, except that the 1917 immigration law that created the Asiatic Barred Zone made it impossible for men to bring their wives in anymore. This presented immigrants with a dilemma— even going back home to visit family might mean they would never be able to return to the United States. As Bagga Singh Sunga of El Centro, California, put it, "I knew that if I went back to India to join her [his wife], we would never be allowed to come back to the United States."

Many Indian Sikhs would ultimately marry Mexican women instead as a result. In central California, roughly seventy-six percent of Sikh men had a Mexican American wife. Partially this was because they had met through their shared work. It also presented a way for Sikh men to purchase land and start farming independently in California. The Alien Land Act of 1913 did not allow aliens who were ineligible for citizenship to purchase land, which would exclude Indians, but not Mexicans. These relationships were not always easily accepted by families back in India. Sucha Singh noted that he had not told his family about his decision to marry a Mexican woman, but "I suppose others have told them about it, but I do not care even if they should be 'sour' about it." A blending of cultures resulted from these intermarriages. Families ate a mixture of Mexican and Punjabi food, spoke a combination of Spanish, Punjabi, and English at home, and might give their children an Indian name, but a Spanish nickname, for instance.

The Great Depression

Ultimately, immigration only proceeded normally under the National Origins Act for a few years, before global events intervened to change immigration dramatically. The Great Depression of the 1930s resulted in far fewer people entering the country than had during the 1920s. In fact, during four years of the Depression (1932–1935), more people actually left the United States than entered it. This was not unprecedented. Fewer people always came to the U.S. during economic downturns, when high unemployment made the nation seem like an unattractive place to seek work. Potential migrants often found it easier to be poor in their home countries, where they had family support networks that could help them survive difficult times.

The United States also took action to encourage some who were already resident to leave. In particular, the government targeted Mexican Americans for "repatriation" back to Mexico. Although the government framed this as a voluntary government-funded repatriation, and not as deportation, many migrants had little choice but to accept. One man who repatriated from Indiana Harbor, Indiana, described his experience:

> So they told you, " You are making $7.00 or $8.00 per payday for your family. You can't feed them, you can't do nothing. So we are going to take you off welfare." "Oh, God, what are you going to do, take us off welfare? We'll starve." "No, no, you have an alternative...go to Mexico. We have a train available. A train full of Mexican people...." So actually they weren't forcing you to leave, they gave you a choice, starve or go back to Mexico.

In this "repatriation", the government made no distinction between citizens and non-citizens, or between Mexican immigrants and native-born Mexican Americans. The Los Angeles Chamber of Commerce estimated that perhaps as much as sixty percent of those "repatriated" from that county were children who were native-born American citizens who left "without very much hope of ever coming back into the United States." One such child, Emilia Castañeda of Los Angeles, remembered how her family had to move to Mexico after her mother died and her father lost his job in 1935. "We cried and cried," she said. "I had never been to Mexico." In fact, she did not even speak Spanish fluently, since her elementary school had forbidden children to speak it. [Document 21] Mary Lou, a fifteen-year old girl born in Wayne, Michigan had her fate decided by a social worker who decided she would be better off if she repatriated, despite the fact that she said she "did not wish to *return* to Mexico." [emphasis mine] We have no good numbers on exactly how many Mexican Americans repatriated during the 1930s—estimates range from five hundred thousand to one million.

Repatriates did not find an easy life in Mexico. Unemployment was also very high there, as were food prices. Many Mexicans worried that the returnees would be unhappy with their lot, and might potentially threaten Mexico's political stability. Others worried they might put on airs or think they were too good for Mexico now. The transition was particularly difficult for children. Many who had been attending school in the United States found that their education was at an end, since many small Mexican villages did not have schools for them to attend. Children also sometimes made fun of the American-born children, calling them pochos, gringos, and yanquis, and mocking them for not speaking Spanish very well, or using Tex-Mex slang.

The government also attempted a campaign of voluntary repatriation with the Filipinos. Supporters portrayed sending Filipinos back home at government expense as a humanitarian effort. Filipinos, however, were skeptical. To convince them to go, a propaganda campaign ensued, promising migrants that they would be traveling on "luxuriant ocean liners with Uncle Sam paying their passage and all expenses and wishing them bon voyage...[to be] greeted in Manila by brass bands and songs of welcome." Nonetheless, only about 157 had taken advantage of this program by the end of 1936, far from the thousands that program advocates had promised would go. By 1938, *Time* magazine was calling the program the "Philippine Flop." In total, about 2,190 went back to the Philippines.

World War II

Refugees during World War II

As Hitler rose to power prior to World War II, most in the U.S. paid little attention to the plight of Jewish refugees fleeing persecution in Germany. The country in general was preoccupied with the Great Depression, which had worsened in 1937, raising unemployment to twenty percent. As a result, in the spring of 1938, there was little support for admitting refugees. Aside from granting temporary visas to a few prominent individuals, the U.S. government took no significant action regarding refugees until 1944, when President Franklin D. Roosevelt created the War Refugee Board to assist refugees in camps in neutral or allied nations, and ordered one thousand refugees brought in from Italy outside of normal immigration procedures. But in general, before and throughout the war, refugees had to produce all of the same paperwork to get a visa as any other immigrant, and would have to be assigned a quota slot to be able to enter the country.

Restrictionists justified this by saying that they did not want to undermine the quota system by letting refugees in above the quota or not requiring them to have the correct papers. Antisemitism clearly played a role in this opposition. Even a proposal to admit twenty thousand Jewish children was defeated in Congress. Congress was representing the will of most Americans on this issue—a Gallup poll showed that sixty-six percent of Americans did not want to admit the children. Furthermore, during these years, the U.S. did not even fill all of the quota spaces assigned to Germany—about 150,000 German Jews immigrated, but the quota slots for the years 1933–1940 were actually over 211,000. Because of this lack of action, in 1979 Vice President Walter Mondale declared that the United States and other nations that had refused to help had "failed the test of civilization."

Braceros

During World War II, attitudes towards Mexican immigration reversed, as almost overnight, the United States went from the high unemployment of the Great Depression to a severe labor shortage. To meet this need, government and industry encouraged women not in the labor force to enter it, and allowed women and people of color to work in industries that previously would never have hired them. Particularly for women of color, this work was generally much higher paying than the work in sweatshops, fields, and domestic service that they previously performed. This does not mean that a sense of patriotism did not also motivate their actions. For instance, Lupe Purdy, a Mexican citizen who had been living in the U.S. since 1922, got naturalized so she could get a war job. As she recalled, "I didn't go to work because I wanted more money. I wanted to help my country. It was tough. It was hard work, very hard work. Riveting is hard work...I just felt very strongly that I should do my part." For others, it was a matter of personal pride, and expanding the boundaries of their lives. Beatrice Morales, for instance, had lived her entire life with her father or her husband. The latter did not like it when she took a war job, but she said, "I was just a mother of four kids, that's all. But I felt proud of myself and felt good being that I had never done anything like that. I felt good that I could do something, and being that it was war, I felt that I was doing my part."

The U.S. government wanted to encourage short-term migration to fill jobs as well. In 1942, the U.S. and Mexican governments created a guest worker program to let Mexican workers enter the U.S. as short-term contract laborers. Known as braceros, after the Spanish word "brazos" meaning arms, these manual laborers received contracts to work in agriculture and transportation. Quite a few Mexicans were ready to sign up, given that both population growth and government decisions that prioritized economic production over jobs left many with difficulties supporting their families. Although the program promised them a way to help their families, it did so by dividing them, sometimes for long periods. The bracero program only hired men, and their families were not able to come along with them to the U.S.

By the end of 1947, when the initial program ended, about 215,000 braceros had come to the U.S. to work in agriculture and another 75,000 for the railroads, doing track and right of way maintenance. The program started up again in 1951, due to labor shortages during the Korean War, and continued until 1964. During that later period, about 200,000 braceros were hired each year, working in twenty-six different states.

Despite protections insisted upon by the Mexican government, braceros found themselves being exploited in many situations. The process of entering the United States was itself not easy, and quite humiliating. All braceros had to undergo a medical examination, particularly checking for venereal disease and tuberculosis. They were then stripped naked and "disinfected" with DDT or other insecticides. Once at their new job, braceros often had very rudimentary living conditions, living in shacks with no running water, heat or electricity. Although in theory government officials were supposed to inspect farms and rail sites where braceros were working, this seldom happened. As one former bracero remembered,

I saw one [government official] come by the farm in the twenty months I worked for that particular rancher. He never said a word to any of us; he just talked to the farmer, stared at us and laughed. We could only smile; none of us had any idea what they could be saying or thinking. I only know that our conditions did not change from the time we first arrived to the time we left.

At times, braceros filed formal complaints with the Mexican consul in their area, reporting violations of their contracts. They also sought to organize collectively to protect their rights, forming organizations like the Alianza de Braceros Nacionales de en los Estados Unidos. Over two dozen strikes took place during the first three years of the program, pushing for better wages, food, and housing.

When conditions on their contracts did not improve, some braceros chose to "skip out." Since they were only approved to be in the United States as part of the program, leaving their contract without returning to Mexico made them into unauthorized immigrants. For some, this was a worthwhile risk. One former bracero, Carlos Morales, maintained it was sometimes better to be a "wetback" than a bracero. As he put it, "As a wetback, alone, safely across the border, I may find a farmer who needs one man. He will pay me honestly, I think. But as a bracero, I am only a number on a paycheck...and I am treated like a number...not like a man."

Zoot Suit Riots

Despite general wartime messages of unity, mob violence against people of color took place during World War II, with one of the worst examples being the Los Angeles Zoot Suit Riots of 1943. Community belief that there was a juvenile delinquency problem in the nonwhite population of Los Angeles increased after José Díaz, a young Mexican American man, was beaten to death at the Sleepy Lagoon, an old gravel pit used for swimming, in August 1942. During the subsequent investigation, hundreds of innocent young men and women were brought in and questioned, in what essentially represented a show of force to make the white middle class feel like something was being done about Mexican American youth violence.

The mark of these supposed delinquents, sometimes referred to as pachucos, was the zoot suit. Inspired by jazz musicians and popular with African American, Mexican American, and Asian American youth, zoot suits featured wide brimmed hats, long double-breasted jackets with wide padded shoulders and narrow waists, and pants that were wide at the hips and narrow at the ankles. Women who adopted the style generally wore the coat with either a short skirt that fell just above the knee or pants (both considered immodest at the time), dark lipstick, and pompadoured hair. Despite the assumptions of middle-class whites, many wore this style without identifying as pachucos or being juvenile delinquents.

In June of 1943, navy men on shore leave rioted in Mexican neighborhoods, attacking people wearing zoot suits, as well as young people of color generally. Some claimed that the rioting started because of Mexican American street gangs—i.e. that whites were tired of all the gang activity, and were fighting back. In reality, most of the "gangsters" who were beaten during the riots were in their teens, and not involved in any kind of crime at all. Journalist Carey McWilliams described the scenes he witnessed during the riots in his book, *North from Mexico*. He referred to the riots as a "mass lynching," describing how "Street cars were halted while Mexicans, and some Filipinos and Negroes, were jerked out of their seats, pushed into the streets, and beaten with sadistic frenzy. If the victims wore zoot suits, they were stripped of their clothing and left naked or half-naked on the streets, bleeding and bruised." Similarly, Al Waxman, the editor of *The Eastside Journal*, described how a group of men "stopped a streetcar, forcing the motorman to open the door and proceeded to inspect the clothing of the male passengers. 'We're looking for zoot-suits to burn,' they shouted." The rioting continued for ten days, essentially condoned by the police, and even encouraged by some newspaper coverage. Hundreds of people were injured during the riots, and although some Mexican Americans were arrested for fighting back, none of the rioters faced prosecution.

Japanese internment

When the U.S. entered World War II in 1941, the noncitizen Germans, Japanese, and Italians living in America were declared enemy aliens. Although Americans made a distinction between "good" and "bad" Germans and Italians, the Japanese were all considered enemy aliens, even if they were not aliens at all, but native-born American citizens. Starting in February 1942, the U.S. government forced 120,000 Japanese Americans, more than two-thirds of whom were native-born American citizens, into ten concentration camps across the West. To justify this, supporters maintained that the Japanese were different from other groups due to their race, which predisposed them to be loyal to Japan, even if they had been born in America. Earl Warren, the attorney general of California, explained the necessity of internment by saying "we believe that when we are dealing with the Caucasian race we have methods that will test the loyalty of them....But when we deal with the Japanese we are in an entirely different field and cannot form any opinion that we believe to be sound." General John L. DeWitt, the commanding general of the Western Defense Command, maintained that "the Japanese race is an enemy race" and that even if they were citizens or Americanized, "the racial strains are undiluted."

People had very little time to settle their affairs before being evacuated, with the result that most of them lost much or all of their possessions. They were allowed to take with them only what they could carry, and only given a few days to deal with the rest, forcing people to sell homes and businesses quickly at a loss or simply abandon them. In the 1980s, a government commission estimated that Japanese Americans had suffered between one and three billion dollars in direct property losses because of internment.

The internment camps were generally located in desert areas, and were thus hot, dusty, and bleak. Housing provisions were basic, with families living in retrofitted barns or quickly constructed barracks. Louise Ogawa, a young Japanese American woman who was interned in the camp at Poston, Arizona, remembered how when she woke up her first morning in the camp, "I looked up at the ceiling and a funny strange feeling came over me. I knew I was not at home and had a terrible yearning to go home. A little boy next door was crying asking his mother to take him home. That day I felt so lost I was as blue as the deep blue sea." Life in the camps was highly regimented and tedious. There was work to do, but this was dispiriting as well, as people who had been self-employed as shopkeepers or farmers now found themselves doing menial wage work for the government. The presence of guards was a reminder of the unnaturalness of the situation. "I was too young to understand," George Takei remembered, "but I remember soldiers carrying rifles, and I remember being afraid." [Document 22]

Resistance did take place, despite how difficult conditions in the camps made it. Some people launched court challenges to the process of internment itself. Minoru Yasui, Gordon Hirabayashi, and Fred Korematsu refused to go to the camps and challenged their arrests in court. Each of these cases went all the way to the Supreme Court, and in each instance, the court upheld the legality of internment. A minority did dissent—in Korematsu's case, for instance, three justices said that internment clearly violated his rights as a U.S. citizen and represented racial discrimination—but the majority was willing to allow it to occur.

Protests also emerged in the camps, particularly in response to the loyalty questionnaire that all camp residents were required to complete if they were over seventeen. Two questions in particular caused controversy—the first asked if they would be willing to fight in the U.S. military, and the second if they would pledge their allegiance to the U.S. and renounce any allegiance to Japan. Most answered yes to both questions, but some chose to not answer the questions, or to say no, as a form of protest. Those who answered no faced segregation to separate camps and, potentially, the loss of their citizenship and deportation to Japan. Frank Emi, at the Heart Mountain internment camp, said about the loyalty questionnaire that "the more I looked at it the more disgusted I became" since "we were treated more like enemy aliens than American citizens." Emi posted his answer to the questionnaire on the mess hall door—"Under the present conditions and circumstances, I am unable to answer these questions." An angry resident of the Manzanar internment camp reported that

Well if you want to know, I said "no" and I'm going to stick to "no." If they want to segregate me they can do it. If they want to take my citizenship away, they can do it. If this country doesn't want me they can throw me out. What do they know about loyalty?

Other Japanese Americans disagreed with this tactic, however, and saw enlisting as a way to demonstrate their commitment to the United States. Ultimately, 33,000 Japanese Americans served in the armed forces during the war.

Japanese internment served no militarily useful purpose. Even before it took place, the FCC and the FBI had concluded that claims that Japanese Americans were signaling to ships off the coast or acquiring stockpiles of weapons or other contraband were without basis. Many Japanese Americans lived in these camps for almost four years, and when they left, had to start their lives over from scratch, since the businesses and farms they had owned were gone. Years later, a Congressional committee investigating internment reached the conclusion that it "was not justified by military necessity, and the decisions which followed from it...were not driven by analysis of military conditions" but rather motivated by "race prejudice, war hysteria and a failure of political leadership."

Long-term changes to immigration

During and after World War II, Americans began to question and to dismantle some of the structures for regulating immigration that the 1924 Immigration Act had created. One change, in the wake of the Holocaust, was increased support for a system that would allow the admission of more refugees. Right after the war, President Truman used executive action, sometimes referred to as the Truman Directive, to admit 23,000 Jewish refugees. Eventually, Congress passed legislation in response to Truman's call, creating the Displaced Persons Act of 1948. This was the first piece of specifically refugee legislation the U.S. ever created. Truman signed it, despite his disappointment with its limits. In particular, eligibility criteria worked against certain groups, particularly Jews and Catholics from communist countries, and refugees were not admitted separately from the quota system, instead "mortgaging" quotas into the future to allow the admission of eligible refugees. The bill allowed 200,000 refugees to enter the country over two years, and then Congress reauthorized it in 1950 for another two years, and raised the total to 415,000.

There was also a gradual erosion of support for racially based immigration quotas after the war. Some of the first signs of this were the repeal of the Chinese Exclusion Act in 1943 and the extension of an immigration quota and naturalization rights to Filipinos and South Asians in 1946. China was a U.S. ally and support for ending Chinese exclusion increased during the war as a result, although supporters primarily focused on exclusion's impact on relations with China, rather than its effect on the Chinese American population. Many maintained that removing the insult of having no quota at all was more important than the practical issues of whether or not people could migrate to the U.S. or reunite with their families. Supporters of repeal saw it as a way to reward an ally and counter Japanese propaganda maintaining that the U.S. was anti-Asian. [Document 23] Ultimately, the government ended Chinese exclusion with the Magnuson Act, signed December 17, 1943. It repealed the exclusion act, gave China a quota of 105, and made Chinese immigrants eligible for naturalization. Similarly, the service and sacrifices of Filipinos during the war resulted in both President Truman officially declaring the Phillipines independent in 1946 and in the Luce-Cellar Act, which gave the Philippines a quota of one hundred and made Filipinos eligible for naturalization. South Asians also gained a quota and naturalization rights through this act in recognition of their service with the British.

Conclusion

World War II thus marked the beginning of the dismantling of the National Origins system, although not necessarily the racism that lay behind it. Americans in the wake of World War II were more willing to admit refugees to the nation, and less willing to make overtly racial arguments to justify immigration restrictions. Nonetheless, those same racial judgements would continue to shape Americans' reactions to immigrants, as well as the immigration legislation that would replace the 1924 Act. Support for a racially neutral immigration program existed, but was not yet widespread.

6 Immigration during the late twentieth century

After World War II, pressure to reform U.S. immigration policy was mounting, not only to eliminate the racism that so marked the National Origins Quota System, but also to create an immigration system that would better help the United States in its emerging conflict—the Cold War with the USSR. In 1952 and 1964, the United States gradually eliminated the racial basis of immigration law. Measures were also implemented to try to help the United States' allies in the global struggle against communism, and refugees from communism were given priority for entry. These reforms resulted in more immigration than advocates had expected, however, and the origin of immigrants changed dramatically, with most coming from Asia or Latin America. As a result, mid-twentieth century immigration reform did not avoid issues of race, as a new generation of nativists expressed concern about how the face of America was changing.

Immigration reform for the Cold War

Even as World War II was ending, the next international conflict for the United States became clear—the Cold War with the Soviet Union and the effort to contain the spread of communism. Immigration policy during the post-World War II era was shaped by an emerging sense of cultural pluralism and the foreign policy objectives of the Cold War. The United States hoped to aid the enemies of communism and to reduce the racism of federal policy, which communist nations used as ammunition against the United States. Immigration reform, when it came, was more limited than these ambitions might suggest, however.

The Immigration and Nationality Act of 1952 (also known as the McCarran-Walter Act) essentially maintained the racial hierarchies of the old National Origins System, while getting rid of its most overt racism. It left the quota system intact, but replaced the Asiatic Barred Zone with an Asian-Pacific Triangle, in which each nation was given an extremely small quota (roughly one hundred in most cases), with an overall regional cap of two thousand. These quotas were also implemented in a racist way—people of European descent counted against the quota of the country where they lived, while a person of Chinese descent counted against China's tiny quota, regardless of where they were born. Although this was the first time that every nation received a quota, about eighty-five percent of those quota slots were allocated to Northwestern Europe, with two-thirds of those going to just three nations—Great Britain, Germany, and Ireland. The act also eliminated the category of aliens ineligible for citizenship, meaning that for the first time since 1790, naturalization was not tied to race.

President Truman vetoed this act, on the grounds that it essentially left the racist hierarchy of the 1924 law intact. In his veto message, Truman addressed Asian Americans in particular, to explain why he was vetoing the bill that would finally have allowed them to naturalize and given quotas to their homelands. As he put it

> I want our residents of Japanese ancestry, and all our friends throughout the Far East, to understand this point clearly. I cannot take the step I would like to take, and strike down the bars that prejudice has erected against them, without, at the same time, establishing new discriminations against the peoples of Asia and approving harsh and repressive measures directed at all who seek a new life within our boundaries.

Nonetheless, Congress passed the bill over Truman's veto.

In response, Truman created a commission to study immigration. Originally framed as a general inquiry into the subject, Truman ultimately hoped that its findings would be able to undermine the McCarran-Walter Act. Its report, titled "Whom Shall We Welcome," recommended replacing quotas with an overall cap on immigration. The commission recommended prioritizing asylum seekers, family reunification, and labor needs in admissions. Senator Pat McCarran, one of the authors of the 1952 act, denounced this report as being communist-inspired, and claimed, rather disingenuously, that "the rock of truth is that the [McCarran-Walter] Act does not contain one iota of racial or religious discrimination."

Immigration during the Cold War

Pressure to admit refugees outside of normal immigration procedures increased during the Cold War, with "refugee" specifically referring to people fleeing communist persecution. Refugees from European communism, like those fleeing Hungary after the Soviet Union sent in troops to crush the Hungarian Revolution of 1956, were generally welcomed. In this case, President Eisenhower used the President's parole power to admit about 38,000 Hungarian refugees between December 1956 and May 1957. The treatment of nonwhite refugees from communism varied, however. In particular, the government was still unwilling to encourage immigration from Asia, and raised questions regarding whether refugees from communist China were "genuine refugees" fleeing persecution or only "rice refugees" seeking economic improvement. About 32,000 Chinese immigrants arrived in the U.S. between 1948 and 1966, but it would not be until the Vietnam War that the U.S. offered significant resettlement opportunities to Asians.

Closer to home, the U.S. also saw an influx of refugees from Cuba, following the revolution led by Fidel Castro in 1959. More than 400,000 came to the U.S. between Castro's rise to power and the interruption of daily flights from Cuba in 1973. These Cuban refugees were disproportionately middle class and white. Nonetheless, many white Americans still perceived them as nonwhite due to anti-Latino prejudices. One Cuban refugee, Carlos Eire, who came to the U.S. at age eleven, reported that "We Cubans tended to be viewed by the locals as nonwhite intruders, even if we had blond hair and blue eyes." Classmates asked him questions that demonstrated their assumptions about life in Cuba, including what it felt like to wear shoes for the first time, whether his house had a toilet, and why his skin was not dark if he was Cuban. Despite this prejudice, Americans as a whole supported the admission of Cuban refugees and were willing to give them additional government aid, such as assistance in finding a home or job.

Immigration and the civil rights movement

The experience of World War II prompted Americans of color to renew their fight for equality in the United States. Black, Latino, and Asian Americans fought in the war and pointed out the hypocrisy of claiming to fight overseas for freedom and democracy, when people of color did not really have these things at home. They hoped that they could win a "double victory" over fascism abroad and discrimination at home. As Sabine R. Ulibarri of New Mexico put it—"Those of us who went to war didn't return the same. We had earned our credentials as American citizens. We had paid our dues on the counters of conviction and faith. We were not about to take any crap." Eva Hernandez added the experiences of women to this, saying

> When our young men came home from the war, they didn't want to be treated as second-class citizens anymore. We women didn't want to turn the clock back either regarding the social positions of women before the war. The war had provided us the unique chance to be socially and economically independent, and we didn't want to give up this experience simply because the war ended. We, too, wanted to be first-class citizens in our communities.

Civil rights movements also gained some support due to the Cold War, as some argued that overt displays of racism hurt the ability of the United States to be an international leader—and in particular, to appeal to newly independent nations in Africa and Asia. As Acting Secretary of State Dean Acheson put it in a letter to the chair of the Fair Employment Practices Commission, "[T]he existence of discrimination against minority groups in this country has an adverse effect upon our relations with other countries. ….Frequently we find it next to impossible to formulate a satisfactory answer to our critics in other countries."

In the eyes of the U.S. government, the civil rights movement primarily referred to what they called "the Negro problem," although other people of color were fighting for rights as well. Some civil rights activists sought to win victories through the court system, and some major victories were achieved this way, like the 1947 case of Mendez v. Westminster School District of Orange County that declared forcing Mexican Americans to attend segregated schools unconstitutional, the 1948 case of Oyama v. California that overturned California's Alien Land Law, allowing Japanese people to purchase land, and the 1954 Supreme Court decision Brown v. Board of Education that struck down school segregation nationwide. But given the slow pace of change, some activists shifted their attention from the courts to the community. Engaging in acts of civil disobedience, activists refused to follow segregation ordinances on buses and in public accommodations. People participating in events like the Montgomery Bus Boycott in Alabama, the sit-ins at the Woolworth's lunch counter in Greensboro, North Carolina, and the Freedom Rides during the summer of 1961 faced real danger of physical violence. Nonetheless, the movement continued and grew. Finally, two major legislative victories were achieved, in the form of the Civil Rights Act of 1964, which outlawed segregation in restaurants, schools, and many other public places and forbade employers from discriminating based on race, and the Voting Rights Act of 1965, which outlawed racial discrimination in voter registration.

Despite these victories, many Black Americans were frustrated, both by the slow pace of change and by the violence against Blacks that only increased. The fact that little or nothing was changing about the structural economic inequalities that Black people faced every day angered many. Riots broke out in Watts and Newark, as some activists began calling for more radical strategies and Black Power. By 1966, Black Power had become a national movement, calling for Black pride and Black separation from white America. Activists like Marcus Garvey, Stokely Carmichael and others argued that racial oppression in the United States was the equivalent of colonialism.

Mexican Americans experienced a slightly different struggle, since in addition to segregation, they confronted stereotypes that associated them with unauthorized immigration. This worsened whenever the U.S. government increased efforts to stop illegal entry, as they did during the 1950s. In 1954, the government turned to mass expulsion as a solution, through a U.S. Justice Department-authorized program known as "Operation Wetback." The fact that a federal program included the derogatory term "wetback" in its title demonstrates how mainstream anti-Mexican sentiments were at the time. In this operation, state, county, and municipal police worked with the military and Border Patrol to arrest and deport thousands of undocumented workers. Supporters argued this was necessary to prevent Soviet operatives from sneaking into the United States disguised as farm workers. Although the operation did not succeed in addressing the root causes of unauthorized immigration, it did demonstrate to many native-born Mexican Americans that they could not avoid immigration issues in their civil rights struggle.

During the 1960s, as the Black Power movement grew among Black Americans, young Mexican American activists created the Chicano movement to fight for Mexican American rights. They called themselves Chicanos as a way of expressing their pride in their Mexican (and particularly indigenous) roots, and emphasized that they were not immigrants like the Germans or Irish, but rather descended from conquered people living in their ancient homeland of Aztlán, a term referring to the American Southwest. As with the Black civil rights movement, the young activists of the Chicano movement became more radical by the late 1960s and early 1970s, as they decided that their parents' efforts to work within the political system were failing. Students organized at universities across the Southwest, forming El Movimiento Estudiantil Chicano de Aztlán (MEChA). [Document 24] Student activists led by José Angel Gutiérrez and Mario Compeán also sought to form a new mass-based political party to serve as an alternative to the two major parties in Texas. Unlike older groups, like the League of United Latin American Citizens, which often sought to work through the Democratic Party, La Raza Unida Party sought to run its own candidates and take more radical stands on Chicano issues. As Gutiérrez put it, "We are fed up. We are going to move to do away with the injustices to the Chicano and if the 'gringo' doesn't get out of our way, we will stampede over him." Their goal was to take control of local city and county governments, and then work their way up from there, ultimately hoping to "decolonize" the economy of Texas and achieve economic independence for Mexican Americans. The party declined quickly in the 1970s, however, partly due to the difficulties all third parties face in the United States due to the winner-takes-all political system.

As African Americans and Mexican Americans fought for rights during the 1960s, so too did Chinese, Japanese, and Filipino Americans. In doing so, they created a shared identity for essentially the first time, becoming Asian Americans. This terminology was an important marker of the new identity that was being developed. As Richard Aoki, best known for being one of the few non-African American Black Panthers, put it, "Up to that point, we had been called Orientals. Oriental was a rug that everyone steps on, so we ain't no Orientals. We were Asian American." Not everyone agreed with this identity, of course, with some objecting that it erased their strongly held national or ethnic identity—i.e. they were Chinese Americans, not Asian Americans. The term first came into use in 1968, with the founding of the Asian American Political Alliance at the University of California, Berkeley. At the same time, students at the University of California, Los

Angeles founded the Asian American Studies Center and started publishing *Gidra: The Monthly of the Asian American Experience*. At San Francisco State College and the University of California, Berkeley, the Third World Liberation Front—a group that included Blacks, Latinos, Asians, and Native Americans—went on strike, protesting the lack of diversity in academia. It was no coincidence that these things were happening during the Vietnam War. The antiwar movement was at its peak by 1968, and many Asian Americans found they could identify with the Vietnamese, particularly given the amount of racist language used to discuss the war in the U.S.

Native American activists were also strongly engaged in civil rights struggles during the 1960s and 1970s. In their case, the existence of the Black civil rights movement and others presented both opportunities and challenges. On the one hand, such movements made white Americans more aware of the grievances of racial minorities in the nation, and created space for their discussion. On the other hand, these other movements put forward a certain vision of activism and civil rights that did not always match the Native American situation. In particular, if civil rights meant integration and sameness, many Native American activists were uninterested in it, pushing for respect for tribal sovereignty instead of integration into American society. As with other civil rights movements of the time, Native American youth were very active, forming the National Indian Youth Council (NIYC) in 1961. A group of students from across the United States met at Gallup, New Mexico, to found this organization and launch what was generally referred to as the Red Power movement. Other groups soon followed, like the American Indian Movement (AIM) founded in Minneapolis in 1968. AIM's initial focus was on urban issues, including police violence and discrimination in cities, although they soon broadened their focus to encompass issues facing Native Americans in rural areas as well. AIM was involved in some of the most notable protests of the 1970s, including the Trail of Broken Treaties and the occupation of the Bureau of Indian Affairs in Washington, D.C., in 1972, and the standoff with federal agents at Wounded Knee in 1973. Native American women were active in all of these groups, and also founded one of their own—Women of All Red Nations (WARN), which was very active in the 1970s.

All of these organizations emphasized the importance of tribal sovereignty, treaty rights, self-determination, and the preservation of Native American culture. Clyde Warrior, a young Ponca leader and president of the NIYC, explained his frustration with Native Americans' lack of sovereignty in a speech, titled "We Are Not Free," to the President's National Advisory Commission on Rural Poverty in February 1967. As Warrior put it,

> We are not free. We do not make choices. Our choices are made for us; we are the poor. For those of us who live on reservations these choices and decisions are made by federal administrators, bureaucrats, and their 'yes men,' euphemistically called tribal governments. Those of us who

live in non-reservation areas have our lives controlled by local white power elites.... We are rarely accorded respect as fellow human beings.

At the same time, women within these movements were often engaged in a second fight—against sexism within the movements themselves. For example, the National Chicano Youth Liberation Conference of 1969 briefly considered the position of women, only to adopt the position that "the Chicana woman does not want to be liberated." Members of the feminist Chicana Caucus were dismayed by this pronouncement. One of them, Enriquita Vásquez, reported

> As a woman who has been faced with living as a member of the Mexican-American minority group, as a breadwinner and a mother raising children, living in housing projects and having much concern for other humans plus much community involvement, I felt this as quite a blow. I could have cried.

Some men and women involved with these civil rights movements believed that it was necessary to fight all levels of oppression, including patriarchy, for the group as a whole to make progress, while others worried that feminism might split and weaken the movement, or that it was a movement dominated by white women who would marginalize their issues.

The Immigration Act of 1965

In many ways, the Immigration Act of 1965, also known as the Hart-Cellar Act, was a product of the same egalitarian period that produced the Civil Rights Act of 1964 and the Voting Rights Act of 1965. The act was intended to undo the legacy of racial discrimination in U.S. immigration policy. It gave 170,000 immigration slots to the eastern hemisphere (Europe, Asia, and Africa) and 120,000 to the western hemisphere (North and South America). No one nation in the eastern hemisphere would be allowed to use more than twenty thousand slots—a condition which was also extended to the western hemisphere in 1976. Priority was given to people with crucial skills and to family reunification, with spouses and unmarried minor children of U.S. citizens being exempt from the quotas.

Although this was vastly more liberal than the previous immigration law, there were ways in which it was more restrictive. In particular, numerical limitations applied to the western hemisphere for the first time. Furthermore, despite the fact that the twenty thousand per country cap was intended to be fair, in practice this did not recognize geographic or historical reality. Nations with small populations, like Iceland, were given the same twenty thousand cap as very large nations, like China. And despite the long, interconnected history between the U.S. and Mexico, they were also limited to only twenty thousand after 1976. As a result, some nations never used many slots at all, while others, including Mexico, India, the Philippines, and China, had visa backlogs that extended for decades.

The Hart-Cellar Act had an immense impact on U.S. immigration, despite the fact that few of those who created it thought it would. When he signed the bill, President Lyndon Johnson even said that "This bill that we sign today is not a revolutionary bill." Most expected that, since family members were given preference, the bill would not dramatically change the origins of immigration. As the *Wall Street Journal* put it, this provision "insured that the new immigration pattern would not stray radically from the old one."

Despite these expectations, the act changed the origin of immigrants profoundly. Under the 1924 Immigration Act, more than half of immigration to the U.S. came from Europe, and much of the rest from Canada. By the 1970s, nearly half of all immigrants were coming from Latin America and another one-third from Asia. The number of immigrants arriving each year also increased dramatically. In theory, the quota set the number of potential immigrants per year at 290,000, but many who entered the country did not count towards that quota. During the late 1970s and early 1980s, immigration averaged 546,000, more than eighty-eight percent higher than the quota.

In addition to those entering the country legally, the act also led to an unexpected increase in illegal immigration. The new quota on western hemisphere migrants in particular contributed to this, given the long history of Mexicans crossing the border for temporary work. In some cases, they might be returning to do the same jobs they had done previously, possibly for years, but now this was illegal unless they went through a time consuming process and waited, possibly for years, to see if they would be admitted. The bracero

Table 6.1 Immigration to the United States after 1965

Region:	1961–1970	1971–1980	1981–1990	1991–2000	2001–2010	2011–2018
Europe:	1,123,492	800,368	761,550	1,359,737	1,317,588	720,577
Asia:	427,642	1,588,178	2,738,157	2,795,672	3,620,937	3,299,975
Canada:	413,310	169,939	156,938	191,987	234,551	149,267
Mexico:	453,937	640,294	1,655,843	2,249,421	1,671,438	1,214,519
Caribbean:	470,213	741,126	872,051	978,787	1,109,108	1,086,443
Central America:	101,330	134,640	468,088	526,915	574,396	383,142
South America:	257,940	295,741	461,847	539,656	887,233	610,559
Africa:	28,954	80,779	176,893	354,939	817,128	829,380
Oceania:	25,122	41,242	45,205	55,845	65,811	47,563

Source: United States Department of Homeland Security, *2018 Yearbook of Immigration Statistics.* (Washington, D.C.: U.S. Department of Homeland Security, Office of Immigration Statistics, 2019), pp. 9–11.

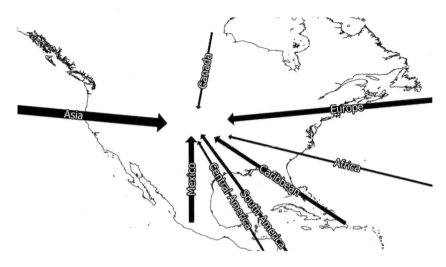

Map 6.1 Immigration to the United States after 1965

program ended at the same time that the act was passed, so some who had been guest workers in that program kept working in the U.S. illegally.

Immigration from Asia

The number of Asian immigrants grew rapidly after 1965. There were 1.54 million Asian Americans in 1970, which grew to 3.5 million by 1980, and 6.9 million by 1990. The Asian American population also became much more diverse. Prior to 1965, the majority of Asian Americans were either Japanese (52%), Chinese (27%), or Filipino (20%). After 1965, they were joined by more migrants from South Korea, India, Vietnam, Laos, Cambodia, Malaysia, Indonesia, Burma, Bangladesh, Sri Lanka, and Pakistan. By 1990, twenty-one percent of the Asian American population was Chinese, twenty-one percent Filipino, fifteen percent Japanese, twelve percent Vietnamese, eleven percent Korean, ten percent Indian, four percent Laotian, and three percent Cambodian. One exception to the general increase was Japan—as with many nations in Western Europe, Japan's economy was doing well by the mid-1960s, giving Japanese people few economic incentives to leave the country. As a result, Japanese Americans went from being more than half of the Asian American population in 1960 to only fifteen percent in 1990.

Southeast Asia

Some Asian immigrants fled war in Southeast Asia. Very few migrants had come to the U.S. from this region prior to the 1970s. However, the Vietnam

War, which lasted from the 1950s through the fall of Saigon in 1975, spurred more migration within and from this region. Millions of people were displaced by war—roughly twelve million people in South Vietnam, about half the country's population, were forced to leave their homes. As one refugee remembered, "I was born in Vietnam into a world at war. Our life was war. We lived and breathed war. We waited for peace, longing night after night...only to see flares burst into bombs and hear the weeping of people who had lost their relatives." Ultimately, nearly three quarters of a million Vietnamese people came to the U.S. between 1975 and 2000.

The U.S. war effort in Vietnam ended in a chaotic scramble to get out at the end as the situation deteriorated rapidly. A week before the South Vietnamese government collapsed, about 10,000–15,000 people were evacuated, and during the second half of April, the U.S. airlifted out another 86,000. Many evacuees were people who had collaborated with the U.S. or served in the South Vietnamese government. Many had to leave on very short notice, not knowing where they were going or if they would ever be able to return. One Vietnamese woman described trying to get on a plane, saying, "I saw people jamming the door and women and children could not get on. The shelling came closer and then the plane took off with people still hanging at the door." Another girl, who tried to leave on a boat,

Figure 6.1 South Vietnamese refugees arriving on board a U.S. Navy vessel during Operation Frequent Wind after the fall of Saigon in 1975

Source: United States Naval Institute

recalled how "As soon as the ship lowered one of its stairs, everybody climbed up the stairs without any order. Men, women, and children were pushed aside and dropped into the sea. Some were crushed between boats. I carried my youngest brother and went up that stairs with fear." Refugees continued fleeing Vietnam in the years to come, many by boat, despite the great risk of being attacked by pirates—nearly two-thirds of boats were, some more than once. Many of these individuals initially wound up in refugee camps in Thailand, before going to Australia, Canada, France, or the United States.

Cambodian refugees were part of this exodus as well. In addition to U.S. bombings in an attempt to destroy North Vietnamese supply lines, Cambodia suffered through a long civil war, as supporters of the U.S. backed Lon Nol government fought with the communist Khmer Rouge. In April of 1975, the Khmer Rouge came to power. During the three and a half years of their reign, nearly two million people died (almost one-third of Cambodia's population). During this time as well as after the overthrow of Pol Pot in 1979, many Cambodians fled to Thailand. Over 100,000 would ultimately come to the U.S.

Laos, the nation between Thailand and Vietnam, also became involved in the war in the 1960s. The Ho Chi Minh Trail, the supply line for North Vietnam, ran through Laos. The North Vietnamese also supported the Pathet Lao, a communist political movement which had sought to overthrow French colonialism. In addition to bombing Laos heavily, the United States received assistance from the Hmong population there, arming and training Hmong guerillas to attack the North Vietnamese. By 1970, roughly one in four Laotians (about 600,000) were displaced due to the war, some of them multiple times, making Laos into the country with the most displaced population in the world. After the Pathet Lao took power in 1975, U.S. supporting groups fled, including about 70,000 Lao, 10,000 Mien, and 60,000 Hmong.

Once in the United States, many Southeast Asian refugees found themselves underemployed. After being in the United States nearly three years, only seven percent of Vietnamese household heads worked as professionals, although thirty percent of them had been in Vietnam. Similarly, only two percent worked in management positions, although fifteen percent of them used to be managers. As one refugee put it, "In Vietnam I was a history and geography teacher" but "Here I worked on many different jobs—brick layer, carpenter, clerk typist, salesman, truck driver, delivery man. I felt frustrated and depressed because I had social status and possessions in Vietnam. Here I didn't have anything." Similarly, Hmong immigrants tended to be poorer than the general U.S. population, partially because they had generally found work in manufacturing, an economic sector which was in decline. In 2010, about twenty-seven percent of Hmong families lived in poverty.

The Philippines

So many Filipinos migrated to the U.S. after 1965 that by 1990, they were the second largest Asian group in the United States. Nearly 102,000 Filipinos moved to the U.S. during the 1960s, 360,000 in the 1970s, and almost 500,000 in the 1980s. Some came due to the repression of President Ferdinand Marcos's regime. For others, economics played a major role. There were many well educated, middle class Filipinos who were not able to find good jobs. A Filipino accountant remembered that "It is common [in the Philippines] for middle-class Filipinos to work at two or even three jobs because of the high cost of living....In the United States, hard work is rewarded. In the Philippines, it is part of the struggle to survive."

Compared to earlier Filipino migrants, these late twentieth century ones were more likely to be from cities and to intend to stay permanently in the U.S. They were also disproportionately women—during 1966–1971, 66,517 women entered the country and only 47,599 men. More of them were professionals—in fact, sixty-five percent of those who entered between 1966 and 1970 were technical workers or professionals, particularly in the medical field. Despite their education and experience, many Filipinos still were underemployed in the U.S. As one college-educated Filipino immigrant remembered, the government employment office agent "simply asked me if I were a Filipino and without opening my folder, he gave me an address of a vegetable grower."

Korea

Some Koreans had immigrated to the U.S. in the 1950s because of the Korean War, many as military brides or adopted children. As with other immigration from Asia after 1965, Korean arrivals were also more likely to be middle class and college educated. South Korean industrialization accelerated greatly after 1960, but it still took several decades for the nation to recover from the Korean War. As a result, economic problems, combined with population growth, led some South Koreans to migrate elsewhere, seeking higher pay or a better standard of living. During the 1970s, about 268,000 Koreans moved to the U.S., and about 334,000 during the 1980s. Overall, more than a million people moved from South Korea to the United States during the years 1970 to 2010. More than one-third of these entered the U.S. based on job skills, although over time as the Korean American population grew, family reunification became an increasingly common type of immigration.

Although many Korean immigrants had technical skills, they sometimes still struggled in the United States or were underemployed. In some cases, they had a certification that was not accepted, while in other cases, their lack of English language skills held them back. Some Koreans sought to open their own businesses as an alternative, attracted to the stability owning one's own business could provide. Credit-rotating organizations known as *kae* helped migrants finance the purchase of grocery stores or other small businesses. Running a small business with mostly family labor was hard work—as one Korean American business owner remarked, he operated his store "from 8:00 a.m. to 8:00 p.m., seven days a week, three hundred sixty five days a year." The benefit of such an arrangement, as he put it, was that "I am my own boss....Nobody tells me what to do." By 1997, there were about 136,000 Korean-American owned businesses in the U.S., and nearly twenty percent of Koreans owned businesses, more than double the rate of business ownership of other immigrant groups, or of Americans generally. Koreans were thus found on both sides of the class spectrum in the U.S. Some were professionals or business owners who were doing very well financially, while others were living in poverty.

South Asia

Immigration from South Asia became more numerous and diverse after 1965. Earlier South Asian migrants had come predominately from the Punjab region of India, whereas afterwards, migrants came from all over India and from other South Asian nations. As with other groups of Asian migrants, earlier migration from India had been more male dominated and temporary in nature, while those after 1965 were more likely to intend to stay permanently and had a more even gender balance. [Document 25] Later migrants were also less likely to work in agriculture or settle in the West. The immigrants themselves perceived a major difference between earlier and later migrants. As one later migrant explained it, "It is a class thing. They came from the farming, the lower class. We came from the educated middle class. We spoke English. We went to college. We were already assimilated in India, before we came here." Like Korea, India experienced a growing economy, but had a greater supply of educated and skilled workers than high paying jobs for them. Many of these migrants found jobs in the medical or technical fields. Not all Indian migrants were professionals, however, and jobs in retail, gas stations, or motels were also common.

Immigration from Pakistan, Bangladesh, and Sri Lanka also increased in the late twentieth century, particularly after 1990. The Pakistani population increased by at least eighty-eight percent during the 1990s—over 134,000 arrived during that ten-year period. Over 70,000 Bangladeshis arrived during those same years. By 2010, the census showed over 409,000 Pakistanis and over 147,000 Bangladeshis living in the U.S. Although they were less likely to have a college degree or be working as professionals than Indians, Bangladeshi migrants still tended to be at least middle class, since only relatively privileged Bangladeshis could afford to emigrate.

After arriving in the U.S., many Bangladeshi migrants experienced a general decline in their work status, having to take lower status positions that they had previously held—i.e. driving a taxi or waiting tables instead of being a lawyer or architect. In some cases, limited English skills prevented them from finding higher status work, while in others, they faced employers who did not value the Bangladeshi credentials they held. And some Bangladeshi immigrants were in the U.S. illegally, having overstayed a tourist or student visa, and had to take what work they could find. For some Bangladeshi women, this status decline was not based in paid labor, but in having to do housework. In Bangladesh, due to low labor costs, it was still common for even lower middle-class families to be able to hire servant women to do the housework. As one Bangladeshi immigrant put it, "At home I had my own life, my own car, driver, cook....I had a small business, a tailoring shop that I owned. Now in this country I stay at home all day. I have become the family's domestic servant, cooking and cleaning for them, taking care of their clothes, cleaning their toilets. You know at home I used to cook maybe once in ten years, and here I cook three times a day. I never cleaned a toilet before in my life. My daughters have become memsahibs and I have become a domestic servant. They get dressed up in their *bideshi* [Western] clothes in the morning and say, 'Bye, *Amma* [mother], see you later.' When they come back, I have washed their clothes and cooked their dinner."

China

Many Chinese migrants also came to the U.S. after 1965. Roughly 419,000 did so in the first twenty years, and the U.S. Chinese population grew from 250,000 in 1966 to 1.6 million in 1990. Most Chinese immigration in the immediate aftermath of the 1965 law came not from mainland China, but from either Hong Kong or Taiwan, where the governments were friendly to the United States. After 1979, when the U.S. government normalized relations with the People's Republic of China, people were able to migrate to the U.S. from mainland China as well. As in the immediate aftermath of the communist revolution, some were fleeing conflict and political instability in China. After the Tiananmen Square massacre in Beijing in 1989, even more Chinese people left Hong Kong and Taiwan. Others sought a higher standard of living or better education.

Despite their hopes of economic betterment, many Chinese immigrants still faced poverty. In 1968, Chinese men in the San Francisco Bay area only earned about sixty-eight percent of white men's wages, and Chinese women only thirty-six percent of what white women earned. In particular, migrants who struggled with English often had difficulty obtaining decent paying work. Chinese women often found work in the textile industry, and Chinese men in restaurants, neither of which paid well. Historian Ronald Takaki describes the result of this economically diverse immigration as a "bipolar Chinese-American community," in which there was a "Downtown Chinese" population that worked in low skilled service or manufacturing jobs, as well as an "Uptown Chinese" population that worked as professionals or in high skilled technical jobs.

Immigration from the Middle East

Immigration from the Middle East to the United States started increasing in 1965, although it was not that visible until the 1990s. The majority of migrants from the Middle East after 1965 were Arab, many of them coming from Egypt, Lebanon, Iraq, or Jordan. However, not all immigrants from the region were from Arabic or Islamic cultures. Some were Jews or various types of Christians, including Egyptian Copts and Armenian Christians. A sizable number of them were aided in their immigration by their marketable skills or higher education, and some had attended school in the United States. Many of these worked as lawyers, teachers, doctors, or engineers after immigrating.

The number of Iranians immigrating to the U.S. increased greatly after 1978, when the Shah of Iran was overthrown and a religious revolution followed. Roughly 36,000 Iranian students were attending school in the United States at the time, many of whom chose to stay and later brought their family to join them. Since the government of the United States considered Iran to be a hostile power after 1979, Iranians were entitled to apply for asylum. About 300,000 Iranians came to the U.S. between the late 1970s and 2010, of whom roughly 100,000 entered as refugees or were offered protection as asylees. Those who entered as regular immigrants were more likely to have resources available to them, in terms of money, education, and English language skills. A similar exodus of the middle class and well educated took place in Afghanistan, after Soviet troops entered that nation to support a communist government.

Immigration from Africa

After the initial forced migration of the slave trade, very few immigrants entered the United States from Africa until the 1970s. Beginning in that decade, African students began coming to American universities to study. Some went home, and became leaders in their native nation, while others chose to stay in the U.S. and became immigrants. Others were refugees, fleeing civil wars in Nigeria, Somalia, and Liberia during the late twentieth century. As with migration from other parts of the world, some African migrants were professionals who were seeking higher pay or a better standard of living elsewhere. In some cases, these migrants had moved to their nation's former colonizer first, only to come to the United States when they did not experience a warm welcome there.

Even in the late twentieth century, Africans remained a relatively small proportion of the migration stream, making up about four percent of the immigrant population in 2009, but their numbers were growing. The number of immigrants from Africa doubled in the 1980s, and then again in the 1990s. By 2000, there were almost one million African-born people living in the United States, and nearly 1.5 million by 2009, whereas there had been only 35,000 in 1970. Many of these migrants were Black, but not all were. Some were South African whites who had rejected apartheid for instance, or other African whites who fled newly independent African nations out of fear that whites would be persecuted. In general, the proportion of Black migrants increased after 1990, so that by 2012, about 1.1 million of the African immigrant population were identified as Black.

Immigration from the western hemisphere

The Latino population of the U.S. increased from 78,000 in 1848 to nearly forty million today. Mexican Americans were by far the single largest group, with perhaps thirty million people of Mexican descent in the U.S. But the category of "Latino" is a diverse one, that also includes more than four million Puerto Ricans living on the mainland, 1.4 million Cuban Americans, more than 1.2 million Dominicans, 1.1 million from Colombia, one million from Honduras, 323,000 from Ecuador, 230,000 from Brazil, 220,000 from El Salvador, 180,000 from Venezuala, 150,000 from Peru, 125,000 from Argentina, 110,000 Costa Ricans, 110,000 from Guatemala, 75,000 from Chile, 70,000 from Panama, and 60,000 from Nicaragua.

Mexico

Immigration from Mexico was the most numerous source of immigration to the United States during the last third of the twentieth century, increasing from 450,000 during the 1960s to 2.2 million in the 1990s. The Mexican American population increased from 4.5 million in 1970 to 25.3 million in 2000. Despite the high rates of immigration from Mexico, the vast majority of Mexican Americans are native-born—roughly seventy-four percent in 1990, and more than sixty percent in 2000.

Many late twentieth century migrants from Mexico had been displaced by changes in Mexico's economy, and were attracted by the higher standard of living available across the U.S. border. Industrialization in Mexico enriched a small group of elites, but did not provide enough jobs to ensure full employment. Even those with jobs often did not earn enough to be able to purchase the new manufactured goods, placing limits on the growth of domestic markets. Furthermore, Mexico's economy was hit hard in the 1980s, sometimes referred to as Mexico's lost decade, when the nation suffered from hyperinflation. At the same time, Mexico experienced major population growth, rising from 26.3 million people in 1950 to 69.7 million in 1980. Finally, the North American Free Trade Agreement in the 1990s brought American investment into Mexico, particularly along the northern border, but only served to destabilize the economy in other areas. About 2.8 million agricultural jobs were lost, while only about 700,000 new manufacturing jobs were added.

There were many more Mexicans who wanted to come to work in the U.S., whether seasonally or permanently, than there were slots available for them under the new immigration law, and unauthorized immigration became more common. For people who were desperate for work, the well-established labor recruitment patterns and increasingly long wait to enter the U.S. legally made it very tempting to try to cross the border illegally. In 1969, it took nine months to get a visa from Mexico, a number which increased steadily until in 1999, the wait was nine years. By 2018, there were 1.2 million Mexicans waiting for a visa.

Central America

Between 1961 and 2000, approximately 1.2 million people came to the United States from Central American nations. In particular, during the 1970s and 1980s, right wing dictatorships in a number of Central American nations, including Honduras, El Salvador, and Guatemala, sent people fleeing.

In Guatemala, for example, the U.S. had helped organize the 1954 overthrow of Jacobo Arbenz Guzmán, who had advocated confiscating unused agricultural lands from international corporations to give to the peasants. Fighting continued for years and was very bloody. As Colonel Carlos Arana Osorio, who became head of state in 1970, put it, "If it is necessary to turn the country into a cemetery in order to pacify it, I will not hesitate to do so." Despite the desperate conditions from which they fled, these immigrants were not recognized as refugees, because of the exigencies of the Cold War. The U.S. was often supporting the right-wing dictators from whom they fled, making it politically problematic to recognize them as refugees. The very definition of refugee in U.S. law included language about fleeing communism.

This was finally changed in 1980, when Congress passed a new Refugee Act which said that anyone could qualify for political asylum if they had a "well-founded fear of persecution based on race, religion, nationality, membership in a particular social group, or political opinion." However, after President Ronald Reagan took office, fighting communists in Central America was a major part of his foreign policy, and he ordered the INS to put all Central Americans applying for political asylum in detention centers. This did not deter refugees from coming, however, since even an uncertain future in a detention center was often better than no future because of death squads. Many Guatemalans settled in Los Angeles, while many Hondurans and Salvadorans settled in Texas along the Gulf Coast. Other Hondurans made the longer trip to New York City, as did some migrants from Panama.

The Caribbean

A fresh influx of Cuban refugees arrived in 1980, when Castro announced that anyone who wanted to leave Cuba could do so from the port of Mariel.

Tens of thousands took to the sea in boats, and Cuban Americans headed out to sea to help. In the end about 130,000 people crossed during the Mariel boatlift over the course of six months.

The United States was not ready to receive such an influx of refugees. These migrants were more likely to be unskilled workers and nonwhites than previous Cuban refugees, making them less desirable in the eyes of white Americans. As a result, President Carter refused to grant them the full resettlement benefits that Cubans usually received. Special treatment for Cuban migrants ultimately ended entirely in 1994, when a new wave of Cubans on boats and makeshift rafts began arriving in Florida. With the Cold War over, President Clinton announced that Cubans caught trying to reach the U.S. illegally would receive no special treatment.

There were also many Caribbean migrants from places besides Cuba. Many Puerto Ricans, as U.S. citizens, moved to the mainland seeking better economic conditions. Migration from Puerto Rico had been down between 1965 and 1980, with more returning to the island than leaving in some years, due to increasing wages in Puerto Rico and fiscal troubles in New York. However, more were migrating again in the 1980s, due to the continuing wage gap between the mainland and the island and problems in Puerto Rico's agricultural economy, which often provided only seasonal employment. It was fairly cheap to go to the mainland by that point as well, costing less than fifty dollars to fly to New York City. By 2010, there were about 2.8 million Puerto Ricans living in the mainland U.S.

Many migrants came from Haiti and the Dominican Republic as well. These nations share an island, but have very different living conditions, with Haiti being much poorer than the Dominican Republic. Both experienced political instability and repression in the late twentieth century that led to emigration. Very few Dominicans immigrated prior to 1961, since the dictatorship of Rafael Leónidas Trujillo was generally unwilling to issue people passports to leave. After he was assassinated in 1961, more Dominicans left, with ten times more coming to the U.S. in the 1960s than in the 1950s. At first, some were people associated with his regime, but after a coup d'état deposed President Juan Bosch, even more people fled. The U.S. was involved with these disruptions, helping Joaquin Balaguer, a longtime assistant to Trujillo, hold onto power in the face of a popular uprising seeking to restore Bosch to office. Economic crises in the 1970s and 1980s resulted in even more Dominicans migrating, including more who were lower class or not white. Nearly 100,000 Dominicans left for the U.S. during the 1960s, many of whom ended up in New York City, where many ran bodegas—small grocery stores that had often been run by other groups of immigrants before them. Many Haitians emigrated during the 1960s and 1970s, particularly the latter decade due to the repression of the government of Francois Duvalier's son, "Baby Doc" Duvalier. About 35,000 Haitians left during the 1960s, and more than 55,000 during the 1970s. Neither group received refugee status, as they were fleeing from non-communist, and U.S. allied, governments. As a result, any who entered illegally were routinely sent back—only about one hundred Haitians were granted asylum during the 1970s. This did change somewhat in 1999, when Congress passed the Haitian Fairness Refugee Act, which set up procedures that let over twenty thousand Haitians claim asylum. Caribbean migrants increased the standard of living of their family who stayed behind by sending earnings home. This was especially pronounced for Haiti, where emigrants sent home about one billion dollars each year, amounting to nearly twenty percent of Haiti's GDP.

War and genocide

Even as the Cold War ended, new crises displaced people, some of whom sought safety in the United States. In August 1990, war broke out in the Middle East after Iraq invaded and annexed the nation of Kuwait. After Iraq's loss, sectarian conflict worsened as the Shiite majority rebelled against the ruling Sunni minority. The Kurdish minority in Iraq also rebelled, trying to gain their independence. Saddam Hussein's government suppressed this dissent violently—as had been done with the Kurds in the 1980s as well—with the result that many people were displaced from their homes. About two million Kurds, Shiites, Assyrians, and Palestinians fled Iraq, with about one million going to Iran, and another 360,000–760,000 to the Turkish–Iraqi border region, where rugged terrain made aiding the refugees difficult. Some refugees ultimately came to the United States—in particular, about 20,000 Kurds relocated there by the end of the 1990s. Nashville, Tennessee became a major center of Kurdish resettlement, with about 13,000 moving there. The U.S. continued to receive some refugees from Iraq due to the Iraq War which began in 2003, over concerns that Saddam Hussain's government might possess weapons of mass destruction. Despite the fact that many of the potential refugees were our allies, U.S. policy towards them was not always generous. In 2007, a single city in Sweden actually accepted more Iraqi refugees than the entire United States did. The United Nations and refugee organizations urged the United States to do more, and in 2008, the U.S. committed to admitting more Iraqi refugees, although the process was still extremely slow. Some members of the Bush administration challenged whether the United States had an obligation to admit refugees due to the war. As John Bolton, President Bush's ambassador to the United Nations put it, the Iraqi refugees had "absolutely nothing to do with our overthrow of Saddam. Our obligation was to give them new institutions and provide security. We have fulfilled that obligation. I don't think we have an obligation to compensate them for the hardships of war."

A major refugee crisis also emerged in Eastern Europe in the 1990s, when political leaders in Yugoslavia tried to undercut reform efforts by stoking ethno-religious conflict. The result was a series of wars in several of the constituent republics of Yugoslavia, including Slovenia, Croatia, and Bosnia. Conditions were particularly bad in Bosnia, where the war lasted more than three years. The Bosnian Serb minority, seeking to form a new state with Serbia and Montenegro, sought to "ethnically cleanse" the territory— essentially a euphemism for genocide—by removing all non-Serbs, using both deportation and executions to accomplish this. The end result was one of the largest population movements in Europe since World War II. By 1992, there were about 1.3 million displaced people, and over 3.5 million by 1995. About 125,000 Bosnians settled in the U.S. between 1993 and 2000, with St. Louis having the largest concentration, with about 35,000.

Conclusion

Despite efforts to remedy the problems and injustices of the National Origins Quota System, both the 1952 act and the 1965 act had problems and injustices of their own. Refugee status was often politicized to meet the Cold War foreign policy needs of the United States, rather than the needs of migrants. In treating each nation equally, geographic and historical ties between nations were ignored. The relative size of nations was also not taken into account, as each was given the same overall immigration cap. As a result, waits for visas from nations like Mexico and China were many years long, and growing longer all the time. The futility of trying to immigrate legally from these nations encouraged illegal immigration, which became a new problem for the U.S. Few Americans who condemned illegal immigration recognized either the ways U.S. immigration law and employment practices had contributed to it, or the futility of being told to wait your turn in a line that had more than a million people in it. Concern about unauthorized immigration would only grow as the U.S. moved into the twenty-first century, and concerns about terrorism joined it at center stage in U.S. immigration debates.

7 Immigration at the dawn of the twenty-first century

Immigration continued to play a major role in American society and politics at the end of the twentieth century and the start of the twenty-first. Relatively high immigration rates, combined with periods of economic downturn and stagnant wages resulted in new waves of economic, cultural, and racial nativism. Concerns about unauthorized immigration continued and grew in the late twentieth and early twenty-first century, becoming for many Americans the main focus of their anti-immigrant sentiments. The September 11, 2001, attack on the World Trade Center and the War on Terror provided new impetus to nativism as well, much of it anti-Muslim in tone. The tensions between inclusion and exclusion that marked so much of U.S. immigration history have thus not vanished, but still shape how Americans react to immigration in the twenty-first century.

Concern about unauthorized immigration

Concern about unauthorized immigration continued to grow in the late twentieth century, until Congress passed the Immigration Reform and Control Act (IRCA) in 1986 to try to address the issue. The act contained a fairly generous amnesty program for those who were currently in the country illegally, allowing anyone who had lived in the United States since January 1, 1982, to legalize their status, provided they could pass a U.S. history test, speak English, and paid the associated fees. About three million undocumented migrants were legalized after 1986. To prevent future unauthorized immigration, the IRCA made it illegal to employ someone in the country illegally. This provision was rendered nearly toothless, however, by the fact that although employers were required to check their workers' documents when hiring them, they were not required to verify that those documents were legitimate. Although the number of illegal border crossings went down for the first three years after the program's creation, by 1989 they were already increasing again.

Concern about immigration grew even greater in the late 1980s and early 1990s, fueled in part by the way the federal government reported immigration figures—in particular, the numbers of people who legalized their status under the IRCA. These individuals were counted as entering in the year they were legalized, with the result that the data shows 5.4 million people entering the country between 1989 and 1992, although more than three million of these had been in the country since at least 1982, and many much longer. Nonetheless, immigration in the 1990s and early 2000s was higher than it had been earlier in the century. By 2012, the foreign-born made up thirteen percent of the U.S. population—typical by U.S. history overall, but far greater than during the 1970s, when it had been less than five percent. These immigrants were also more likely to be dispersed throughout the country than previous immigrants, who were mostly located in large coastal cities, making it more likely that people in all regions of the country would encounter immigrants during their daily life. Combined with the inflated numbers, the impression created was that an epic surge of immigration was taking place. Nativists increasingly portrayed U.S. borders as being out of control, and described immigration as an invasion. In general, nativists denounced the presence of "illegal immigrants" rather than any one race or nationality. However, this accomplished essentially the same thing, since the term "illegal immigrant" was effectively racialized due to the strong association in Americans' minds of Mexican Americans with unauthorized entry, regardless of the fact that most Mexican Americans are native-born and many unauthorized immigrants are not Mexican.

During his time in office, President Bill Clinton authorized another $540 million for additional construction of barriers at the border and more than one thousand new Border Patrol agents. As he put it in a 1993 speech on immigration, "We must not, and we will not, surrender our borders to those who wish to exploit our history of compassion and justice....We will make it tougher for illegal aliens to get into our country." Several major operations, including Operation Gatekeeper in California and Operation Safeguard in Arizona, were conducted along the U.S.–Mexico border during the 1990s, adding thousands of new immigration agents to the border as well as new surveillance equipment and additional border fencing. These operations made it more difficult to cross the border, but failed to halt illegal entry, since the economic conditions that induced migrants to come still existed. Instead of crossing near urban areas like San Diego, which were now heavily guarded, migrants were pushed to cross in desert areas, like the Imperial Valley Desert. This not only made migrants more dependent on smugglers, who could guide them through these areas, but crossing there was also much more dangerous. By 2000, nearly 1,700 people had died of heat stroke, dehydration, and hypothermia trying to cross the Imperial Valley.

By 1994, polls showed that two-thirds of Americans agreed that "immigrants today are a burden on our country because they take our jobs, housing, and health care." To address the issue of illegal immigrants using state services, in 1994, California adopted Proposition 187, known as the "Save Our State" initiative. Written by the California Coalition for Immigration Reform, this proposition made undocumented migrants ineligible for any public social services, public health care, and public education, and required state and local government agencies to report anyone they thought might be in the U.S. illegally. It passed with sixty percent of the vote. [Document 26] This measure was only in effect for a few days before a district judge issued an injunction against it, which was ultimately made permanent in 1997. The court ruled that Proposition 187 violated the federal government's exclusive power over immigration and contradicted previous Supreme Court rulings, including one in 1982 that had ruled that undocumented children could attend public schools. Nonetheless, even during that brief period, the measure resulted in a considerable amount of vigilante harassment of Latinx people suspected of being in the U.S. illegally, including many who were U.S. citizens or legal residents.

The use of deportation and detention as methods of immigration enforcement increased steadily in the early twenty-first century. Between 1975 and 1995, the U.S. on average formally deported about 29,000 people per year. In 2000, they deported 188,000, and 410,000 in 2012. The U.S. thus deported more people in the first ten years of the twenty-first century than they had in the previous 110 years, disproportionately men from Latin America. Operation Streamline, which began in 2005 during President George W. Bush's administration, detained people caught crossing the border for future prosecution, and President Bush additionally sent six thousand National Guards to assist on the border.

Some Americans criticized this level of militarization along the border, as did an editorial in the *San Francisco Chronicle*, which accused Bush of "chasing a mirage" by trying to stop unauthorized immigration with militarization without eliminating the conditions that gave rise to it. Others, however, saw it as appropriate, as did the civilian groups who took the fight against unauthorized immigration into their own hands, including most notably the Minutemen Project. Although President Bush characterized the members of this group as vigilantes, most Minutemen saw themselves as patriots and border soldiers defending the nation from a Mexican invasion.

During President Barack Obama's administration, some Bush era programs were eliminated, but many others continued or even expanded. In particular, many people were deported during the Obama administration, including a record 1.5 million during his first term, most of them Mexicans. The threat of deportation was particularly concerning to undocumented migrants who had come to the United States as children. There are roughly two million undocumented children in the U.S. under the age of eighteen, forming about one-sixth of the undocumented population. Some did not even know they were undocumented until they became older, and encountered problems in applying for jobs, driver's licenses, or scholarships. As one Latina recalled, "I was my class Valedictorian. I had perfect grades. I was all set to get a full scholarship to any school of my choice. It was then that they said there was a problem with my social security number. I went home and my mother said she made it up. I didn't have one." Another undocumented youth, Sandy Rivera, remembered how when she started high school,

> I realized that I would not be able to have my first job, my license, and my first car, all things that were considered milestones for the typical American high school student...but most importantly I realized that despite all the sacrifices and efforts made by my parents, I would fail to grasp onto the opportunity and dreams that they hoped I would be able to attain by bringing me to the United States.

Since 2001, these young people and their allies have been lobbying Congress for the Development, Relief, and Education for Alien Minors Act—known as the DREAM Act. This act, if passed, would put these minors on a path to citizenship or permanent residency, provided they met the eligibility requirements and completed either a college degree or two years of military service. In 2012, a small step was taken to provide some assistance to these young people in the form of the Deferred Action for Childhood Arrivals program (DACA). [Document 27] This program allowed people to apply for a two-year deferral of deportation and eligibility for a driver's license and work permit, provided they were under the age of thirty-one, had arrived in the U.S. before age sixteen, were in school or had graduated from it, and did not have a criminal record. Sandy Rivera maintained that "DACA created a pathway for me attain all the dreams I thought were far beyond my reach. Through DACA I was not only able to bring benefit upon myself, but I was also able to give back to the only country I have ever known as home."

Despite the portrayal of "illegal immigrants" as invaders, in actuality many U.S. citizens have family members, sometimes multiple, who are undocumented. There are at least 16.7 million people in the U.S. who are part of mixed-status families, in which some members of the family are U.S. citizens or permanent residents, and others are not. The undocumented status of some members of the family affects all of them, even those who are native-born. They experience not only the threat of having their family torn apart if some members are deported, but also can have difficulty traveling or accessing resources, if not all of their family members have the correct documents. In many cases, the dividing lines are generational, with one or both parents being undocumented and the children being native-born citizens, while in other cases, undocumented children have younger brothers and sisters who are U.S. citizens. In general, the number of mixed status households has increased during the past two decades, as border militarization made it more difficult for seasonal workers to return to Mexico regularly. Instead of having a family in Mexico while they came to the U.S. to work, these workers have had to settle permanently, either forming new families or bringing an existing family to the U.S.

Figure 7.1 President Donald Trump examining border wall prototypes near San Diego, California, in 2018

Source: "Loopholes in Child Trafficking Laws Put Victims—and American Citizens—At Risk." 5 April 2018. https://www.whitehouse.gov/articles/loopholes-child-trafficking-laws-put-victims-american-citizens-risk/

When President Donald Trump was elected in 2016, one of the first things he pushed for was the construction of a wall along the border with Mexico. As this chapter demonstrates, his position on immigration was not completely new—instead, he was drawing on sentiments and ideas that had been growing in popularity for decades. Trump summed these attitudes up by saying "When Mexico sends its people, they're not sending their best," claiming that "They're bringing drugs. They're bringing crime. They're rapists. And some, I assume are good people." Trump's fixation on the wall as a solution represents a misunderstanding of how both drug smuggling and illegal immigration work. Most drugs enter the U.S. through legal ports of entry, not the open spaces between that would be secured by a wall, and two-thirds of "illegal" migrants did not cross the border illegally, but rather entered legally on a temporary visa and then overstayed. Nonetheless, constructing a physical barrier at the border remains a powerful symbol for opponents of unauthorized immigration.

The War on Terror and Islamophobia

Before the attacks on the World Trade Center and Pentagon on September 11, 2001, when agents of Al Qaeda hijacked four jet planes and flew them into important buildings, most immigration restrictionists focused their concern on the cultural and economic impact of immigration, as migrants took jobs, used public services, and changed the cultural and racial composition of the nation. Afterwards, anti-immigrant sentiment came increasingly to focus on the impact immigration could have on U.S. national security, portraying immigrants as potential terrorists.

This was not an entirely new phenomenon—immigration restrictionists had feared that Eastern European migrants might be bomb-throwing anarchists in the late nineteenth century. The association of terrorism with immigrants is inaccurate, however. Most acts of terrorism in the U.S. are carried out by domestic terrorists, not immigrants. Nonetheless, the attacks of 9/11, as it came to be called, were such a shock in their scale that they had an impact analogous to the bombing of Pearl Harbor that drew the Americans into World War II. In response, the federal government reorganized its agencies related to terrorism, creating the Department of Homeland Security, which combined twenty-one different agencies and departments under one leadership, with the goal of preventing future terrorist attacks.

In the weeks after 9/11, attacks on people who "looked Middle Eastern" increased greatly. An elderly woman in Los Angeles was pulled from her car and beaten for wearing a hijab. Also in L.A., a Chicano man was followed home and beaten by two whites who thought he "looked Arab." A mosque was burned and worshippers shot at in Seattle. And across the country, people attacked Middle Easterners and South Asians, calling them "rag-heads" and "sand niggers." Along with violent attacks on individuals, some preached against the entire religion of Islam, maintaining that it was a political ideology rather than a legitimate religion and that its adherents thus did not deserve freedom of religion. A Bangladeshi American cardiologist, although he reportedly had never experienced racism or hostility towards his religion before 9/11, experienced so much trouble with hate mail and patients being uncomfortable with him that he actually changed his name (from Dr. Niaz Hussain to Dr. Niaz) to seem less Muslim. As one Bangladeshi woman put it in a letter published in the *New York Times* the week after 9/11:

> Before last week, I had thought of myself as a lawyer, a feminist, a wife, a sister, a friend, a woman on the street. Now I begin to see myself as a brown woman who bears a vague resemblance to the images of terrorists we see on television and in the newspapers...as I become identified as someone outside the New York community, I feel myself losing the power to define myself and losing that wonderful sense of belonging to this city.

President George W. Bush made some effort to stem the tide of hatred towards Muslim Americans after 9/11. He visited the Islamic Center in Washington, D.C., not long after the attacks, where he met with Muslim leaders. He characterized Islam as a religion of peace, quoted from the Quran, and said that "Those who feel like they can intimidate our fellow citizens to take out their anger don't represent the best of America, they represent the worst of humankind, and they should be ashamed of that kind of behavior."

Nonetheless, government actions since 9/11 have had major negative impacts on the lives and rights of Muslims in the U.S., particularly Arabs and South Asians, making this official repression that went far beyond the actions of private citizens. Several thousand Muslims, some of them U.S. citizens and some not, were arrested for questioning by the FBI, INS, and state and local forces. None of them were found to be terrorists or in any way connected with the attacks. Many of the new security measures undertaken at airports targeted those who "looked Muslim" to white American eyes. As Louisiana Congressmember John Cooksey put it, any passenger wearing "a diaper on his head" should be questioned, since "We know the faces of terrorists and where they're from." Muslims and Sikhs who wear turbans or hijabs are disproportionately likely to face additional screening at airports, for no reason besides their appearance. Other government policies that targeted people from certain nations include the Department of Justice's National Security Entry-Exit Registration System (NSEERS), created in 2002. This program required nonimmigrant men from certain countries to report to immigration officials at regular intervals as well as whenever they took certain actions like changing a job, school, or address. Only twenty-five countries were included, almost all of which are in the Middle East, North Africa, or South Asia, and almost all of which are either majority Muslim or have significant Muslim populations. In creating this program, the government made two assumptions—first that people of certain nationalities and faiths were more likely to be terrorists or know things about terrorism, and second that it was acceptable to subject a large group of people to additional interrogation based solely on their nationality and religion, with no other suspicions being necessary.

In the years following 9/11, anti-Muslim sentiment continued to grow. At the end of his first week in office, President Donald Trump signed Executive Order 13760 "Protecting the Nation from Foreign Terrorist Entry into the United States." The goal of the measure was to keep "radical Islamic terrorists out of the United States of America." The measure banned entry from a number of predominantly Muslim countries for ninety days, characterizing migration from these nations as "detrimental to the interests of the United States." The order also suspended refugee admissions for 120 days and banned Syrian refugees permanently. Although the ban was overtly based on geography, not religion, President Trump's comments about it make it clear that it was intended achieve, as he put it, a "total and complete shutdown of Muslims entering the United States." Although this travel ban quickly faced challenges in the courts and had its implementation placed on hold, a later travel ban which included a few non-Muslim countries was upheld by the Supreme Court in 2018 in the case of Trump v. Hawaii.

Conclusion

The United States in the twenty-first century is becoming ever more diverse, with most estimates showing that Latinos, Blacks, and Asians will outnumber whites by the mid-twenty-first century, if not sooner. For some whites, this has prompted additional fears about immigration. Peter Brimelow, a naturalized citizen from England, argued in his 1996 book *Alien Nation* that "America will become a freak among the world's nations because of the unprecedented demographic mutation it is inflicting on itself." Nonetheless, immigrants and their children keep maintaining that "We are America." They believe in America's promise, and did so even before they arrived. Immigrants continue to seek entry to the U.S., searching for safety, jobs, and the chance to raise their children in a land with more opportunities.

The U.S. Citizenship and Immigration Service's mission statement, updated in February 2018, demonstrates the current negative tone toward immigration in the U.S. While it had previously sought to ensure "America's promise as a nation of immigrants," the statement now said that the service "administers the nation's lawful immigration system, safeguarding its integrity and promise by efficiently and fairly adjudicating requests for immigration benefits," all while "protecting Americans, securing the homeland, and honoring our values." Instead of seeing immigrants as part of the promise of America, they have become a threat against which America needed to be safeguarded, protected and secured. In time, perhaps this contemporary nativism will give way to a renewed appreciation of the major role immigrants have played in American history.

Part 2
Documents

Document 1

Richard Ffrethorne. Letter to His Father and Mother, March 20, April 2 and 3, 1623.

Indentured servants left behind few written records, but those that exist demonstrate their desperation. In this letter from 1623, Richard Frethorne appealed to his parents to redeem his contract and free him from servitude. If they attempted to do so, however, they were too late, since Frethorne died within the year.

Loveing and kind father and mother my most humble duty remembred to you hopeing in God of yor good health, as I my selfe am t at the makeing hereof, this is to let you vnderstand that I yor Child am in a most heavie Case by reason of the nature of the Country is such that it Causeth much sicknes, as the scurvie and the bloody flix, and divers other diseases, wch maketh the bodie very poore, and Weake, and when wee are sicke there is nothing to Comfort vs; for since I came out of the ship, I never at anie thing but pease, and loblollie (that is water gruell) as for deare or venison I never saw anie since I came into this land, ther is indeed some foule, but Wee are not allowed to goe, and get yt, but must Worke hard both earelie, and late for a messe of water gruell, and a mouthfull of bread, and beife, a mouthfull of bread for a pennie loafe must serve for 4 men wch is most pitifull if you did knowe as much as I, when people crie out day, and night, Oh that they were in England without their lymbes and would not care to loose anie lymbe to bee in England againe, yea though they beg from doore to doore, for wee live in feare of the Enimy eu^{9}ie hower...

...[Mr. Jackson] he much marvailed that you would send me a servaunt to the Companie, he saith I had beene better knockd on the head, and Indeede so I fynd it now to my greate greife and miserie, and saith, that if you love me you will redeeme me suddenlie, for wch I doe Intreate and begg, and if you cannot get the marchaunte to redeeme me for some litle money then for Gode sake geta a gathering or intreat some good folke to lay out some little Sum̃ of moneye, in meale, and Cheese and butter, and beife...

...good ffather doe not forget me, but haue m^{9}cie and pittye my miserable Case. I know if you did but see me you would weepe to see me...therefore if you loue or respect me, as yor Child release me from this bondage, and saue my life...

Source: *The Records of the Virginia Company of London, volume IV*, edited by Susan Myra Kingsbury. Washington, D.C.: Government Printing Office, 1935, pages 58–60.

Document 2

Excerpt from Boyrereau Brinch and Benjamin F. Prentiss,
The Blind African Slave, or Memoirs of Boyrereau Brinch.

In this slave narrative, Boyrereau Brinch, who was born in West Africa around 1742, describes how he was enslaved and the experience of the Middle Passage.

...we flew to the wood with precipitation. But Lo! when we had passed the borders and entered the body thereof, to our utter astonishment and dismay, instead of pursuers we found ourselves waylayed by thirty or forty more of the same pale race of white Vultures, whom to pass was impossible, we attempted without deliberation to force their ranks. But alas! we were unsuccessful, eleven out of fourteen were made captives, bound instantly, and notwithstaning our unintelligible intreaties, cries & lamentations, were hurried to their boat, and within five minutes were on board, gagged, and carried down the stream like a sluice; fastened down in the boat with cramped jaws, added to a horrid stench occasioned by filth and stinking fish; while all were groaning, crying and praying, but poor creatures to no effect. I after a siege of the most agonizing pains describable, fell into a kind of torpid state of insensibility which continued for some hours. Towards evening I awoke only to horrid consternation, deep wrought misery and woe, which defies language to depict. I was pressed almost to death by the weight of bodies that lay upon me; night approached and for the first time in my life, I was accompanied with gloom and horror.

Thus in the 16th year of my age, I was borne away from native innocence ease, and luxury, into captivity, by a christian people, who preach humility, charity, and benevolence....

...ON the fourth day, about four o'clock, in the afternoon we arrived at the ship, and were carefully taken out of the boat, and put on board; even this momentary relief seemed to cheer my desponding spirits, and at least eased the pains I endured, by relieving me of those galling cords with which I was bound. I was suffered to walk upon the deck for a few minutes under a strong guard, which gave my blood an opportunity in some degree to assume its usual circulation. But in a short time I was forced into the hole, where I found my comrades, with about thirty more poor African wretches whom the ships crew had stolen from a neighboring tribe. These poor creatures were screaming, crying and wringing their hands, with prayers and ejaculations to the great Father for their deliverance. This group was composed of men, women and children, some little girls and boys, not more than six or seven years of age were shut up in a pen or stye, crying for food and water and their fathers and mothers....

As soon as we had fairly got under way, and about bidding adieu to the African coast forever, the captain and many of the officers made choice of such of the young women as they chose to sleep with them in their Hammocks, whom they liberated from chains and introduced into their several apartments. After the officers had provided themselves with mistresses of color, they made arrangements for the keeping and feeding the slaves. We were fastened in rows, as before observed, so that we could set upon our ramps or lie upon our backs, as was most convenient, and as our exercises were not much, we, it was concluded, could do with little food; our allowance was put at two scanty meals per day, which consisted of about six ounces of boiled rice and Indian corn each meal, with the addition of about one gill of fresh water…

> Source: Boyrereau Brinch and Benjamin F. Prentiss, *The Blind African Slave, or Memoirs of Boyrereau Brinch, Nick-Named Jeffrey Brace*. Printed by Harry Whitney, 1810. *Documenting the American South*, https://docsouth.unc.edu/neh/brinch/brinch.html

Document 3

Excerpt from Alexander Thomson, News from America, *1774.*

Alexander Thomson wrote a series of five letters about his experiences in America to a friend back home in Glasgow, which were subsequently published as a pamphlet. The following is an excerpt from the first and second letters.

Corkerhill in Pensilvania, August 16th, 1773

Dear Sir,

I know well that after the promises I made you, you could not have thought that so much time would pass, before you had any letter from me. Indeed I did not forget my promise, but after I had got an agreeable settlement to myself, I was desirous to have some particular knowledge of this country, before I should undertake to write any account of it to you.

In July 1771, I and my wife and twelve of our children went aboard the Friendship in the harbour of Greenock: It was after the middle of that month when we set sail for North-America, and happily we arrived at the city Boston on the tenth of September, all in perfect health.

I believe that some of my neighbours and acquaintance thought it strange, that one of my age should forsake his native country: but I thought I had but too much reason to do as I have done: as I was blessed with a numerous family, (and I have had another child since I left Scotland) I was very desirous to provide for them: All my sons who were able to work were brought up to the business of farming, and it was by their labour that I was assisted to gain any money I have: I therefore endeavoured to have one or two of the eldest of my sons settled in farms at home; and with that view I employed myself for the space of five years, in looking out for such farms as might answer my purpose. I travelled through the country for twenty miles round the place where I lived; but tho' I found plenty of vacant farms, I told you before, and I declare it again on the word of an honest man, that I could see no farm for which the laird did not ask more than double the rent it was worth; so that if I had meddled with any of them I saw well that my sons would never be able to pay the rent, and that in three or four years I would not have had one shilling to rub upon another.

After I had spent so much time and labour to no purpose, I confess that at length I conceived a sort of distaste for the lairds: I imagined that as they knew I had a little money, they wanted to get it from me as fast as they could; and in truth some of my neighbours observed a change in my temper, and alledged that I was turned so obstinate that I would not stay in the country, even though some laird should offer me a farm or two on reasonable terms: and I dare not say they were altogether in the wrong...

It was in April 1772, that I settled on this plantation: it is situate at the distance of 150 miles from Philadelphia, and it is just as far from Fort-Pit; it lies in a large and beautiful valley which runs thro' all Pensilvania, Maryland, and Virginia; it consists of about 430 acres, and there was a house of two stories high, and officehouses upon it: The house is built of square blocks of wood nocked or indented into one another; it is well plaistered, so that it is warm enough, and I have six convenient rooms in it.

My plantation which I have called Corkerhill, after the name of the farm where my father lived and died, and where I lived so long; My plantation consists wholly of limestone-land, and in general limestone-land is reckoned the best in this country. There is plenty of limestone for manure in every field, and it doth not cost much labour or expence to come at it; and it can be burned with the wood which we grub out when we clear the ground. Our greatest labour is to cut the wood into small pieces when we are to burn the lime.

Dear Sir, I do assure you I am well pleased with the country, and with my situation in it. I bless God that I came here, and I heartily thank every man who encouraged me and helped me to get the better of that fear which a man is under when he is to venture over so wide a sea, and indeed when, excepting my eldest son, I was to carry along with me all that was dear to me in the world, I could not but be anxious about them; but I was determined in my mind, and providence hath been very favourable to us. We are all at present in good health; and blessed be God, we have always been so since we came into this country....

Source: *News from America: Letter I / from Alexander Thomson, late tenant at Corkerhill in the Parish of Paisley, now proprietor of a considerable estate in Pensylvania. To a gentleman near Glasgow.* Glasgow: printed and sold by John Bryce, 1774. Princeton University Library, Princeton, N.J.

Document 4

Naturalization Law of 1790

This statute was the first law governing naturalization in the United States, and set precedents that would be followed for centuries.
    An Act to establish an uniform Rule of Naturalization.

Section 1. *Be it enacted by the Senate and House of Representatives of the United States of America in Congress assembled*, That any alien, being a free white person, who shall have resided within the limits and under the jurisdiction of the United States for the term of two years, may be admitted to become a citizen thereof....And the children of such persons so naturalized, dwelling within the United States, being under the age of twenty-one years at the time of such naturalization, shall also be considered as citizens of the United States. And the children of citizens of the United States, that may be born beyond sea, or out of the limits of the United States, shall be considered as natural born citizens

Source: 1 Stat. 103–104.

Document 5

Letter from Hannah Curtis to John Curtis, April 21, 1847.

In this letter Hannah Curtis writes to her brother John, who had emigrated to America, to inform him about conditions in Ireland as the Potato Famine continued and to request that he send money to help finance her own emigration.

Mountmellick April 21ˢᵗ 1847

My Dear Brother John
    ...I related to you the state of the Country in that letter therefore I need not go over it any more only the distress that was amongst the people at that time was nothing to what it is at present the people are in a starving state the poor house is crowded with people and they are dying as fast as they can from 10 to 20 a day out of it there is come kind of a strange fever in it and it is the opinion of the Doctor it will spread over town and country when the weather grows warm no person can be sure of their lives one moment the times are so sudden you would scarcely see as many people with a funeral as would take it to the grave in fact I would not describe the aweful state of Ireland at present you all may think the people are not so bad on account of all the provision that is coming into it but only for it the country could be a good deal worse of but there is no trade of any kind doing nor no money in

the country went is gone to America from every one that can go to America is going this year as there is no prospect of any think here but poverty and distress the Revd Father Healy is after getting I think above 50 letters and mony in them all they were sent to his care by people in America to their friends at home to take them out to them...

...Many time my father let money behind the back of a ditch to neighbours and got it again and I am sure he nor you could not turn it to better use than sending for me now it was my Aunt Arthurs sent Aunt Hannah and family every one is getting mony but me I am quite jealous and ashamed of you all you are as I think behaving so bad as I can say nothing else to you if yous attempt to forgot one on the present occasion mind I don't [t]hink you will have me to trouble you long...

> Source: Hannah Curtis to John Curtis, April 21, 1847, Curtis
> family papers (MSS072), Historical Society of Pennsylvania.

Document 6

Excerpt from The 1842 Diary of Julia Turnau: Sailing from Bremen to New Orleans

Julia Turnau kept this journal during her voyage from Bremen to the United States at the age of twenty-three to marry Reverend George W. Wall. In the following excerpts she describes life on board the ship and some of her fellow passengers.

We went to bed early, scarcely able to get undressed alone. A very bad night followed. The wind blew hard so that the ship rolled from one side to the other, and our trunks, chests, etc. in the cabins and storeroom banged together with great noise. Way down below, one could hear the dull thud of the water striking the ship.

The groaning and creaking of the ship, even when it was moving forward on the water, the rattling of the planks and doors in the ship and down in the hold; the trampling feet of the sailors right above our heads; the beating, falling, flapping of the sails and hawsers; the loud calls and the shouting of orders—all of this, in pitch black night in a narrow berth, dizzy from the constant tossing from side to side, makes an impression which doesn't let a sea voyage appear in the most favorable light. It appeared to me as though I were being driven about in the belly of some huge sea monster, and I had to think really vividly of poor Jonah, of the great distress which he must have suffered in the belly of the great fish, and of how fervently he must have implored the Lord for deliverance....

...The food here on the ship is very good. However, I can't get used to the breakfast, for which we get coffee at eight o'clock without milk. The men mix an egg yolk with it. We three womenfolk can't drink it at all in any form.

Likewise we don't drink any tea. It is remarkable that especially coffee is so repugnant after seasickness. Besides black bread, ship biscuit, and butter we get: soft boiled eggs, sausage, ham (raw and boiled), cheese, meat, etc., and sometimes ham and eggs. I usually eat simply a piece of buttered bread, and with Louise I drink watery oatmeal gruel with it, of which she is very fond. And she it was who had the idea of using it as an ordinary beverage.

We also drink a lot of water. So far it has been pretty good. In the heat, however, it will probably not be potable any more without further ingredients. Good wine, beer, and seltzer water are also on board for the use of the passengers.

At noon we always first have soup. In the early part of the trip it was made with fresh meat, now with wine or chicken, of which five dozen were taken along. Then, after the soup, come smoked meat, ham, beef tongue with vegetables, etc., pudding, fruit, pancakes, etc., and wine. In short, we can be satisfied; and for me it is more than three times enough, which is to say, usually too much.

In the afternoon the gentlemen now drink coffee, while we eat maybe a piece of cake or something like that. Our evening meal usually consists of tea with wine, rum, beer, water (for us), bread and butter with all sorts of things on it, warmed-up meat, hash, and if some of it is left over, we'll produce a salad....

...We have all types on board. There is an old couple that, I believe, is devout Christians. The husband is the same who first requested Nollau [the Reverend Louis Nollau, one of her travelling companions] to conduct religious services.

Then there is a family from the Black Forest, fourteen of them, all told. The wife was quite ill when she came on board. Now she is much better. The daughters, all of them grown, are pretty girls and conspicuous by their strange folk costumes as well as their dialect, which is scarcely understandable to us. Also adult sons are with them....

...Then there is also a deaf mute, a handsome looking young man who with his sister wants to seek his luck in America. I don't understand what such a person intends to do.

The prisons of Ranover have added to the number of our traveling companions by releasing three individuals and sending them out of the country. They are robust looking men, addicted to drink, and in their features one may read the name of their most recent sojourn....

...A very old woman with her two grown granddaughters attracted our attention right at the start. We felt sorry that at her age she should have to endure the hardships of a sea voyage; but when we learned the reasons for her emigration we could enter into her soul's joy....

...You see, she showed Nollau a letter from her son living near St. Louis who is very well off there and who begs her urgently to come over. The letter was charmingly beautiful. In it he expressed a great love for his mother.

The son wrote that he could not bear the thought that his aged mother in Germany should be working and had to eat black bread while he had white bread and roast beef. She should please come over. She would be well taken care of and could take it easy in her old age. On reading this we could really enter into the deeply felt joy of the old lady.

Source: *The 1842 Diary of Julia Turnau: Sailing from Bremen to New Orleans*, translated by Armin L. Saeger and edited by Julie Saeger Nierenberg. CreateWrite Enterprises, 2013. Reproduced with the permission of Julie Saeger Nierenberg.

Document 7

The Treaty of Guadalupe Hidalgo, February 2, 1848

This treaty, which ended the Mexican–American War, contained important safeguards for those Mexican citizens living on territory annexed by the United States. In practice, however, these rights were often not enforced.

ARTICLE VIII
Mexicans now established in territories previously belonging to Mexico, and which remain for the future within the limits of the United States, as defined by the present treaty, shall be free to continue where they now reside, or to remove at any time to the Mexican Republic, retaining the property which they possess in the said territories, or disposing thereof, and removing the proceeds wherever they please, without their being subjected, on this account, to any contribution, tax, or charge whatever.

Those who shall prefer to remain in the said territories may either retain the title and rights of Mexican citizens, or acquire those of citizens of the United States. But they shall be under the obligation to make their election within one year from the date of the exchange of ratifications of this treaty; and those who shall remain in the said territories after the expiration of that year, without having declared their intention to retain the character of Mexicans, shall be considered to have elected to become citizens of the United States.

In the said territories, property of every kind, now belonging to Mexicans not established there, shall be inviolably respected. The present owners, the heirs of these, and all Mexicans who may hereafter acquire said property by contract, shall enjoy with respect to it guarantees equally ample as if the same belonged to citizens of the United States.

Source: Treaty of Guadalupe Hidalgo, February 2, 1848, *Treaties and Conventions between the United States of America and Other Powers since July 4, 1776*. Washington, DC: Government Printing Office, 1871. Yale Law School Avalon Project: Documents in Law, History, and Diplomacy.

Document 8

*Proclamation by Juan Cortina regarding the treatment of
Mexicans in Texas, 1859.*

*In the following excerpt, Juan Cortina calls on Mexicans to resist the loss
of property and violence they have faced since Texas statehood, as well as
on the Texas government to live up to its stated commitment to enforce
the laws.*

Mexicans! When the State of Texas began to receive the new organization
which its sovereignty required as an integrant part of the Union, flocks
of vampires, in the guise of men, came and scattered themselves in the
settlements, without any capital except the corrupt heart and the most per-
verse intentions. Some, brimful of laws, pledged to us their protection against
the attacks of the rest; others assembled in shadowy councils, attempted and
excited the robbery and burning of the houses of our relatives on the other
side of the river Bravo; while others, to the abusing of our unlimited confidence, when we intrusted them with our titles, which secured the future of
our families, refused to return them under false and frivolous pretexts; all,
in short, with a smile on their faces, giving the lie to that which their black
entrails were meditating. Many of you have been robbed of your property,
incarcerated, chased, murdered, and hunted like wild beasts, because your
labor was fruitful, and because your industry excited the vile avarice which
led them. A voice infernal said, from the bottom of their soul, "kill them; the
greater will be our gain!" Ah! this does not finish the sketch of your situation. It would appear that justice had fled from this world, leaving you to
the caprice of your oppressors, who become each day more furious towards
you; that, through witnesses and false charges, although the grounds may be
insufficient, you may be interred in the penitentiaries, if you are not previously deprived of life by some keeper who covers himself from responsibility
by the pretence of your flight. There are to be found criminals covered with
frightful crimes, but they appear to have impunity until opportunity furnish
them a victim; to these monsters indulgence is shown, because they are not of
our race, which is unworthy, as they say, to belong to the human species....

Mexicans! Is there no remedy for you? Inviolable laws, yet useless, serve,
it is true, certain judges and hypocritical authorities, cemented in evil and
injustice, to do whatever suits them, and to satisfy their vile avarice at the
cost of your patience and suffering; rising in their frenzy, even to the taking
of life, through the treacherous hands of their bailiffs. The wicket way in
which many of you have been oftentimes involved in persecution, accompanied by circumstances making it the more bitter, is now well known; these
crimes being hid from society under the shadow of a horrid night, those
implacable people, with the haughty spirit which suggests impunity for a life

of criminality, have pronounced, doubt ye not, your sentence, which is, with accustomed insensibility, as you have seen, on the point of execution.

Mexicans! My part is taken; the voice of revelation whispers to me that to me is entrusted the work of breaking the chains of your slavery, and that the Lord will enable me, with powerful arm, to fight against our enemies, in compliance with the requirements of that Sovereign Majesty, who, from this day forward, will hold us under His protection. On my part, I am ready to offer myself as a sacrifice for your happiness; and counting upon the means necessary for the discharge of my ministry, you may count upon my coöperation, should no cowardly attempt put an end to my days. This undertaking will be sustained on the following bases:

First. A society is organized in the State of Texas, which devotes itself sleeplessly until the work is crowned with success, to the improvement of the unhappy conditions of those Mexicans resident therein; exterminating their tyrants, to which end those which compose it are ready to shed their blood and suffer the death of martyrs.

Second. As this society contains within itself the elements necessary to accomplish the great end of its labors, the veil of impenetrable secrecy covers "The Great Book" in which the articles of its constitution are written; while so delicate are the difficulties which must be overcome that no honorable man can have cause for alarm, if imperious exigencies require them to act without reserve.

Third. The Mexicans of Texas repose their lot under the good sentiments of the governor elect of the State, General Houston, and trust that upon his elevation to power he will begin with care to give us legal protection within the limits of his powers.

Mexicans! Peace be with you! Good inhabitants of the State of Texas, look on them as brothers, and keep in mind that which the Holy Spirit saith: "Thou shalt not be the friend of the passionate man; nor join thyself to the madman, lest thou learn his mode of work and scandalize thy soul."

Juan N. Cortinas
> Source: House Executive Documents, 36th Congress, 1st session.
> H. Executive Document 55a, U.S. Congressional Serial Set 1050,
> pages 80–82.

Document 9

Excerpt from Reminiscences *by Huie Kin.*

Huie Kin moved to the U.S. from China in 1868 at the age of 14. He converted to Christianity and worked his way through college, becoming a minister and founding New York City's first Chinese Christian church. He published this memoir of his life in 1932.

On a clear, crisp, September morning in 1868, or the seventh year of our Emperor T'ung Chih, the mists lifted, and we sighted land for the first time since we left the shores of Kwangtung over sixty days before. To be actually at the "Golden Gate" of the land of our dreams! The feeling that welled up in us was indescribable. I wonder whether the ecstasy before the Pearly Gates of the Celestial City above could surpass what we felt at the moment we realized that we had reached our destination. We rolled up our bedding, packed our baskets, straightened our clothes, and waited.

In those days there were no immigration laws or tedious examinations; people came and went freely. Somebody had brought to the pier large wagons for us. Out of the general babble, some one called out in our local dialect, and, like sheep recognizing the voice only, we blindly followed, and soon were piling into one of the waiting wagons. Everything was so strange and so exciting that my memory of the landing is just a big blur. The wagon made its way heavily over the cobblestones, turned some corners, ascended a steep climb, and stopped at a kind of clubhouse, where we spent the night. Later, I learned that people from the various districts had their own benevolent societies, with headquarters in San Francisco's Chinatown. As there were six of them, they were known as the "Six Companies." Newcomers were taken care of until relatives came to claim them and pay the bill. The next day our relatives from Oakland took us across the bay to the little Chinese settlement there, and kept us until we found work.

In the sixties, San Francisco's Chinatown was made up of stores catering to the Chinese only. There was only one store, situated at the corner of Sacramento and Dupont streets, which kept Chinese and Japanese curios for the American trade. Our people were all in their native costume, with queues down their backs, and kept their stores just as they would do in China, with the entire street front open and groceries and vegetables overflowing on the sidewalks. Forty thousand Chinese were then resident in the bay region, and so these stores did a flourishing business. The Oakland Chinatown was a smaller affair, more like a mining camp, with rough board houses on a vacant lot near Broadway and Sixteenth Street. Under the roof of the houses was a shelf built in the rear and reached by a ladder. Here we slept at night, rolled in our blankets much in the manner of Indians.

Source: Huie Kin, *Reminiscences* (Peiping, China: San Yu Press, 1932), pages 24–25. Reprinted with permission of William Trigg and other descendants of Reverend Huie Kin.

Document 10

Address of the Convention of Native American Democrats of the City of Brooklyn, in the County of Kings, to the Native American Democrats of Kings County, 1835.

The "Native American" in this document's title refers not to American Indians, but to native-born American citizens and even as early as 1835, lays out the arguments that became the core of the Know Nothing Party.

FELLOW-CITIZENS—

When in the course of events, a new Party, acting on a new combination of established principles, is from necessity or choice called into being, it is due as well to the projectors as to the rest of their fellow-citizens, that the motives and objects of the one, and the manner in which it affects the other, should be clearly and candidly defined.

We therefore declare to you, and to the world, that the objects which we, as a new party, seek to accomplish, are mainly these two:

First—Such an alteration in the Naturalization Laws as to require all foreigners who shall come to this country with a view to make it their permanent residence, to declare upon oath within one year after their arrival, their attachment to the Constitution, and that it is their intention to become citizens of the United States; and that after such declaration shall be made, they shall evince the sincerity and soundness of their principles, and intention by a due observance of the Constitution and laws for a much longer period than five years, before they shall be admitted to citizenship;—and we are of the opinion that twenty-one years probation should be required.

Secondly—To oppose the elevation of Foreigners to office.

The necessity and propriety of accomplishing these objects are manifest from the following facts:

1st. That Almost the whole body of emigrants to this country for some years past, and at present, are persons attached to the Roman Catholic Church.

2d—That all the Bishops and Priests of that Church in this, as in all other countries, are appointed by the Pope, and under his direction and control.

3d—That Religion and Politics are inseparably united in the published creeds and standard works of the Roman Catholic Church,—the Pope claiming to be the Supreme Ruler of both Church and State,—King of Kings, and Lord of Lords, and to have the rightful authority to forgive all sins, and to absolve the members of his Church from their oath of allegiance to any government which will not submit to his authority and control.

Source: Native American Democrats, Brooklyn, N.Y. *The American Cause. Proceedings, &c. of the Native American Democrats of Brooklyn.* Brooklyn, Office of the Native American Citizen, 1835. Library of Congress. https://www.loc.gov/item/ca10005004/

Document 11

Interview with Miriam Gether Krasnow, November 29, 1983, interviewed by Dennis Cloutier with the Ellis Island Oral History Project.

Miriam Gether Krasnow, who immigrated to the U.S. in 1910 at age eleven from Russia, tells about her family's experience of migration and Ellis Island in this oral history interview from 1983.

CLOUTIER: Were you traveling alone, or with anyone?

KRASNOW: No. I was traveling, my father and two sisters and a grandmother.

CLOUTIER: Your mother didn't come.

KRASNOW: My mother was left in Antwerp because one of my younger sister got sick there. So she was left in Antwerp, and we went on our journey.

CLOUTIER: Did she ever come to America?

KRASNOW: Yes. About four months later she came to America, to Ellis Island. And then my sister again was sick in Ellis Island. My mother didn't want to get off without her, so she stayed there about four weeks, and then they both got off from Ellis Island. My sister was in the hospital, and my mother was in Ellis Island.

CLOUTIER: What was wrong with your sister?

KRASNOW: She had eczema, which is not a sickness, but they told her it was a sickness and until it cleared up they wouldn't let her off....

CLOUTIER: Do you remember much about the trip?

KRASNOW: The trip was terrible. We were a day, about a day-and-a-half on the boat when I, when we all got very sick. Not my father, but the three of us, the three sisters. And funny as it may seem to you, when I went down to my cabin I already couldn't find it, and somehow I got into a cabin of the crew. And the funniest part is, when I got into that cabin and all the luxuries that was there, I said, "Gee, whiz, it's good to be in with an American. Look all the things he's getting." And they really looked for me and couldn't find me. I went to bed and slept quite a bit, and they were worried about it. But meanwhile I saw nobody showing up. Somehow I got out of the cabin, and I saw them standing, my two sisters crying, and my father said, "Where were you? Why were you in there?" I said, I told him, "It was my cabin." (Mr. Cloutier laughs) And then, of course, we were sick. The whole trip, my father had traveled with us. In fact, we couldn't even eat at all. But he, we couldn't even get out on the deck. He used to pay off the help to take us up on the deck for at least a few hours until we got to America....

CLOUTIER: And how was Ellis Island?

KRASNOW: When we got in?

CLOUTIER: Uh-huh.

KRASNOW: Crowded with people, beautiful. It looked beautiful. Of course, we were anxious to look around, you know. And I don't think we were very long. They just called us over to the desk, and they asked us to read. And each one of us knew how to read Russian. We read a line, and they let us go....

CLOUTIER: So why did you come to America? How was it in Russia in those days?

KRASNOW: Well, we came right after the war. It wasn't any honey at all. You know, it was pogroms and every day there was a different government, and you had to have ten different kinds of money to know what, to go out to shop with. And you really were in danger if you didn't know who was in the power that day. But money was (?), Kerenska [ph], Nicholai, you know, the czar's money. And, of course, they all preferred the czar's money. So we really, were really in trouble when we went out shopping. We didn't know what government was ruling that day. Very bad. And we came to America because my mother had nobody left in Europe. My father was in America. The whole family was in America. And when he came for us, we went. But the trip wasn't a easy trip. Went through a lot.

> Source: Interview with Miriam Gether Krasnow, November 29, 1983, interviewed by Dennis Cloutier, Ellis Island Oral History Project. Reproduced with permission from the Statue of Liberty-Ellis Island Foundation. https://www.statueofliberty.org/

Document 12

Excerpt from Out of the Shadow *by Rose Cohen*

In this excerpt from her biography, Rose Cohen, a Russian Jewish immigrant, describes her experiences at her first job, as she and her father worked to save money to bring her mother and siblings to America.

About the same time that the bitter cold came father told me one night that he had found work for me in a shop where he knew the presser. I lay awake long that night. I was eager to begin life on my own responsibility but was also afraid. We rose earlier than usual that morning for father had to take me to the shop and not be over late for his own work. I wrapped my thimble and scissors, with a piece of bread for breakfast, in a bit of newspaper, carefully stuck two nedles into the lapel of my coat and we started.

The shop was on Pelem Street, a shop district one block long and just wide enough for two ordinary sized wagons to pass each other. We stopped at a door where I noticed at once a brown shining porcelain knob and a half rubbed off number seven. Father looked at his watch and at me.

"Don't look so frightened," he said. "You need not go in until seven. Perhaps if you start in at this hour he will think you have been in the habit of beginning at seven and will not expect you to come in earlier. Remember, be independent. At seven o'clock rise and go home no matter whether the others go or stay."

He began to tell me something else but broke off suddenly, said "goodbye" over his shoulder and went away quickly. I watched him until he turned into Monroe Street.

Now only I felt frightened, and waiting made me nervous, so I tried the knob. The door yielded heavily and closed slowly. I was half way up when it closed entirely, leaving me in darkness. I groped my way to the top of the stairs and hearing a clattering noise of machines, I felt about, found a door, and pushed it open and went in. A tall, dark, beardless man stood folding coats at a table. I went over and asked him for the name (I don't remember what it was). "Yes," he said crossly. "What do you want?"

I said, "I am the new feller hand." He looked at me from head to foot. My face felt so burning hot that I could scarcely see.

"It is more likely," he said, "that you can pull bastings than fell sleeve lining." Then turning from me he shouted over the noise of the machine: "Presser, is this the girl?" The presser put down the iron and looked at me. "I suppose so," he said, "I only know the father."

The cross man looked at me again and said, "Let's see what you can do." He kicked a chair, from which the back had been broken off, to the finisher's table, threw a coat upon it and said raising the corner of his mouth: "Make room for the new feller hand."

One girl tittered, two men glanced at me over their shoulders and pushed their chairs apart a little. By this time I scarcely knew what I was about. I laid my coat down somewhere and pushed my bread into the sleeve. Then I stumbled into the bit of space made for me at the table, drew in the chair and sat down. The men were so close to me on each side I felt the heat of their bodies and could not prevent myself from shrinking away. The men noticed and probably felt hurt. One made a joke, the other laughed and the girls bent their heads low over their work. All at once the thought came: "If I don't do this coat quickly and well he will send me away at once." I picked up the coat, threaded my needle, and began hastily, repeating the lesson father impressed upon me. "Be careful not to twist the sleeve lining, take small false stitches."

My hands trembled so that I could not hold the needle properly. It took me a long while to do the coat. But at last it was done. I took it over to the boss and stood at the table waiting while he was examining it. He took long, trying every stitch with his needle. Finally he put it down and without looking at me gave me two other coats. I felt very happy! When I sat down at the table I drew my knees close together and stitched as quickly as I could....

...All day I took my finished work and laid it on the boss's table. He would glance at the clock and give me other work. Before the day was over I knew that this was a "piece work shop," that there were four machines and sixteen people were working. I also knew that I had done almost as much work as "the grown-up girls" and that they did not like me. I heard Betsy, the head feller hand, talking about "a snip of a girl coming and taking the very bread out of your mouth...."

...Seven o'clock came and every one worked on. I wanted to rise as father had told me to do and go home. But I had not the courage to stand up alone. I kept putting off going from minute to minute. My neck felt stiff and my back ached. I wished there were a back to my chair so that I could rest against it a little. When the people began to go home it seemed to me that it had been night a long time.

The next morning when I came into the shop at seven o'clock, I saw at once that all the people were there and working as steadily as if they had been at work a long while. I had just time to put away my coat and go over to the table, when the boss shouted gruffly, "Look here, girl, if you want to work here you better come in early. No office hours in my shop." It seemed very still in the room, even the machines stopped. And his voice sounded dreadfully distinct. I hastened into the bit of space between the two men and sat down. He brought me two coats and snapped, "Hurry with these!"

From this hour a hard life began for me. He refused to employ me except by the week. He paid me three dollars and for this he hurried me from early until late. He gave me only two coats at a time to do. When I took them over and as he handed me the new work he would say quickly and sharply, "Hurry!" And when he did not say it in words he looked at me and I seemed to hear even more plainly, "Hurry!" I hurried but he was never satisfied. By looks and manner he made me feel that I was not doing enough. Late at night when the people would stand up and begin to fold their work away and I too would rise feeling stiff in every limb and thinking with dread of our cold empty little room and the uncooked rice, he would come over with still another coat.

"I need it the first thing in the morning," he would give as an excuse. I understood that he was taking advantage of me because I was a child. And now that it was dark in the shop except for the low single gas jet over my table and the one over his at the other end of the room, and there was no one to see, more tears fell on the sleeve lining as I bent over it than there were stitches in it.

I did not soon complain to father. I had given him an idea of the people and the work during the first days. But when I had been in the shop a few weeks I told him, "The boss is hurrying the life out of me." I know now that if I had put it less strongly he would have paid more attention to it. Father hated to hear things put strongly. Besides he himself worked very hard. He never came home before eleven and he left at five in the morning.

He said to me now, "Work a little longer until you have more experience; then you can be independent."

"But if I did piece work, father, I would not have to hurry so. And I could go home earlier when the other people go."

Father explained further, "It pays him better to employ you by the week. Don't you see if you did piece work he would have to pay you as much as he pays a woman piece worker? But this way he gets almost as much work out of you for half the amount a woman is paid."

I myself did not want to leave the shop for fear of losing a day or even more perhaps in finding other work. To lose half a dollar meant that it would take so much longer before mother and the children would come. And now I wanted them more than ever before. I longed for my mother and a home where it would be light and warm and she would be waiting when we came from work. Because I longed for them so I lived much in imagination. For so I could have them near me. Often as the hour for going home drew near I would sit stitching and making believe that mother and the children were home waiting. On leaving the shop I would hasten along through the street keeping my eyes on the ground so as to shut out everything but what I wanted to see. I pictured myself walking into the house. There was a delicious warm smell of cooked food. Mother greeted me near the door and the children gathered about me shouting and trying to pull me down. Mother scolded them saying, "Let her take her coat off, see how cold her hands are!" but they paid no attention and pulled me down to them. Their little arms were about my neck, their warm faces against my cold cheeks and we went tumbling all over each other. Soon mother called, "Supper is ready." There was a scampering and a rush to the table, followed by a scraping of chairs and a clattering of dishes. Finally we were all seated. There was browned meat and potatoes for supper.

I used to keep this up until I turned the key in the door and opened it and stood facing the dark, cold, silent room.

Source: Rose Cohen, Out of the Shadow. New York:
George H. Doran Company, 1918.

Document 13

"The New Colossus" by Emma Lazarus

This poem by Emma Lazarus epitomizes the welcoming view of American immigration, and is engraved on the base of the Statue of Liberty.

> Not like the brazen giant of Greek fame,
> With conquering limbs astride from land to land;
> Here at our sea-washed, sunset gates shall stand
> A mighty woman with a torch, whose flame
> Is the imprisoned lightning, and her name
> Mother of Exiles. From her beacon-hand
> Glows world-wide welcome; her mild eyes command
> The air-bridged harbor that twin cities frame.
> "Keep, ancient lands, your storied pomp!" cries she
> With silent lips. "Give me your tired, your poor,
> Your huddled masses yearning to breathe free,
> The wretched refuse of your teeming shore.
> Send these, the homeless, tempest-tost to me,
> I lift my lamp beside the golden door!"

Source: The Poems of Emma Lazarus in Two Volumes: Volume 1.
Boston and New York: Houghton, Mifflin and
Company, 1889, pages 202–203.

Document 14

"Unguarded Gates" by Thomas Bailey Aldrich

In this poem, Thomas Bailey Aldrich warned of the potential dangers of unrestricted immigration.

> Wide open and unguarded stand our gates,
> Named of the four winds, North, South, East, and West;
> Portals that lead to an enchanted land
> Of cities, forests, fields of living gold,
> Vast prairies, lordly summits touched with snow,
> Majestic rivers sweeping proudly past
> The Arab's date-palm and the Norseman's pine—
> A realm wherein are fruits of every zone,
> Airs of all climes, for lo! throughout the year
> The red rose blossoms somewhere—a rich land,
> A later Eden planted in the wilds,
> With not an inch of earth within its bound
> But if a slave's foot press it sets him free!
> Here, it is written, Toil shall have its wage,
> And Honor honor, and the humblest man
> Stand level with the highest in the law.
> Of such a land have men in dungeons dreamed,
> And with the vision brightening in their eyes
> Gone smiling to the fagot and the sword.
>
> Wide open and unguarded stand our gates,
> And through them presses a wild motley throng—
> Men from the Volga and the Tartar steppes,
> Featureless figures of the Hoang-Ho,
> Malayan, Scythian, Teuton, Kelt, and Slav,
> Flying the Old World's poverty and scorn;
> These bringing with them unknown gods and rites,
> Those, tiger passions, here to stretch their claws.
> In street and alley what strange tongues are these,
> Accents of menace alien to our air,
> Voices that once the Tower of Babel knew!
> O Liberty, white Goddess! is it well
> To leave the gates unguarded? On thy breast
> Fold Sorrow's children, soothe the hurts of fate.
> Lift the down-trodden, but with hand of steel
> Stay those who to thy sacred portals come
> To waste the gifts of freedom. Have a care
> Lest from thy brow the clustered stars be torn

And trampled in the dust. For so of old
The thronging Goth and Vandal trampled Rome,
And where the temples of the Caesars stood
The lean wolf unmolested made her lair.

> Source: Thomas Bailey Aldrich, "Unguarded
> Gates," *Atlantic Monthly*, July 1892, page 57.

Document 15

Excerpt from **Some Reasons for Chinese Exclusion. Meat vs.
Rice. American Manhood Against Asiatic Coolieism. Which
Shall Survive?,** *1902.*

*In this document, prepared to try to convince Congress to renew the Chinese
Exclusion Act again in 1902, the American Federation of Labor argues that
Chinese workers have caused a degradation of labor conditions for white
workers.*

CHINESE LABOR DEGRADES LABOR JUST AS SLAVE LABOR DID.
For many years it was impossible to get white persons to do the menial
labor usually performed by Chinese. It was Chinamen's labor, and not fit
for white. In the agricultural districts a species of tramp has been created,
known as the blanket man. White agricultural laborers seldom find permanent employment; the Chinese are preferred. During harvest time the
white man is forced to wander from ranch to ranch and find employment
here and there for short periods of time, with the privilege of sleeping in
the barns or haystacks. He is looked upon as a vagabond, unfit to associate
with his employer or to eat from the same table with him. The negro slave
of the South was housed and fed, but the white trash of California is placed
beneath the Chinese.

The white domestic servant was expected to live in the room originally
built for John, generally situated in the cellar and void of all comforts, frequently unpainted or unpapered, containing a bedstead and a chair. Anything
was good enough for John, and the white girl had to be satisfied as well. Is
it any wonder that self-respecting girls refused to take service under those
conditions? And what is true of agricultural laborers and domestics equally
applies to the trades in which Chinese were largely employed. Absolute ser-
vility was expected from those who took the place of the Chinaman, and
it will take years to obliterate these traces of inferiority and reestablish the
proper relations of employer and employee.

From the report of the special committee on Chinese immigration to the
California State senate, 1878, we quote the following in this connection:

"A serious objection to slavery, as it existed in the Southern States, was
that it tended to degrade white labor. The very same objection exists against
Chinese labor in this State...."

"The employment of Chinese as agricultural laborers is most generally in droves, held in some sort of dependence by a head man or agent of the Chinese companies. The workmen live in sheds or in straw stacks, do their own cooking, have no homes, and are without interest in their work or the country. The white laborer who would compete with them must not only pursue the same kind of life, but must, like them, abdicate his individuality. The consequence would be lamentable, even if the white laborer should succeed by such means in driving the Asiatic from the field. We would in that event have a laboring class without homes, without families, and without any of the restraining influences of society."

Source: American Federation of Labor, *Some Reasons for Chinese Exclusion. Meat vs. Rice. American Manhood Against Asiatic Coolieism. Which Shall Survive?*. Washington D.C.: Government Printing Office, 1902.

Document 16

Departure paper of Jung Kee Hoe, 1898

After exclusion, Chinese Americans who wanted to leave the United States and be able to return had to carry documents vouching that they were not new immigrants, but rather had been living in the United States before exclusion. The following document is the departure paper of Jun Kee Hoe, vouching for her residency status and the citizenship of her five children.

Know Ye All Men By This Instrument: That We, the Undersigned, residents of the County of Monterey, and vicinity of Pajaro, Cal., do hereby certify that we have been acquainted with JUNG KEE HOE, who is the wife of Dong Kee Hoe, a merchant residing in and doing business in Chinatown, near Pajaro, in the County of Monterey, California; that we have known said Jung Kee Hoe for Five Years or more; and we further certify that from said marriage there are five children, namely:

> #Dong How Soon, boy, age about 14 years;
> #Dong Yuk Lon, girl, age about 12 years;
> #Dong Yuk Sue, girl, age about 10 years;
> #Dong How Lun, boy, age about 8 years;
> #Dong How Chun, boy, age about 1 year;
> All Born in the State of California:

And we further certify that the photograph hereto attached is a true and correct likeness of the said Jung Kee Hoe.

Dated and Signed this 23rd day of May, A.D. 1898.

Source: Immigration Arrival Investigation Case File for Tsai Cho Ming. Series: Immigration Arrival Investigation Case Files, 1884–1944. Record

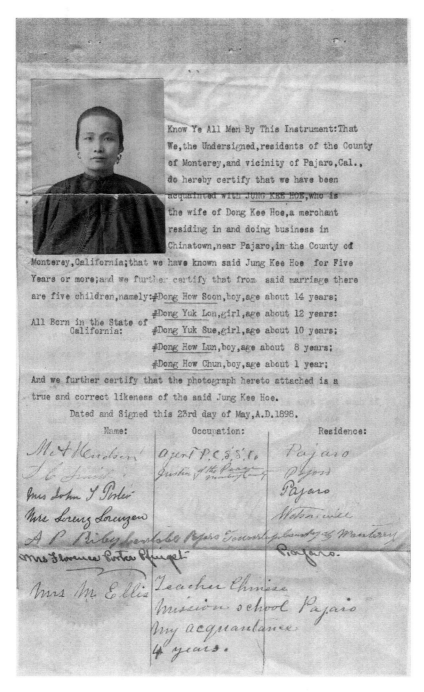

Know Ye All Men By This Instrument:That
We,the Undersigned,residents of the County
of Monterey,and vicinity of Pajaro,Cal.,
do hereby certify that we have been
acquainted with JUNG KEE HOE,who is
the wife of Dong Kee Hoe,a merchant
residing in and doing business in
Chinatown,near Pajaro,in the County of
Monterey,California;that we have known said Jung Kee Hoe for Five
Years or more;and we further certify that from said marriage there
are five children,namely:#Dong How Soon,boy,age about 14 years;
                        #Dong Yuk Lon,girl,age about 12 years:
All Born in the State of
California: #Dong Yuk Sue,girl,age about 10 years;
                        #Dong How Lun,boy,age about 8 years;
                        #Dong How Chun,boy,age about 1 year;
And we further certify that the photograph hereto attached is a
true and correct likeness of the said Jung Kee Hoe.
     Dated and Signed this 23rd day of May,A.D.1898.

Name:	Occupation:	Residence:
M.H Hudson	Agent P.C.S.S.Co	Pajaro
J.C Smith	Justice of the Peace monterey co	Pajaro
Mrs John T Porter		Pajaro
Mrs Lorenz Lorenzen		Watsonville
A.P Riley constable Pajaro Township county of Monterey		Pajaro.
Mrs Florence Porter Pfingst		
Mrs M. Ellis	Teacher Chinese Mission school Pajaro my acquaintance 4 years.	

Figure D16 Departure paper of Jung Kee Hoe, 1898

Group 85: Records of the Immigration and Naturalization Service, 1787–2004. National Archives. https://catalog.archives.gov/id/296461

Document 17

"A Letter from Mrs. Tape," Daily Alta California, *April 16, 1885*

In 1884, at the age of eight, Mamie Tape was denied entry to the all-white Spring Valley School in San Francisco due to her race. Her parents, Joseph and Mary Tape, sued, on the grounds that they were being denied access to the public schools. They won their case before the California Supreme Court (Tape v. Hurley, 1885), although the outcome was not the admission of Chinese students to the white schools, but rather the creation of a separate public school system for the Chinese. In the following letter, which was published in the San Francisco Daily Alta California, *Mary Tape defends the right of her daughter to attend her neighborhood school instead of the segregated school for the Chinese.*

The following is a verbatim copy of a letter received from Mrs. Tape, in regard to her children at present attending the Chinese school:

1769 Green Street
San Francisco, April 8, 1885.

To the Board of Education—DEAR SIRS: I see that you are going to make all sorts of excuses to keep my child out off the Public schools. Dear sirs, Will you please to tell me! Is it a disgrace to be Born a Chinese? Didn't God make us all!!! What right! have you to bar my children out of the school because she is a chinese Decend. They is no other worldly reason that you could keep her out, except that. I suppose, you all goes to churches on Sundays! Do you call that a Christian act to compell my little children to go so far to a school that is made in purpose for them. My children don't dress like the other Chinese. They look just as phunny amongst them as the Chinese dress in Chinese look amongst you Caucasians. Besides, if I had any wish to send them to a chinese school I could have sent them two years ago without going to all this trouble. You have expended a lot of the Public money foolishly, all because of a one poor little Child. Her playmates is all Caucasians ever since she could toddle around. If she is good enough to play with them! Then is she not good enough to be in the same room and studie with them? You had better come and see for yourselves. See if the Tape's is not same as other Caucasians, except in features. It seems no matter how a Chinese may live and dress so long as you know they Chinese. Then they are hated as one. There is not any right or justice for them.

You have seen my husband and child. You told him it wasn't Mamie Tape you object to. If it were not Mamie Tape you object to, then why didn't you let her attend the school nearest her home! Instead of first making one pretense Then another pretense of some kind to keep her out? It seems to me Mr. Moulder has a grudge against this Eight-year-old Mamie Tape. I know they is no other child I mean Chinese child! care to go to your public Chinese school. May you Mr. Moulder, never be persecuted like the way you have persecuted little Mamie Tape. Mamie Tape will never attend any of the Chinese schools of your making! Never!!! I will let the world see sir What justice there is When it is govern by the Race prejudice men! Just because she is of the Chinese decend, not because she don't dress like you because she does. Just because she is decended of Chinese parents I guess she is more of a American then a good many of you that is going to prewent her being Educated.

Mrs. M. Tape

Source: "A Letter from Mrs. Tape," Daily Alta California,
April 16, 1885, page 1, column 3. From the California Digital
Newspapers Collection. https://cdnc.ucr.edu/

Document 18

Mary Church Terrell, "What It Means to Be Colored in the Capital of the United States"

In this speech presented at the United Women's Club in Washington, D.C., on October 10, 1906, noted African American educator and activist Mary Church Terrell explains the difficulties Black Americans encountered when living in or traveling through cities across the U.S., including the national capital.

Washington, D.C., has been called "The Colored Man's Paradise." Whether this sobriquet was given to the national capital in bitter irony by a member of the handicapped race, as he reviewed some of his own persecutions and rebuffs, or whether it was given immediately after the war by an ex-slave-holder who for the first time in his life saw colored people walking about like freemen, minus the overseer and his whip, history saith not. It is certain that it would be difficult to find a worse misnomer for Washington than "The Colored Man's Paradise" if so prosaic a consideration as veracity is to determine the appropriateness of a name.

For fifteen years I have resided in Washington, and while it was far from being a paradise for colored people when I first touched these shores it has been doing its level best ever since to make conditions for us intolerable. As a colored woman I might enter Washington any night, a stranger in a strange land, and walk miles without finding a place to lay my head. Unless I happened to know colored people who live here or ran across a chance acquaintance who could recommend a colored boarding-house to me, I should be obliged to spend the entire night wandering about. Indians, Chinamen, Filipinos, Japanese and representatives of any other dark race can find hotel accommodations, if they can pay for them. The colored man alone is thrust out of the hotels of the national capital like a leper.

As a colored woman I may walk from the Capitol to the White House, ravenously hungry and abundantly supplied with money with which to purchase a meal, without finding a single restaurant in which I would be permitted to take a morsel of food, if it was patronized by white people, unless I were willing to sit behind a screen. As a colored woman I cannot visit the tomb of the Father of this country, which owes its very existence to the love of freedom in the human heart and which stands for equal opportunity to all, without being forced to sit in the Jim Crow section of an electric car which starts from the very heart of the city—midway between the Capitol and the White House. If I refuse thus to be humiliated, I am cast into jail and forced to pay a fine for violating the Virginia laws....

As a colored woman I may enter more than one white church in Washington without receiving that welcome which as a human being I have a right to expect in the sanctuary of God....

Unless I am willing to engage in a few menial occupations, in which the pay for my services would be very poor, there is no way for me to earn an honest living, if I am not a trained nurse or a dressmaker or can secure a position as teacher in the public schools, which is exceedingly difficult to do. It matters not what my intellectual attainments may be or how great is the need of the services of a competent person, if I try to enter many of the numerous vocations in which my white sisters are allowed to engage, the door is shut in my face....

And so I might go on citing instance after instance to show the variety of ways in which our people are sacrificed on the altar of prejudice in the Capital of the United States and how almost insurmountable are the obstacles which block his path to success....

It is impossible for any white person in the United States, no matter how sympathetic and broad, to realize what life would mean to him if his incentive to effort were suddenly snatched away. To the lack of incentive to effort, which is the awful shadow under which we live, may be traced the wreck and ruin of score of colored youth. And surely nowhere in the world do oppression and persecution based solely on the color of the skin appear more hateful and hideous than in the capital of the United States, because the chasm between the principles upon which this Government was founded, in which it still professes to believe, and those which are daily practiced under the protection of the flag, yawn so wide and deep.

Source: Mary Church Terrell, "What It Means to Be Colored in the Capital of the United States," *The Independent*, January 24, 1907, pages 181–186.

Document 19

Photo of immigrants at Ellis Island suspected of being
"mental defectives," early twentieth century.

This photo is taken from a manual prepared by officers of the U.S. Public Health service who worked at Ellis Island inspecting immigrants for disabilities that might justify their exclusion. Intended to educate inexperienced officers, the manual included both photos like the one below as well as detailed descriptions of how to identify different types of "mental defects." As the caption notes, the photo below shows a group of people who were singled out for further inspection on the suspicion that they were "mental defectives." Some of them were ultimately allowed to enter the country, while others were certified as "feeble-minded" and turned back.

Source: *Manual of the Mental Examination of Aliens*
(Washington, D.C.: Government Printing Office,
1918), page 13.

Figure D19 Photo of immigrants at Ellis Island suspected of being "mental defectives," early twentieth century

Document 20

Excerpt from Alfred P. Schultz, Race or Mongrel?

In this book, Alfred Schultz warned that the U.S. was destined to decline unless immigration restriction was used to defend the country's racial purity. The excerpt below covers his beliefs on equality and the impact of education.

The principle that all men are created equal is still considered the chief pillar of strength of the United States. It is a little declamatory phrase, and only one objection can be raised against it, that it does not contain one iota of truth. Every man knows that the phrase is a falsehood. The truth is that all men are created unequal. Even the men of one and the same race are unequal; the inequalities, however, are not greater than the inequalities existing between the individual leaves of one tree, for they are variations of one and the same type. The differences between individuals of distinct races are essential, and, as they are the differences that exist between one species and another, they are lasting. The attempts at creating perfect man, man pure and simple, or "The American," by a fusion of all human beings, is similar to the attempt of creating the perfect dog by a fusion of all canine races. Every animal breeder knows that it cannot be done....

The friends of universal uniformity and of eternal peace will say: "Well, as soon as we are equally worthless, we will not know it, and happiness and peace will prevail." The conclusion is false. The mongrels are equally worthless, but there is no harmony in the depraved lot. The instincts of the different races do not entirely disappear, but they cannot develop. The result is internal unhappiness as far as the individual is concerned, and discord, chronic civil war, as far as the state is concerned. Anarchy within the individual, anarchy in the state.

And why should promiscuousness in the United States have a different effect than it had in Rome and elsewhere? The opinion is advanced that the public schools change the children of all races into Americans. Put a Scandinavian, a German, and a Magyar boy in at one end, and they will come out Americans at the other end. Which is like saying, let a pointer, a setter, and a pug enter one end of a tunnel and they will come out three greyhounds at the other end.

Public schools are in our time not educational institutions, but information bureaus, and the cultivation of the memory predominates. The children of every race can be trained to the cultivation of the memory, but they cannot all be educated alike. The instincts of the different races are too much out of harmony. It is for this reason that the schools give information, with very little education. Schools cannot accomplish the impossible. To express the same opinion biologically, "All animals cannot be fed with the same fodder."

Source: Alfred P. Schultz, *Race or Mongrel: A Brief History of the Rise and Fall of the Ancient Races of Earth: A Theory that the Fall of Nations is Due to Intermarriage with Alien Stocks: A Demonstration that a Nation's Strength is Due to Racial Purity: A Prophecy that America Will Sink to Early Decay Unless Immigration is Rigorously Restricted*. Boston: L.C. Page and Co., 1908, pages 259–261.

Document 21

Excerpt from oral history with Mrs. Emilia Castañeda de Valenciana, interviewed by Christine Valenciana on September 8, 1971.

In this oral history from 1971, Emilia Castañeda de Valenciana remembers how despite being a native-born American citizen, she was forced to move to Mexico when her father was repatriated, after her mother died and he lost his job, during the Great Depression.

CV: Tell me what you think your dad's financial situation was before the Depression?

EV: Well, since he had a trade I think his financial situation was very good. He told me that he worked in constructing buildings here in Los Angeles. I guess he traveled to other cities in the United States. He said that he missed out on going to work in New York City. I guess my mother got sick, and this stopped him from going to New York City to work. He was probably going to work on some of those skyscrapers.

I remember us owning the home on Folsom Street right next to the Malabar Street School. He owned a duplex and our house was very well furnished. My dad, from what I remember used to like to dress well and he had quite a bit of jewelry. It was a pretty nice lot that we had, plus the house. We had fruit trees and turkeys. I think we had chickens and rabbits. My mother and dad used to take care of them....

CV: Tell me how you originally got to Mexico.

EV: After my mother died, I guess my dad was pretty sad. Here he was left with a family, a couple of children to raise, no wife, no work and living off of welfare. He had a trade and could work if the work was available. Maybe he thought that he should go back to his country....

Anyway, we went to Mexico because my dad asked the county to send him back to Mexico. He told me that he asked to be sent....He knew he could get work there and that he wouldn't be living off welfare. So he asked us if we wanted to go with him, and we told him, "Yes, our place is with you." He was our father and we weren't going to be left here to be made wards of the state....

Anyway, we arrived at my Tía Santitos' house. It wasn't really her house because she lived there with her married son. His name was

Salvador. I think his last name was Villalobos, or Villanueva; I've even forgotten, now. It's been so many years since I've seen him....

This family that we lived with had six children, three girls, then three boys. The oldest boy used to call me <u>repatriada</u>. I don't think I felt that I was a <u>repatriada</u> because I was an American citizen. Maybe we were <u>repatriados</u>.

CV: How could you be if you were born in the United States?

EV: Well, maybe they kicked us out of our country to get rid of us and to make room for Anglos. How do I know? I'll never know.

CV: What did you think about that kid telling you all that?

EV: Well, it wasn't nice, especially from a relative of your own. He must have heard it from the parents. Why else would he say it? After all, his mother wasn't that friendly. We used to have to sleep outdoors while we lived there. If it rained we couldn't go into the house. Boy, it rains in Mexico!...They were crowded as it was. They had just one room there, a great big room that was their bedroom and their living room. It was one great big long room, maybe a little bit longer than this room here, which is about twenty feet wide. So they didn't have any room for us to go in. Even if they had had a little space, I felt that they didn't have the heart to tell us, "Well, come in and get out of the rain...."

CV: You were telling me that you and your brother were a novelty.

EV: Yes, we were a novelty, because, I guess, we spoke mostly English. We used to go to the store and we used to refer to the money as pennies, not centavos. So you know, the people used to laugh at us. They didn't really laugh at us, but, they used to get a kick out of it. So I think we spoke more English than Spanish.

On the other hand, I remember several times that the school teachers at Malabar Street School [in Los Angeles] used to reprimand us on the playground for speaking Spanish. The school teachers used to tell us that we shouldn't be speaking Spanish....In a way it was nice because I didn't grow up really with too much of an accent....

CV: Well, do you remember having trouble understanding the people when you went to Mexico.

EV: Yes I do. I remember that I didn't understand a lot of what they said to me, and they didn't understand what I said. I remember there were little kids who followed us, probably because my brother and I talked in English, and they were getting a big kick out of this. We were like a circus I guess, a novelty to them.

Source: Mrs. Emilia Castañeda de Valenciana, interviewed by Christine Valenciana on September 8, 1971. Oral History Program. O.H. 700, Mexican American Project. Reproduced courtesy of the Lawrence de Graaf Center for Oral and Public History, California State University Fullerton.

Document 22

Report from an embittered Nisei on why he answered "no" to the loyalty questionnaire, 1944

In addition to being forced to move to internment camps during the war, Japanese Americans, whether they were citizens or not, were asked to complete a loyalty questionnaire. Those who answered "no" to questions twenty-seven and twenty-eight, which asked if the respondent would be willing to serve in the military or Women's Army Auxiliary Corps and if they would be willing to swear unqualified allegiance to the U.S. and forswear any allegiance to Japan or any other foreign government, were segregated to separate camps like the one at Tule Lake, California, and potentially faced loss of citizenship and deportation to Japan. Some Nisei—native-born Americans of parents born in Japan—refused to answer these questions based on principle. The excerpt below is from an interview conducted by anthropologist and community analyst Morris Opler with a Nisei at the Manzanar internment camp in California, explaining why he is being sent to Tule Lake for answering "no".

Yes, I'm going. It's no sudden decision with me. I've been "no" from the beginning. Everyone of the children in our family who was of age said "no." I'm from Venice. Lots of the people who lived around Venice said "no" and are going to Tule. It's on account of the dirty deal we got. We haven't asked for repatriation or expatriation. We are just going on "no" answers....It was bad enough without registration and question 28 but when that came along it turned the minds of about half of the nisei. Up to that time we had some hope. But we took the stand that the government had no right to ask us such a question; it showed that they were regarding us as aliens. If you had left us outside you could have asked us anything you wanted. Even if some of us had been attacked, even if a few had been killed, it would have been better. It would have been up to us. If we wanted to stay we would have been taking our own chances. Even if the aliens had been made to move, the citizens should have been allowed to remain. It would have showed that this government was treating its citizens alike, regardless of ancestry. I grew up in this country. I can speak Japanese pretty well but I can't read or write it. I've never been to Japan. But if citizenship and hard work and a good record don't bring you any consideration; if they can still do this to you, there's no use talking about loyalty. A man's got to go where there is some security and chance for him and where his face won't be against him.

Source: Morris E. Opler, "Why So Many of the Venice People Are Tule Lake Bound (From An Evacuee)." Manzanar Relocation Center, Community Analysis Section, February 11, 1944, Report No. 172. Quoted in Harlan D. Unrau, *Evacuation and Relocation of Persons of Japanese*

Ancestry During World War II: A Historical Study of the Manzanar War Relocation Center. Historical Resource Study/Special History Study, Volume 2 (United States Department of the Interior, National Park Service, 1996), page 722.

Document 23

Speech by President Franklin D. Roosevelt regarding the repeal of the Chinese exclusion laws, October 11, 1943.

In this message to Congress, President Roosevelt calls for an end to Chinese exclusion, based on their status as an ally during World War II.

There is now pending before the Congress legislation to permit the immigration of Chinese people into this country and to allow Chinese residents here to become American citizens. I regard this legislation as vital to the winning of the war and the establishment of a secure peace.

China is our ally. For many long years she stood alone in the fight against aggression. Today we fight at her side. She has continued her gallant struggle against the greatest odds.

China has understood that the strategy of victory in this global war first required the concentration of our strength upon the European front. She has understood that the amount of supplies we could make available to her has been limited by difficulties of transportation. She knows that substantial aid will be forthcoming as soon as possible—aid not only in the form of weapons and supplies. For plans are already under way for offensive, effective action. We and our allies will aim our forces at the heart of Japan—in ever-increasing force until the common enemy is driven from China's soil.

But China's resistance does not depend alone on guns and planes and on attacks on land, sea and from the air. It is based more in the spirit of her people and her faith in her allies. We owe it to the Chinese to strengthen that faith. One step in this direction is to wipe from the statute books those anachronisms in our law which forbid the immigration of Chinese people into this country and which bar Chinese residents from American citizenship.

Nations like individuals make mistakes. We must be big enough to acknowledge our mistakes of the past and to correct them.

By the repeal of the Chinese Exclusion Laws, we can correct a historic mistake and silence the distorted Japanese propaganda. The enactment of legislation now pending before the Congress would put Chinese immigrants on a parity with those from other countries. The Chinese quota would, therefore, be only about 100 immigrants a year. There can be no reasonable apprehension that any such number of immigrants will cause unemployment or provide competition in the search for jobs.

The extension of the privileges of citizenship to the relatively few Chinese residents in our country would operate as another meaningful display of friendship. It would be additional proof that we regard China not only as a partner in waging war but that we shall regard her as a partner in days of peace. While it would give the Chinese a preferred status over other Oriental people, their great contribution to the cause of decency and freedom entitles them to such preference.

Action by the Congress now will be an earnest [expression] of our purpose to apply the policy of the good neighbor to our relations with other peoples...

Source: Message to Congress re Repeal of Chinese Exclusion Laws (speech file 1490), October 1943, Box 75, Franklin D. Roosevelt, Master Speech File, 1898–1945. Franklin D. Roosevelt Presidential Library & Museum. http://www.fdrlibrary. marist.edu/_resources/images/msf/msfb0116

Document 24

Proposal for Chicano Educational Development at the University of Washington, submitted by the United Mexican American Students (UMAS), May 5, 1969.

Calls for ethnic studies programs like the following became common during the late 1960s and early 1970s at American universities. In the excerpt below, UMAS explains why a program in Chicano Studies is necessary, and how such a program would benefit not only Chicano students but the university as a whole.

What is a Chicano? Most persons, particularly Anglo-Americans, could not begin to answer this question. This much afflicted individual has been referred to throughout history by many names, some not very flattering, and many of them misguided at best. His history and his culture have been placed at a low level of priority by the educational and cultural processes of the majority.

Not only have his historical achievements and cultural traits been made unavailable to him, but at the same time he has been faced with a misdirected educational process that does not prepare him for nor direct him toward taking full advantage of the American economic system. This partial education frequently results in what the sociological census-oriented professionals call "lower-income Spanish-speaking peoples."

The most frustrating link in this dehumanizing chain of events is the fact that the Mexican American population is impotent to determine the functions and directions of those institutions which govern and attempt to serve it. There has been little encouragement to organize and participate in the political process.

The added phenomenon of the Chicano being largely a regionally-based population has resulted in many American institutions passing him by, taking no note of his existence, his achievements and his contributions to the whole society, nor making a concentrated effort to solve the unique problems stemming from the interface of his culture and the American society.

The need to combat this ignorance and deprivation is imperative if this country is to arrest and correct the many destructive attitudes and courses of action that such ignorance foments. At the same time the opportunity must be given to the young Chicano to learn and fully participate in the educational process, to take pride in his heritage and to develop the confidence and skills necessary for him to realize his full potential as a member of this society.

Systematic study of the relationship between our people and American society is urgently needed. There are two broad considerations: One, the understanding of American society by members of our ethnic group and two, the understanding of the Mejicanos by the members of the larger dominant society. This calls for intensive and extensive programs of study designed to expand our knowledge about social interaction between this little known ethnic group and American society. Programs of this type could produce competent scholars of Mexican identity.

Finally, it is estimated that by Fall quarter 1969 over 200 Chicano students will be attending this university. In order to make the educational process relevant to their needs and the needs of the Chicano community as a whole, a new, bold and vigorous approach must be immediately implemented. The present course in Mexican American History and Culture is a good example of the positive results that are possible when a fresh, vigorous, imaginative approach to education is taken. However, that course has but increased our thirst for learning about that civilization, that history, that has shaped our own beings. The university as an institution of learning must respond to this need, and the manner it is able to so respond will determine its worth as an institution of education.

The essence of education is to forever question the present, the accepted method of doing things, and thus to challenge the imagination to seek a better world....

Source: Proposal for Chicano Educational Development, submitted to Dean Phillips, Arts & Sciences, at the University of Washington, by the United Mexican American Students, May 5, 1969. MEChA de UW Collection, Chicano/a Movement in Washington State History Project, Seattle Civil Rights and Labor History Project, University of Washington.

Document 25

Interview with Sarabjit Sikand, interviewed by Justin Nordstrom, 29 October 1998.

In the following oral history interview, Sarabjit (Beenu) Sikand, an Indian Sikh who immigrated to the U.S. in the 1990s, talks about the cultural differences between India and the United States and her experiences raising her young children as she pursues her M.B.A.

N: So, you mentioned before you came to the U.S. because of marriage. Can you say a little bit more about that, how the, what it was like to come to the U.S., and also what your marriage was like, what the decision was like to get married?

S: I was the one who made the decision. Bobby and me, we met each other. We liked each other and then we said, "Yes." I got married and after six-and-a-half months, because of the visa, then I came here. It was very hard for me. I can speak English. I can do Westernized stuff, but then also it's two different cultures from India to USA. My way of thinking is totally different. My husband's way of thinking is totally different because he was raised here. So the first one and a half years were very, very tough, but then after that now, it's fine for me. Sometimes I feel like that I'm an outsider. It's like I take my son to the school or something. There are some things to this date that I can't understand, like double meaning stuff, some jokes or some things, but everything else if fine. I'm doing everything. Everything else is OK....

N: Would you say that attitudes work or towards in education are different from folks that were, that are sort of native-born Americans, as opposed to folks that immigrated from India or from another country for that matter? Do you think that there are different attitudes toward work or schooling?

S: You are talking about the Indians who were born here or who were coming from India?

N: Or comparing Indian immigrants to America at large, native-born Americans.

S: Yes, I think so, you guys take everything very lightly. We don't. When I was growing up, my dad, he told me, "I want you to get graduated, at least graduate, and then after that you can do anything you want to." So that's what we did, all of us. My brothers and sisters, we have bachelor's, and after that we did one more course over there. When I came here, my husband wanted me to become a...gosh what...dentist. But I told him, "No, I can't study for the next ten years." But, yes that kind of thing, we really take it seriously, studies and business, professions, we do. We stick with one profession instead of just going to different ones.

N: I know this is thinking really far into the future, but when you retire from work, later in your life, do you ever see yourself returning to India to live?

S: No, never, because my husband, he cannot go back. He went back when we got married. He went back after twenty years. And now I don't know when he'll go back. Because once you are raised here, it's just totally different. He cannot eat that food. When he goes to India, he cannot drink that water. My kids, they cannot go either. So I don't think we will ever go and settle there....

N: What languages do you speak at home?

S: I speak Hindi, Punjabi, English. And my son, now he has started English, so he doesn't want to speak Indian language. But he understands everything. And my husband, most of the time he speaks English, but he understands Hindi and Punjabi.

N: Is it important to you that your children maintain that sort of language or is it not really important?

S: Yes, it's very important. That's why I speak it, yes....

N: What can you say about the—you mentioned a little bit about this before, about the sort of cultural differences between the U.S. and India, in terms of raising your children or in terms of day to day life, what sorts of differences are there between your experiences growing up in India and raising your children here?

S: I would like to take my kids to India and raise them there [laughter] [inaudible], because in India it's a very protective life, and children, they listen to you, and then...I don't know, it's just totally different. Over here, kids are more independents. And then peer pressure in schools and colleges, they tend to do wrong things. In India, those things are not there yet. Dating, and those things, I'm against dating and everything. In India those things are not there. So, yes there are differences....

N: We talked about this a little before, but what do you feel you've lost or gained by coming to the U.S.? What is it that's, what's been good and what's been bad about coming there instead of say, staying in India?

S: I miss my family. And because I came here, it's not easy to see them every year. And then, but the good part is, I like freedom over here. It's just totally different. I mean in India, there's an age limit, like you can only do your bachelor's until twenty one. After that, no university will let you do that. So, I mean that kind of thing, I mean so over here, I'm raising my kids and I'm going to school. I'm getting my master's. I like that. It's, it's different. More freedom, I believe and everything....

Source: Interview with Sarabjit Sikand, interviewed by Justin Nordstrom, 29 October 1998. OHRC accession #98-20-1. Oral History Research Center, Indiana University.

Document 26

Argument in favor of California Proposition 187

This excerpt from the ballot information for California Proposition 187 presents the argument in favor of the proposition by the "Save Our State" Committee.

Argument in Favor of Proposition 187

California can strike a blow for the taxpayer that will be heard across America; in Arizona, in Texas and in Florida in the same way Proposition 13 was heard across the land.

Proposition 187 will go down in history as the voice of the people against an arrogant bureaucracy.

WE CAN STOP ILLEGAL ALIENS.

If the citizens and the taxpayers of our state wait for the politicians in Washington and Sacramento to stop the incredible flow of ILLEGAL ALIENS, California will be in economic and social bankruptcy.

We have to act and ACT NOW! On our ballot, Proposition 187 will be the first giant stride in ultimately ending the ILLEGAL ALIEN invasion.

It has been estimated that ILLEGAL ALIENS are costing taxpayers in excess of 5 billion dollars a year.

While our own citizens and legal residents go wanting, those who choose to enter our country ILLEGALLY get royal treatment at the expense of the California taxpayer.

IT IS TIME THIS STOPS!

Welfare, medical and educational benefits are the magnets that draw these ILLEGAL ALIENS across our borders.

Senator Robert Byrd (D-West Virginia), who voted against federal reimbursement for state funds spent on ILLEGAL ALIENS, said "states must do what they can for themselves."

PROPOSITION 187 IS CALIFORNIA'S WAY.

Should those ILLEGALLY here receive taxpayer subsidized education including college?

Should our children's classrooms be over-crowded by those who are ILLEGALLY in our country?

Should our Senior Citizens be denied full service under Medi-Cal to subsidize the cost of ILLEGAL ALIENS?

Should those ILLEGALLY here be able to buy and sell forged documents without penalty?

Should tax paid bureaucrats be able to give sanctuary to those ILLEGALLY in our country?

If your answer to these questions is NO, then you should support Proposition 187.

The federal government and the state government have been derelict in their duty to control our borders. It is the role of our government to end the benefits that draw people from around the world who ILLEGALLY enter our country. Our government actually entices them.

Passage of Proposition 187 will send a strong message that California will no longer tolerate the dereliction of the duty by our politicians.

Vote YES on Proposition 187.

The Save Our State Coalition is comprised of Democrats, Republicans and Independents. It includes all races, colors and creeds with the same common denominator. We are American, by birth or naturalization; we are Americans!

We were outraged when our State Legislature voted on July 5th to remove dental care as a medical option and force the increase of the cost of prescription drugs for Senior Citizens. Then, as a final slap in the face, they voted to continue free pre-natal care for ILLEGAL ALIENS!

Vote YES ON PROPOSITION 187. ENOUGH IS ENOUGH!

ASSEMBLYMAN DICK MOUNTJOY
Author of Proposition 187

RONALD PRINCE
Chairman of the "Save Our State" Committee

MAYOR BARBARA KILEY
Co-Chair of the "Save Our State" Committee
> Source: California Proposition 187. Illegal Aliens. Ineligibility for Public Services. Verification and Reporting. Initiative Statute. (1994). http://repository.uchastings.edu/ca_ballot_props/1104

Document 27

Remarks by President Barack Obama on immigration, June 15, 2012.

In this speech, President Obama explains both the DREAM Act and Deferred Action for Childhood Arrivals (DACA).

THE PRESIDENT: Good afternoon, everybody. This morning, Secretary Napolitano announced new actions my administration will take to mend our nation's immigration policy, to make it more fair, more efficient, and more just—specifically for certain young people sometimes called "Dreamers."

These are young people who study in our schools, they play in our neighborhoods, they're friends with our kids, they pledge allegiance to our flag. They are Americans in their heart, in their minds, in every single way but one: on paper. They were brought to this country by their parents—sometimes even as infants—and often have no idea that they're undocumented until they apply for a job or a driver's license, or a college scholarship.

Put yourself in their shoes. Imagine you've done everything right your entire life—studied hard, worked hard, maybe even graduated at the top of your class—only to suddenly face the threat of deportation to a country that you know nothing about, with a language that you may not even speak.

That's what gave rise to the DREAM Act. It says that if your parents brought you here as a child, if you've been here for five years, and you're willing to go to college or serve in our military, you can one day earn your citizenship....

In the absence of any immigration action from Congress to fix our broken immigration system, what we've tried to do is focus our immigration enforcement resources in the right places. So we prioritized border security, putting more boots on the southern border than at any time in our history—today, there are fewer illegal crossings than at any time in the past 40 years. We focused and used discretion about whom to prosecute, focusing on criminals who endanger our communities rather than students who are earning their education. And today, deportation of criminals is up 80 percent. We've improved on that discretion carefully and thoughtfully. Well, today, we're improving it again.

Effective immediately, the Department of Homeland Security is taking steps to lift the shadow of deportation from these young people. Over the next few months, eligible individuals who do not present a risk to national security or public safety will be able to request temporary relief from deportation proceedings and apply for work authorization....

Precisely because this is temporary, Congress needs to act. There is still time for Congress to pass the DREAM Act this year, because these kids deserve to plan their lives in more than two-year increments. And we still need to pass comprehensive immigration reform that addresses our 21st century economic and security needs—reform that gives our farmers and ranchers certainty about the workers that they'll have. Reform that gives our science and technology sectors certainty that the young people who come here to earn their PhDs won't be forced to leave and start new businesses in other countries....

We have always drawn strength from being a nation of immigrants, as well as a nation of laws, and that's going to continue. And my hope is that Congress recognizes that and gets behind this effort.

All right. Thank you very much.

Source: Remarks by President Barack Obama on Immigration, June 15, 2012. Press release from President Barack Obama Whitehouse Archives. https://obamawhitehouse.archives.gov/ the-press-office/2012/06/15/remarks-president-immigration

Further reading

The literature on immigration to the United States is as extensive and diverse as the peoples that have come to this nation. The following represents a selection of the major works in the principle subject areas covered in this book.

General overviews

There are many good general overviews of U.S. immigration history, including Roger Daniels, *Coming to America: A History of Immigration and Ethnicity in American Life*, 2d ed. (New York: Harper Perennial, 2002); Paul Spickard, *Almost All Aliens: Immigration, Race, and Colonialism in American History and Identity* (New York: Routledge, 2007); Ronald Takaki, *A Different Mirror: A History of Multicultural America*, rev. ed. (New York and Boston: Back Bay Books, Little, Brown, and Company, 2008).

Migration to Colonial British America

Migration from Europe to the British North American colonies is discussed in: Bernard Bailyn, *The Barbarous Years: The Peopling of British North America: The Conflict of Civilizations, 1600–1675* (New York: Alfred A. Knopf, 2012); Marianne S. Wokeck, *Trade in Strangers: The Beginnings of Mass Migration to North America* (University Park: Pennsylvania State University Press, 1999); and Alan Taylor, *American Colonies: The Settling of North America* (New York: Penguin Books, 2001). Interactions between the colonizers and the Native Americans are discussed in: Richard White, *The Middle Ground: Indians, Empires, and Republics in the Great Lakes Region, 1650–1815*, 20th anniversary ed. (New York: Cambridge University Press, 2011); Roger M. Carpenter, *"Times Are Altered with Us": American Indians from First Contact to the New Republic* (Chichester, West Sussex, UK: John Wiley & Sons, Inc., 2015); Daniel K. Richter, *Facing East from Indian Country: A Native History of Early America* (Cambridge: Harvard University Press, 2001). For the introduction of African slavery into North America and the experiences of the enslaved in colonial America, see: Ira Berlin, *Many Thousands Gone: The First Two Centuries of Slavery in North America* (Cambridge, Mass.: The Belknap Press of Harvard University Press, 1998); Philip D. Morgan, *Slave Counterpoint: Black Culture in the Eighteenth-Century Chesapeake & Lowcountry* (Chapel Hill: University of North Carolina Press, 1998); and T.H. Breen and Stephen Innes,

"Myne Owne Ground": *Race and Freedom on Virginia's Eastern Shore, 1640–1676* (New York: Oxford University Press, 2005).

Migration to nineteenth-century America

German and Irish immigration dominated for most of the nineteenth century. For their experiences, see: Kevin Kenny, *The American Irish: A History* (New York: Longman, 2000); James R. Barrett, *The Irish Way: Becoming American in the Multiethnic City* (New York: The Penguin Press, 2012); Hasia R. Diner, *Erin's Daughters in America: Irish Immigrant Women in the Nineteenth Century* (Baltimore: Johns Hopkins University Press, 1983); Kathleen Neils Conzen, *Immigrant Milwaukee, 1836–1860: Accommodation and Community in a Frontier City* (Cambridge, Mass.: Harvard University Press, 1976); Linda Schelbitzki Pickle, *Contented Among Strangers: Rural German-Speaking Women and Their Families in the Nineteenth-Century Midwest* (Urbana and Chicago: University of Illinois Press, 1996); Regina Donlon, *German and Irish Immigrants in the Midwestern United States, 1850–1900* (Cham, Switzerland: Palgrave Macmillan, 2018).

For the experiences of Mexicans living in the American Southwest after the Mexican–American War, see: Raul A. Ramos, *Beyond the Alamo: Forging Mexican Ethnicity in San Antonio, 1821–1861* (Chapel Hill: Published in association with the William P. Clements Center for Southwest Studies, Southern Methodist University, by the University of North Carolina Press, 2008); Arnoldo De Leon, *They Called Them Greasers: Anglo Attitudes toward Mexicans in Texas, 1821–1900* (Austin: University of Texas Press, 1983); and Linda Heidenreich, *"This Land Was Mexican Once": Histories of Resistance from Northern California* (Austin: University of Texas Press, 2007).

For the experiences of nineteenth-century Chinese immigrants, see: Gordon H. Chang, *Ghosts of Gold Mountain: The Epic Story of the Chinese Who Built the Transcontinental Railroad* (Boston and New York: Houghton Mifflin Harcourt, 2019); Sue Fawn Chung, *In Pursuit of Gold: Chinese American Miners and Merchants in the American West* (Urbana and Chicago: University of Illinois Press, 2011); Sucheng Chan, *This Bittersweet Soil: The Chinese in California Agriculture, 1860–1910* (Berkeley and Los Angeles: University of California Press, 1986); and Huping Ling, *Surviving on the Gold Mountain: A History of Chinese American Women and Their Lives* (Albany: State University of New York Press, 1998).

Immigration in the late nineteenth and early twentieth centuries

For immigration from Southern and Eastern Europe during the late nineteenth and early twentieth centuries, see: Thomas A. Guglielmo, *White on Arrival: Italians, Race, Color, and Power in Chicago, 1890–1945* (New York: Oxford University Press, 2003); Irving Howe, *World of our Fathers: The Journey of the East European Jews to America and the Life They Found and Made* (1976; reprint, New York: Schocken Books, 1989); Matthew Frye Jacobson, *Special Sorrows: The Diasporic Imagination of Irish, Polish, and Jewish Immigrants in the United States* (Cambridge, Mass.: Harvard University Press, 1995); and David R. Roediger, *Working Toward Whiteness: How America's Immigrants Became White: The Strange Journey from Ellis Island to the Suburbs* (New York: Basic Books, 2005). For more information on return migration to Europe, see: Mark Wyman, *Round-Trip to America: The Immigrants Return to Europe, 1880–1930* (Ithaca: Cornell University Press, 1993). For the history of Ellis Island, see Vincent J. Cannato, *American Passage: The History of Ellis Island* (New York: Harper Perennial, 2010).

For the experiences of immigrants with industrialization and urbanization in the late nineteenth century, see: Thomas Mackaman, *New Immigrants and the Radicalization of American Labor, 1914–1924* (Jefferson, N.C.: McFarland and Company, Inc., 2017; Marianne Debouzy, ed., *In the Shadow of the Statue of Liberty: Immigrants, Workers, and Citizens in the American Republic, 1880–1920* (Urbana and Chicago: University of Illinois Press, 1992); Ryan Dearinger, *The Filth of Progress: Immigrants, Americans, and the Building of Canals and Railroads in the West* (Oakland: University of California Press, 2016).

For immigration in the Western United States, see: Arnoldo De Leon, *Racial Frontiers: Africans, Chinese, and Mexicans in Western America, 1848–1890* (Albuquerque: University of New Mexico Press, 2002); Elliott Robert Barkan, *From All Points: America's Immigrant West, 1870s–1952* (Bloomington and Indianapolis: Indiana University Press, 2007) and Richard Edwards, Jacob K. Friefeld, and Rebecca S. Wingo, *Homesteading the Plains: Toward a New History* (Lincoln: University of Nebraska Press, 2017).

For the situation of Puerto Rico and the Philippines after the Spanish–American War, see: Sam Erman, *Almost Citizens: Puerto Rico, the U.S. Constitution, and Empire* (New York: Cambridge University Press, 2019); Rick Baldoz, *The Third Asiatic Invasion: Empire and Migration in Filipino America, 1898–1946* (New York: New York University Press, 2011); and Robert C. McGreevey, *Borderline Citizens: The United States, Puerto Rico, and the Politics of Colonial Migration* (Ithaca: Cornell University Press, 2018).

Nativism and xenophobia

For the history of nativism and xenophobia in the United States, see: Tyler Anbinder, *Nativism and Slavery: The Northern Know Nothings and the Politics of the 1850s* (New York: Oxford University Press, 1992); Erika Lee, *America for Americans: A History of Xenophobia in the United States* (New York: Basic Books, 2019); and Lon Kurashige, *Two Faces of Exclusion: The Untold History of Anti-Asian Racism in the United States* (Chapel Hill: University of North Carolina Press, 2016).

U.S. immigration policy

For a general overview of the history of U.S. immigration policy, see Roger Daniels, *Guarding the Golden Door: American Immigration Policy and Immigrants Since 1882* (New York: Hill and Wang, 2004). For the creation and impact of the Chinese Exclusion Act, see: Lucy E. Salyer, *Laws Harsh as Tigers: Chinese Immigrants and the Shaping of Modern Immigration Law* (Chapel Hill: University of North Carolina Press, 1995) and Estelle T. Lau, *Paper Families: Identity, Immigration Administration, and Chinese Exclusion* (Durham: Duke University Press, 2006). For the creation of the National Origins Act of 1924, see: Katherine Benton-Cohen, *Inventing the Immigration Problem: The Dillingham Commission and Its Legacy* (Cambridge,

Mass.: Harvard University Press, 2018). For the struggle to reform the National Origins Quota System, see Jia Lynn Yang, *One Mighty and Irresistible Tide: The Epic Struggle over American Immigration, 1924–1965* (New York: W.W. Norton and Company, 2020). For the experiences of women and the gendered nature of immigration policy, see Candice Lewis Bredbenner, *A Nationality of Her Own: Women, Marriage, and the Law of Citizenship* (Berkeley and Los Angeles: University of California Press, 1998) and Martha Gardner, *The Qualities of a Citizen: Women, Immigration, and Citizenship: 1870—1965* (Princeton: Princeton University Press, 2005). For the development of border security and unauthorized immigration, see: Mae M. Ngai, *Impossible Subjects: Illegal Aliens and the Making of Modern America* (Princeton: Princeton University Press, 2004); Deirdre M. Moloney, *National Insecurities: Immigrants and U.S. Deportation Policy since 1882* (Chapel Hill: University of North Carolina Press, 2012) and Patrick Ettinger, *Imaginary Lines: Border Enforcement and the Origins of Undocumented Immigration, 1882–1930* (Austin: University of Texas Press, 2009).

Racial theories and segregation

For racial theories at the turn of the twentieth century that contributed to segregation and immigration restriction, see: Ian Haney Lopez, *White by Law: The Legal Construction of Race* (New York: New York University Press, 2006); Thomas C. Leonard, *Illiberal Reformers: Race, Eugenics, and American Economics in the Progressive Era* (Princeton: Princeton University Press, 2016); and Daniel Okrent, *The Guarded Gate: Bigotry, Eugenics, and the Law that Kept Two Generations of Jews, Italians, and Other European Immigrants Out of America* (New York: Scribner, 2019).

Disability and immigration

For the history of disability and immigration, see: Douglas C. Baynton, *Defectives in the Land: Disability and Immigration in the Age of Eugenics* (Chicago: University of Chicago Press, 2016) and Kim E. Nielsen, *A Disability History of the United States* (Boston: Beacon Press, 2012).

Immigration during the Great Depression and World War II

For the "repatriation" of Mexican Americans during the Great Depression, see Francisco E. Balderrama and Raymond Rodriguez, *Decade of Betrayal: Mexican Repatriation in the 1930s*, rev. ed. (Albuquerque: University of New Mexico Press, 2006). For the experiences of bracero laborers during World War II, see: Mireya Loza, *Defiant Braceros: How Migrant Workers Fought for Racial, Sexual, and Political Freedom* (Chapel Hill: University of North Carolina Press, 2016) and Ana Elizabeth Rosas, *Abrazando el Espíritu: Bracero Families Confront the U.S.–Mexico Border* (Oakland: University of California Press, 2014). For an account of the Zoot Suit Riots during World War II, see: Eduardo Orbregón Pagán, *Murder at the Sleepy Lagoon: Zoot Suits, Race, and Riot in Wartime L.A.* (Chapel Hill: University of North Carolina Press, 2003).

Late twentieth-century immigration

For migration from Latin America in the twentieth century, see: Neil Foley, *Mexicans in the Making of America* (Cambridge, Mass.: The Belknap Press of Harvard University Press, 2014); Zaragosa Vargas, *Crucible of Struggle: A History of Mexican Americans from Colonial Times to the Present Era*, 2d ed. (New York: Oxford University Press, 2017); Juan Gonzalez, *Harvest of Empire: A History of Latinos in America*, rev. ed. (New York: Penguin Books, 2011); Roberto Suro, *Strangers Among Us: Latino Lives in a Changing America* (New York: Vintage Books, 1999); and Jorge Duany, *Blurred Borders: Transnational Migration Between the Hispanic Caribbean and the United States* (Chapel Hill: University of North Carolina Press, 2011).

For migration from Asia in the twentieth century, see: Ronald Takaki, *Strangers from a Different Shore: A History of Asian Americans: Updated and Revised* (1989, rev. ed. 1998); Erika Lee, *The Making of Asian America: A History* (New York: Simon and Schuster, 2015). Jane H. Hong, *Opening the Gates to Asia: A Transpacific History of How America Repealed Asian Exclusion* (Chapel Hill: University of North Carolina Press, 2019); and Madeline Y. Hsu, *The Good Immigrants: How the Yellow Peril Became the Model Minority* (Princeton: Princeton University Press, 2015).

For the civil rights movements of the 1960s and 1970s, see: Mary L. Dudziak, *Cold War Civil Rights: Race and the Image of American Democracy* (Princeton: Princeton University Press, 2000); Taylor Branch, *Parting the Waters: America in the King Years, 1954–1963* (New York: Simon and Schuster, 1988); Taylor Branch, *Pillar of Fire: America in the King Years, 1964–1965* (New York: Simon and Schuster, 1998); Jimmy Patiño, *Raza Sí, Migra No: Chicano Movement Struggles for Immigrant Rights in San Diego* (Chapel Hill: University of North Carolina Press, 2017); Carlos Muñoz, Jr. *Youth, Identity, Power: The Chicano Movement*, rev. and expanded ed. (New York: Verso, 2007); Karen L. Ishizuka, *Serve the People: Making Asian America in the Long Sixties* (New York: Verso, 2016); Frederick Hoxie, *This Indian Country: American Indian Activists and the Place They Made* (New York: Penguin Books, 2012); and Bradley G. Shreve, *Red Power Rising: The National Indian Youth Council and the Origins of Native Activism* (Norman: University of Oklahoma Press, 2011).

For U.S. refugee policy in the twentieth century, see: David S. Wyman, *The Abandonment of the Jews: America and the Holocaust, 1941–1945* (New York: Pantheon Books, 1984); Carl J. Bon Tempo, *Americans at the Gate: The United States and Refugees during the Cold War* (Princeton: Princeton University Press, 2008); Laura Madokoro, *Elusive Refuge: Chinese Migrants in the Cold War* (Cambridge, Mass.: Harvard University Press, 2016); Felix Roberto Masud-Piloto, *From Welcomed Exiles to Illegal Immigrants: Cuban Migration to the U.S., 1959–1995* (Lanham, Md.: Rowman and Littlefield Publishers, Inc., 1996) and María Christina García, *The Refugee Challenge in Post-Cold War America* (New York: Oxford University Press, 2017).

Immigration at the dawn of the twenty-first century

The twenty-first century has seen a continued growth of opposition to immigration, particularly focused on unauthorized immigration and Muslim immigrants.

For a general overview of these trends, see Naomi A. Paik, *Bans, Walls, Raids, Sanctuary: Understanding U.S. Immigration for the Twenty-First Century* (Oakland: University of California Press, 2020). For studies of unauthorized immigration, see: Heide Castañeda, *Borders of Belonging: Struggle and Solidarity in Mixed-Status Immigrant Families* (Stanford: Stanford University Press, 2019); Hiroshi Motomura, *Immigration Outside the Law* (New York: Oxford University Press, 2014); and Eileen Truax, *Dreamers: An Immigrant Generation's Fight for Their American Dream* (Boston: Beacon Press, 2015). For studies of anti-Muslim sentiment in the U.S., see: Deepa Iyer, *We Too Sing America: South Asian, Arab, Muslim, and Sikh Immigrants Shape Our Multiracial Future* (New York: The New Press, 2015) and Deepa Kumar, *Islamophobia and the Politics of Empire* (Chicago: Haymarket Books, 2012).

References

Alexander, June Granatir. *Daily Life in Immigrant America, 1870–1920: How the Second Great Wave of Immigrants Made Their Way in America*. Chicago: Ivan R. Dee, 2009.

Allain, Jean. *The Legal Understanding of Slavery: From the Historical to the Contemporary*. New York: Oxford University Press, 2012.

Alroey, Gur. *Bread to Eat and Clothes to Wear: Letters from Jewish Migrants in the Early Twentieth Century*. Detroit: Wayne State University Press, 2011.

Anbinder, Tyler. *Nativism and Slavery: The Northern Know Nothings and the Politics of the 1850s*. New York: Oxford University Press, 1992.

Anderson, Virginia Dejohn. *New England's Generation: The Great Migration and the Formation of Society and Culture in the Seventeenth Century*. New York: Cambridge University Press, 1991.

Axtell, James. *After Columbus: Essays in the Ethnohistory of Colonial North America*. New York: Oxford University Press, 1988.

Bailyn, Bernard, *The Barbarous Years: The Peopling of British North America: The Conflict of Civilizations, 1600–1675*. New York: Alfred A. Knopf, 2012.

Balderrama, Francisco E. and Raymond Rodriguez. *Decade of Betrayal: Mexican Repatriation in the 1930s*, Revised edition. Albuquerque: University of New Mexico Press, 2006.

Baldoz, Rick. *The Third Asiatic Invasion: Empire and Migration in Filipino America, 1898–1946*. New York: New York University Press, 2011.

Baynton, Douglas C. *Defectives in the Land: Disability and Immigration in the Age of Eugenics*. Chicago: University of Chicago Press, 2016.

Berkin, Carol. *First Generations: Women in Colonial America*. New York: Hill and Wang, 1996.

Berlin, Ira. *Many Thousands Gone: The First Two Centuries of Slavery in North America*. Cambridge, Mass.: The Belknap Press of Harvard University Press, 1998.

Berlin, Ira and Leslie M. Harris, editors. *Slavery in New York*. New York: The New Press, 2005.

Bon Tempo, Carl J. *Americans at the Gate: The United States and Refugees during the Cold War*. Princeton: Princeton University Press, 2008.

Bradburn, Douglas. "'True Americans' and 'Hordes of Foreigners': Nationalism, Ethnicity, and the Problems of Citizenship in the United States, 1789–1800." *Historical Reflections/Reflexions Historiques*. Vol. 29, No. 1: 19–41.

Bradford, Anita Casavantes. "'With the Utmost Practical Speed': Eisenhower, Hungarian Parolees, and the 'Hidden Hand' Behind U.S. Immigration and Refugee Policy, 1956–1957." *Journal of American Ethnic History.* Vol. 39, No. 2 (Winter 2020): 5–35.

Bradford, Anita Casavantes. *The Revolution is for the Children: The Politics of Childhood in Havana and Miami, 1959–1962.* Chapel Hill: University of North Carolina Press, 2014.

Breen, T.H. and Stephen Innes. *"Myne Owne Ground": Race and Freedom on Virginia's Eastern Shore, 1640–1676.* New York: Oxford University Press, 2005.

Bulosan, Carlos. *America is in the Heart: A Personal History.* 1946. Reprint, with an introduction by Marilyn C. Alquizola and Lane Ryo Hirabayashi, Seattle: University of Washington Press, 2014.

Calhoun, Charles W., editor. *The Gilded Age: Perspectives on the Origins of Modern America.* New York: Rowman and Littlefield Publishers, Inc., 2007.

Carpenter, Roger M. *"Times Are Altered with Us": American Indians from First Contact to the New Republic.* Chichester, West Sussex, U.K.: John Wiley & Sons, Inc., 2015.

Cashman, Sean Dennis. *America in the Gilded Age: From the Death of Lincoln to the Rise of Theodore Roosevelt,* Third edition. New York: New York University Press, 1993.

Castañeda, Heide. *Borders of Belonging: Struggle and Solidarity in Mixed-Status Immigrant Families.* Stanford: Stanford University Press, 2019.

Cave, Alfred A. *Lethal Encounters: Englishmen and Indians in Colonial Virginia.* Denver: Praeger, 2011.

Chan, Shelly. *Diaspora's Homeland: Modern China in the Age of Global Migration.* Durham: Duke University Press, 2018.

Chan, Sucheng, editor. *Entry Denied: Exclusion and the Chinese Community in America, 1882–1943.* Philadelphia: Temple University Press, 1991.

Chan, Sucheng. *This Bitter-Sweet Soil: The Chinese in California Agriculture, 1860–1910.* Berkeley and Los Angeles: University of California Press, 1986.

Chang, Gordon H. and Shelley Fisher Fishkin, editors. *The Chinese and the Iron Road: Building the Transcontinental Railroad.* Stanford: Stanford University Press, 2019.

Cobb, Daniel, editor. *Say We Are Nations: Documents of Politics and Protest in Indigenous America since 1887.* Chapel Hill: University of North Carolina Press, 2015.

Conzen, Kathleen Neils. *Immigrant Milwaukee, 1836–1860: Accommodation and Community in a Frontier City.* Cambridge, Mass.: Harvard University Press, 1976.

Daniels, Roger. *Coming to America: A History of Immigration and Ethnicity in American Life,* Second edition. New York: Harper Perennial, 2002.

Daniels, Roger. *Guarding the Golden Door: American Immigration Policy and Immigrants since 1882.* New York: Hill and Wang, 2004.

Daniels, Roger. *Not Like Us: Immigrants and Minorities in America, 1890–1924.* Chicago: Ivan R. Dee, 1997.

Daniels, Roger and Otis L. Graham. *Debating American Immigration, 1882–Present.* New York: Rowman and Littlefield Publishers, Inc., 2001.

Dearinger, Ryan. *The Filth of Progress: Immigrants, Americans, and the Building of Canals and Railroads in the West.* Oakland: University of California Press, 2016.

De Leon, Arnoldo. *Racial Frontiers: Africans, Chinese, and Mexicans in Western America, 1848–1890*. Albuquerque: University of New Mexico Press, 2002.

De Leon, Arnoldo. *They Called Them Greasers: Anglo Attitudes toward Mexicans in Texas, 1821–1900*. Austin: University of Texas Press, 1983.

Deverell, William F. "To Loosen the Safety Valve: Eastern Workers and Western Lands." *The Western Historical Quarterly*. Vol. 19, No. 3 (1988): 269–285.

Diner, Hasia R. *Erin's Daughters in America: Irish Immigrant Women in the Nineteenth Century*. Baltimore: Johns Hopkins University Press, 1983.

Dinnerstein, Leonard and David M. Reimers. *The World Comes to America: Immigration to the United States since 1945*. New York: Oxford University Press, 2014.

Donlon, Regina, *German and Irish Immigrants in the Midwestern United States, 1850–1900*. Cham, Switzerland: Palgrave Macmillan, 2018.

Duany, Jorge. *Blurred Borders: Transnational Migration Between the Hispanic Caribbean and the United States*. Chapel Hill: University of North Carolina Press, 2011.

Dudziak, Mary L. *Cold War Civil Rights: Race and the Image of American Democracy*. Princeton: Princeton University Press, 2000.

Edwards, Richard, Jacob K. Friefeld, and Rebecca S. Wingo. *Homesteading the Plains: Toward a New History*. Lincoln: University of Nebraska Press, 2017.

Elliott, J.H. *Empires of the Atlantic World: Britain and Spain in America, 1492–1830*. New Haven: Yale University Press, 2006.

Escobedo, Elizabeth R. *From Coveralls to Zoot Suits: The Lives of Mexican American Women on the World War II Home Front*. Chapel Hill: University of North Carolina Press, 2013.

Espiritu, Yen Le. *Home Bound: Filipino Lives across Cultures, Communities, and Countries*. Oakland: University of California Press, 2003.

Estes, Nick. *Our History is the Future: Standing Rock versus the Dakota Access Pipeline, and the Long Tradition of Indigenous Resistance*. New York: Verso, 2019.

Etulain, Richard W. *Beyond the Missouri: The Story of the American West*. Albuquerque: University of New Mexico Press, 2006.

Evans, James. *Emigrants: Why the English Sailed to the New World*. London: Weidenfeld and Nicolson, 2017.

Fogleman, Aaron Spencer. *Hopeful Journeys: German Immigration, Settlement, and Political Culture in Colonial America, 1717–1775*. Philadelphia: University of Pennsylvania Press, 1996.

Foley, Neil. *Mexicans in the Making of America*. Cambridge, Mass.: The Belknap Press of Harvard University Press, 2014.

Foner, Eric. *Forever Free: The Story of Emancipation and Reconstruction*. Illustrations edited with commentary by Joshua Brown. New York: Vintage Books, 2005.

Franklin, Benjamin. "Observations Concerning the Increase of Mankind, 1751," Founders Online, National Archives, https://founders.archives.gov/documents/Franklin/01-04-02-0080. [Original source: *The Papers of Benjamin Franklin, vol. 4, July 1, 1750, through June 30, 1753*, ed. Leonard W. Labaree. New Haven: Yale University Press, 1961, pp. 225–234.]

Friedman, Saul S. *No Haven for the Oppressed: United States Policy Toward Jewish Refugees, 1938–1945*. Detroit: Wayne State University Press, 1973.

Gabaccia, Donna R. and Vicki L. Ruiz, editors. *American Dreaming, Global Realities: Rethinking U.S. Immigration History*. Urbana and Chicago: University of Illinois Press, 2006.

García, María Christina. *The Refugee Challenge in Post-Cold War America*. New York: Oxford University Press, 2017.

Gardner, Martha. *The Qualities of a Citizen: Women, Immigration, and Citizenship: 1870–1965*. Princeton: Princeton University Press, 2005.

Garrison, Arthur H. "The Internal Security Acts of 1798: The Founding Generation and the Judiciary during America's First National Security Crisis." *Journal of Supreme Court History*. Vol. 34, No. 1 (2009):1–27.

Gjelten, Tom. *A Nation of Nations: A Great American Immigration Story*. New York: Simon and Schuster, 2015.

Goldstone, Lawrence. *Inherently Unequal: The Betrayal of Equal Rights by the Supreme Court, 1865–1903*. New York: Walker and Company, 2011.

Gonzales, Juan. *Harvest of Empire: A History of Latinos in America*. New York: Penguin Books, 2000.

Gonzalez, Manuel G. *Mexicanos: A History of Mexicans in the United States*, Third edition. Bloomington: Indiana University Press, 2019.

Greenwald, Emily. *Reconfiguring the Reservation: The Nez Perces, Jicarilla Apaches, and the Dawes Act*. Albuquerque: University of New Mexico Press, 2002.

Griffin, Patrick. *The People with No Name: Ireland's Ulster Scots, America's Scots Irish, and the Creation of a British Atlantic World, 1689–1764*. Princeton: Princeton University Press, 2001.

Griswold del Castillo, Richard. *The Treaty of Guadalupe Hidalgo: A Legacy of Conflict*. Norman: University of Oklahoma Press, 1990.

Grizzard, Frank E., Jr. and D. Boyd Smith. *Jamestown Colony: A Political, Social, and Cultural History*. Santa Barbara, Calif. and Denver, Colo.: ABC-CLIO, 2007.

Guglielmo, Thomas A. *White on Arrival: Italians, Race, Color, and Power in Chicago, 1890–1945*. New York: Oxford University Press, 2003.

Gyory, Andrew. *Closing the Gate: Race, Politics, and the Chinese Exclusion Act*. Chapel Hill: University of North Carolina Press, 1998.

Halperin, Terri Diane. *The Alien and Sedition Acts of 1798: Testing the Constitution*. Baltimore: Johns Hopkins University Press, 2016.

Heidenreich, Linda. *"This Land Was Mexican Once": Histories of Resistance from Northern California*. Austin: University of Texas Press, 2007.

Heizer, Robert F. and Alan J. Almquist. *The Other Californians: Prejudice and Discrimination under Spain, Mexico, and the United States to 1920*. Berkeley and Los Angeles: University of California Press, 1971.

Helbich, Wolfgang and Walter D. Kamphoefner, editors. *German-American Immigration and Ethnicity in Comparative Perspective*. Madison: Max Kade Institute for German-American Studies and University of Wisconsin-Madison, 2004.

Henderson, Timothy J. *Beyond Borders: A History of Mexican Migration to the United States*. Chichester, U.K: Wiley-Blackwell, 2011.

Henderson, Timothy J. *A Glorious Defeat: Mexico and its War with the United States*. New York: Hill and Wang, 2007.

Hine, Robert V. and John Mack Faragher. *Frontiers: A Short History of the American West*. New Haven: Yale University Press, 2007.

Hirota, Hidetaka. *Expelling the Poor: Atlantic Seaboard States and the Nineteenth-Century Origins of American Immigration Policy.* New York: Oxford University Press, 2017.

Hong, Jane H. *Opening the Gates to Asia: A Transpacific History of How America Repealed Asian Exclusion.* Chapel Hill: University of North Carolina Press, 2019.

Hsu, Madeline Y. "The Disappearance of America's Cold War Chinese Refugees, 1948–1966." *The Journal of American Ethnic History.* Vol. 31, No. 4 (Summer 2012): 12–33.

Ishizuka, Karen L. *Serve the People: Making Asian America in the Long Sixties.* New York: Verso, 2016.

Iyer, Deepa. *We Too Sing America: South Asian, Arab, Muslim, and Sikh Immigrants Shape Our Multiracial Future.* New York: The New Press, 2015.

Jacobson, Matthew Frye. *Whiteness of a Different Color: European Immigrants and the Alchemy of Race.* Cambridge, Mass.: Harvard University Press, 1998.

Jorae, Wendy Rouse. *The Children of Chinatown: Growing Up Chinese American in San Francisco, 1850–1920.* Chapel Hill: University of North Carolina Press, 2009.

Kanazawa, Mark. "Immigration, Exclusion, and Taxation: Anti-Chinese Legislation in Gold Rush California." *The Journal of Economic History.* Vol. 65, No. 3 (Sept. 2005): 779–805.

Kenny, Kevin, ed. *New Directions in Irish-American History.* Madison: University of Wisconsin Press, 2003.

Kenny, Kevin. *The American Irish: A History.* New York: Longman, 2000.

Kibria, Nazli. *Muslims in Motion: Islam and National Identity in the Bangladeshi Diaspora.* New Brunswick: Rutgers University Press, 2011.

King, Desmond. *Making Americans: Immigration, Race, and the Origins of the Diverse Democracy.* Cambridge, Mass.: Harvard University Press, 2000.

Klapper, Melissa R. *Small Strangers: The Experiences of Immigrant Children in America, 1880–1925.* Chicago: Ivan R. Dee, 2007.

Kulikoff, Allan. *From British Peasants to Colonial American Farmers.* Chapel Hill: University of North Carolina Press, 2000.

Kumar, Deepa. *Islamophobia and the Politics of Empire.* Chicago: Haymarket Books, 2012.

Lau, Estelle T. *Paper Families: Identity, Immigration Administration, and Chinese Exclusion.* Durham: Duke University Press, 2006.

Lee, Erika. *America for Americans: A History of Xenophobia in the United States.* New York: Basic Books, 2019.

Lee, Erika. *The Making of Asian America: A History.* New York: Simon and Schuster, 2015.

Lee, Erika. *At America's Gates: Chinese Immigration during the Exclusion Era, 1882–1943.* Chapel Hill: University of North Carolina Press, 2003.

Leonard, Thomas C. *Illiberal Reformers: Race, Eugenics, and American Economics in the Progressive Era.* Princeton: Princeton University Press, 2016.

Levario, Miguel Antonio. *Militarizing the Border: When Mexicans Became the Enemy.* College Station: Texas A&M University Press, 2012.

Levine, Bruce. *The Spirit of 1848: German Immigrants, Labor Conflict, and the Coming of the Civil War.* Urbana and Chicago: University of Illinois Press, 1992.

Lovoll, Odd S. *Promise of America: A History of the Norwegian-American People,* Revised edition. Minneapolis: University of Minnesota Press, 1999.

Loza, Mireya. *Defiant Braceros: How Migrant Workers Fought for Racial, Sexual, and Political Freedom*. Chapel Hill: University of North Carolina Press, 2016.

McWilliams, Carey. *North from Mexico: The Spanish-Speaking People of the United States*. 1948. Reprint, with an introduction by the author, New York: Greenwood Press Publishers, 1968.

Madokoro, Laura. *Elusive Refuge: Chinese Migrants in the Cold War*. Cambridge, Mass.: Harvard University Press, 2016.

Mann, Charles C. *1491: New Revelations of the Americas before Columbus*. New York: Alfred A. Knopf, 2005.

Marinari, Maddalena. "Divided and Conquered: Immigration Reform Advocates and the Passage of the 1952 Immigration and Nationality Act." *Journal of American Ethnic History*. Vol. 35, No. 3 (Spring 2016): 9–40.

Marinari, Maddalena, Madeline Y. Hsu, and Marcia Cristina Garcia, editors. *A Nation of Immigrants Reconsidered: U.S. Society in an Age of Restriction, 1924–1965*. Urbana, Chicago, and Springfield: University of Illinois Press, 2019.

Menchaca, Martha. *Naturalizing Mexican Immigrants: A Texas History*. Austin: University of Texas Press, 2011.

Miller, Brandon Marie. *Good Women of a Well-Blessed Land: Women's Lives in Colonial America*. Minneapolis: Lerner Publications Company, 2003.

Moloney, Deirdre M. *National Insecurities: Immigrants and U.S. Deportation Policy since 1882*. Chapel Hill: University of North Carolina Press, 2012.

Moran, Gerard. *Sending Out Ireland's Poor: Assisted Emigration to North America in the Nineteenth Century*. Dublin: Four Courts Press, 2004.

Morgan, Philip, editor. *African American Life in the Georgia Lowcountry: The Atlantic World and the Gullah Geechee*. Athens: University of Georgia Press, 2010.

Morgan, Philip D. *Slave Counterpoint: Black Culture in the Eighteenth-Century Chesapeake and Lowcountry*. Chapel Hill: University of North Carolina Press, 1998.

Mormino, Gary Ross. *Immigrants on the Hill: Italian-Americans in St. Louis, 1882–1982*. Columbia: University of Missouri Press, 2002.

Nash, Gary B. *Red, White, and Black: The Peoples of Early America*, Fourth edition. Upper Saddle River, N.J.: Prentice Hall, 2000.

Ngai, Mae M. *Impossible Subjects: Illegal Aliens and the Making of Modern America*. Princeton: Princeton University Press, 2004.

Nielsen, Kim E. *A Disability History of the United States*. Boston: Beacon Press, 2012.

Olson, Daron W. *Vikings across the Atlantic: Emigration and the Building of a Greater Norway, 1860–1945*. Minneapolis: University of Minnesota Press, 2013.

Olson, James S. and Heather Olson Beal. *The Ethnic Dimension in American History*, Fourth edition. Chichester, U.K.: Wiley-Blackwell, 2010.

Ordover, Nancy. *American Eugenics: Race, Queer Anatomy, and the Science of Nationalism*. Minneapolis: University of Minnesota Press, 2003.

Pagán, Eduardo Orbregón. *Murder at the Sleepy Lagoon: Zoot Suits, Race, and Riot in Wartime L.A.* Chapel Hill: University of North Carolina Press, 2003.

Paik, A. Naomi. *Bans, Walls, Raids, Sanctuary: Understanding U.S. Immigration for the Twenty-First Century*. Oakland: University of California Press, 2020.

Painter, Nell Irvin. *Standing at Armageddon: A Grassroots History of the Progressive Era*. 1987. Reprint, New York: W.W. Norton & Company, 2008.

Pani, Erika. "Saving the Nation through Exclusion: Alien Laws in the Early Republic in the United States and Mexico." *The Americas*. Vol. 65, No. 2 (Oct. 2008): 217–246.

Parker, Kunal M. *Making Foreigners: Immigration and Citizenship Law in America, 1600–2000*. New York: Cambridge University Press, 2015.

Patiño, Jimmy. *Raza Sí, Migra No: Chicano Movement Struggles for Immigrant Rights in San Diego*. Chapel Hill: University of North Carolina Press, 2017.

Paul, Rodman M. *The Far West and the Great Plains in Transition, 1859–1900*. New York: Harper and Row, 1988.

Peffer, George Anthony. *If They Don't Bring Their Women Here: Chinese Female Immigration before Exclusion*. Urbana and Chicago: University of Illinois Press, 1999.

Piecuch, Jim. *Three Peoples One King: Loyalists, Indians, and Slaves in the Revolutionary South, 1775–1782*. Columbia: University of South Carolina Press, 2008.

Ramos, Raul A. *Beyond the Alamo: Forging Mexican Ethnicity in San Antonio, 1821–1861*. Chapel Hill: Published in association with the William P. Clements Center for Southwest Studies, Southern Methodist University, by the University of North Carolina Press, 2008.

Rees, Jonathan. *Industrialization and the Transformation of American Life: A Brief Introduction*. Armonk, NY: M.E. Sharpe, 2013.

Resendez, Andres. *Changing National Identities at the Frontier: Texas and New Mexico, 1800–1850*. New York: Cambridge University Press, 2005.

Reynolds, David S. *Waking Giant: America in the Age of Jackson*. New York: Harper Collins, 2008.

Richter, Daniel K. *Before the Revolution: America's Ancient Pasts*. Cambridge: The Belknap Press of Harvard University Press, 2011.

Richter, Daniel K. *Facing East from Indian Country: A Native History of Early America*. Cambridge: Harvard University Press, 2001.

Rivera, Sandy. "Undocumented, Yet Hopeful: Dreamer Sandy Rivera's speech at the Indianapolis Women's March." National Immigrant Justice Center, https://immigrantjustice.org/staff/blog/undocumented-yet-hopeful-dreamer-sandy-riveras-speech-indianapolis-womens-march.

Rosas, Ana Elizabeth. *Abrazando el Espíritu: Bracero Families Confront the U.S.–Mexico Border*. Oakland: University of California Press, 2014.

Salyer, Lucy E. *Laws Harsh as Tigers: Chinese Immigrants and the Shaping of Modern Immigration Law*. Chapel Hill: University of North Carolina Press, 1995.

Scherr, Arthur. "Thomas Jefferson, White Immigration, and Black Emancipation: Part II: Jefferson's Symbiosis: White Immigration and Black Emancipation." *Southern Studies: An Interdisciplinary Journal of the South*. Vol. 23, No. 1 (Spring/Summer 2016): 1–26.

Shreve, Bradley G. *Red Power Rising: The National Indian Youth Council and the Origins of Native Activism*. Norman: University of Oklahoma Press, 2011.

Sifuentez, Mario Jimenez. *Of Forests and Fields: Mexican Labor in the Pacific Northwest*. New Brunswick, N.J.: Rutgers University Press, 2016.

Silver, Peter. *Our Savage Neighbors: How Indian War Transformed Early America*. New York: W.W. Norton and Co., 2008.

Sivertsen, Karen. "Babel on the Hudson: Community Formation in Dutch Manhattan." Ph.D. Dissertation. Duke University, N.C., 2007.

Smith, Roger M. *Civic Ideals: Conflicting Visions of Citizenship in U.S. History*. New Haven: Yale University Press, 1997.

Spickard, Paul. *Almost All Aliens: Immigration, Race, and Colonialism in American History and Identity*. New York: Routledge, 2007.

Takaki, Ronald. *A Different Mirror: A History of Multicultural America*, Revised edition. New York and Boston: Back Bay Books, 2008.

Takaki, Ronald. *Strangers from a Different Shore: A History of Asian Americans*, Updated and revised. 1989, rev. ed. 1998.

Taylor, Paul S. "Songs of the Mexican Migration" in *Puro Mexicano*, edited by J. Frank Dobie. Austin: Texas Folklore Society, 1935.

Tong, Benson. *Unsubmissive Women: Chinese Prostitutes in Nineteenth-Century San Francisco*. Norman: University of Oklahoma Press, 1994.

Torget, Andrew J. *Seeds of Empire: Cotton, Slavery, and the Transformation of the Texas Borderlands, 1800–1850*. Chapel Hill: University of North Carolina Press, 2015.

Trachtenberg, Alan. *The Incorporation of America: Culture and Society in the Gilded Age*. 1982. Reprint, New York: Hill and Wang, 2007.

Ueda, Reed. *Postwar Immigrant America: A Social History*. Boston and New York: Bedford Books of St. Martin's Press, 1994.

Urban, Andrew. *Brokering Servitude: Migration and the Politics of Domestic Labor during the Long Nineteenth Century*. New York: New York University Press, 2018.

Van Zandt, Cynthia J. *Brothers Among Nations: The Pursuit of Intercultural Alliances in Early America, 1580–1660*. New York: Oxford University Press, 2008.

White, Richard. *The Middle Ground: Indians, Empires, and Republics in the Great Lakes Region, 1650–1815*. 1991. 20th anniversary edition, New York: Cambridge University Press, 2011.

Wokeck, Marianne S. *Trade in Strangers: The Beginnings of Mass Migration to North America*. University Park: Pennsylvania State University Press, 1999.

Woo, Susie. *Framed by War: Korean Children and Women at the Crossroads of U.S. Empire*. New York: New York University Press, 2019.

Wood, Peter H. *Black Majority: Negroes in Colonial South Carolina from 1670 through the Stono Rebellion*. 1974. Reprint, New York: W.W. Norton and Co., 1996.

Wyman, Mark. *Immigrants in the Valley: Irish, Germans, and Americans in the Upper Mississippi Country, 1830–1860*. 1984. Reprint, Carbondale: Southern Illinois University Press, 2016.

Yang, Jia Lynn. *One Mighty and Irresistible Tide: The Epic Struggle over American Immigration, 1924–1965*. New York: W.W. Norton and Company, 2020.

Young, Elliott. *Alien Nation: Chinese Migration in the Americas from the Coolie Era through World War II*. Chapel Hill: University of North Carolina Press, 2014.

Index

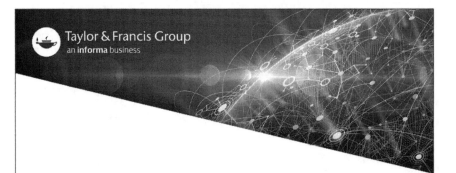